Multiculturalism and Conflict Reconciliation in the Asia-Pacific

Multiculturalism and Conflict Reconciliation in the Asia-Pacific

Migration, Language, and Politics

Edited by

Kosuke Shimizu
Professor, Ryukoku University, Japan

and

William S. Bradley
Professor, Ryukoku University, Japan

Except where otherwise noted, this work is licensed under a Creative Commons Attribution 3.0 Unported License. To view a copy of this license, visit http://creativecommons.org/licenses/by/3.0/

Editorial matter, selection and introduction © Kosuke Shimizu and William S. Bradley 2014

Individual chapters © Respective authors 2014

Foreword © Koichi Iwabuchi 2014

The authors have asserted their rights to be identified as the authors of this work in accordance with the Copyright, Designs and Patents Act 1988.

Open access:

 Except where otherwise noted, this work is licensed under a Creative Commons Attribution 3.0 Unported License. To view a copy of this license, visit http://creativecommons.org/licenses/by/3.0/

First published 2014 by
PALGRAVE MACMILLAN

Palgrave Macmillan in the UK is an imprint of Macmillan Publishers Limited, registered in England, company number 785998, of Houndmills, Basingstoke, Hampshire RG21 6XS.

Palgrave Macmillan in the US is a division of St Martin's Press LLC, 175 Fifth Avenue, New York, NY 10010.

Palgrave Macmillan is the global academic imprint of the above companies and has companies and representatives throughout the world.

Palgrave® and Macmillan® are registered trademarks in the United States, the United Kingdom, Europe and other countries.

DOI 10.1057/9781137403605
E-PDF ISBN 978-1-137-40360-5
E-PUB ISBN 978-1-137-40361-2
Hardback ISBN 978-1-137-40359-9
Paperback ISBN 978-1-137-46462-0

A catalogue record for this book is available from the British Library.

A catalog record for this book is available from the Library of Congress.

Typeset by MPS Limited, Chennai, India.

Transferred to Digital Printing in 2014

Contents

List of Figures and Tables   vii
Foreword by Koichi Iwabuchi   viii
Acknowledgments   xi
Notes on Contributors   xii

1 Introduction   1
  Kosuke Shimizu and William S. Bradley

Part I Theories and Identities

2 Multicultural Coexistence in Japan: Follower, Innovator, or Reluctant Late Adopter?   21
  William S. Bradley

3 A Critical Analysis of Multiculturalism and Deviant Identities: Untold Stories of Japanese Americans without Nations   44
  Takumi Honda

4 Theorizing Multiculturalism: Modeling the Dynamics of Inclusion and Exclusion in School-Based Multicultural Settings   62
  Lee Gunderson

Part II Language and Language Policies

5 Who Owns Our Tongue? English, Academic Life, and Subjectivity   81
  Kosuke Shimizu

6 Preservice and Inservice English as a Foreign Language Teachers' Perceptions of the New Language Education Policy Regarding the Teaching of Classes in English at Japanese Senior High Schools   99
  Toshinobu Nagamine

7 An Alternative Approach to Foreign Language Education in Japan with a View toward Becoming a Multicultural Society   118
  Mitsunori Takakuwa

Part III Migration and Citizenship

8 Female Domestic Workers on the Move: Examining Global Householding and Global De-Householding in Today's World 137
Rieko Karatani

9 Multiculturalism Policies and the Stepwise International Migration of Filipino Nurses: Implications for Japan 162
Maria Reinaruth D. Carlos

10 Who Benefits from Dual Citizenship? The New Nationality Law and Multicultural Future of South Korea 190
Shincha Park

11 "Global *Jinzai*," Japanese Higher Education, and the Path to Multiculturalism: Imperative, Imposter, or Immature? 213
Julian Chapple

Afterword 229
William S. Bradley and Kosuke Shimizu

Index 232

List of Figures and Tables

Figures

4.1	First (C1) and second (C2) cultures and inclusion/exclusion	74
A6.1	Sample concept map (subset)	114
7.1	Total number of registered foreigners in Japan	126
7.2	Percentage of registered foreigners by nationality in 2011	127

Tables

6.1	Participants' biographical information	103
A6.1	Coding sample of Yuji	113
7.1	Japanese population, Japanese nationals overseas, and Japanese overseas travelers	124
7.2	Number of registered foreigners and breakdowns by nationalities	125
7.3	Number of foreign children who require Japanese language instruction	130
7.4	Number of schools hosting foreign children requiring Japanese language instruction	131
A9.1	Stepwise migration pathways of Filipino nurses in Australia, Singapore, and the UAE	184
10.1	Acquisition and loss of nationality in South Korea from 2007 to 2012	200

OPEN

Foreword

In the new millennium, multiculturalism has significantly declined as a policy and social aspiration. While multiculturalism has long been criticized for connoting the mosaic like cohabitation of mutually exclusive cultures and communities, it has come under much stronger attack and critical scrutiny, particularly since September 11, 2001. Multiculturalism is alleged to be nation dividing, a detriment to national unity, and harmful to national security. Thus, the denunciation of multiculturalism has been accompanied by the intensification of national border controls and the reclaiming of national integration; this has resonated in a reactionary fashion, further amplifying people's growing sense of anxiety and longing for a secure and peaceful community in which to live. However, the demise of multiculturalism has diminished neither the dynamics of national border crossings nor cultural diversity within national borders. The speed and scale of transnational mobility and interconnection have become even more intensified. Stuart Hall (2000) famously distinguished the "multicultural question" from multiculturalism, which refers to policy discussion on the management of immigration and cultural diversity. An imperative multicultural issue we need to engage with is "how people from different cultures, different backgrounds, with different languages, different religious beliefs, produced by different and highly uneven histories, live together and attempt to build a common life while retaining something of their 'original identity'" (p. 210). The decline of multiculturalism necessitates that we develop better analytical tools and approaches that seriously tackle the multicultural question by involving a wider strata of people and institutions.

While multiculturalism has come under serious criticism in many Western societies, the management of emerging multicultural situations has come to be officially discussed in East Asian countries such as Japan, Korea, and Taiwan, though the term multiculturalism is not necessarily adopted. In these countries, in addition to long-existing racial and ethnic minorities, the rise in the last few decades of labor migration and transnational marriage, especially involving people from other parts of Asia, has considerably increased the number of foreign-national residents, migrants, and "mixed race" youth. The multicultural question has become a key issue in the Asia-Pacific, though in contrast to Europe and the United States, the experiences of East Asian countries pose the intriguing question of how to engage the multicultural question in a societies that have not addressed multiculturalism and related immigration policy through institutional development at the national level. However, while multiculturalism as policy and liberal political discourse in the Asian region has recently attracted academic attention, the multicultural question remains critically underexplored.

Multiculturalism and Conflict Reconciliation in the Asia-Pacific is a significant attempt to fill this lacuna. The innovativeness of this book lies in its argumentative structure. The first part presents theoretical and conceptual considerations of multiculturalism in a critical manner. Three chapters in this part critically revisit liberal multiculturalism and the essentialist conception of culture in the Asia-Pacific context. The following part deals with issues pertaining to language and education in a multicultural society—some of the most highly contested issues in policy. The final part explores in an empirical manner various sociocultural issues that migrants encounter and negotiate in their moves to host countries. While these three parts appear to deal with diverse issues by using different disciplinary approaches, they are coherently structured according to the key principle of the book: to examine theories, policies, and negotiations in pursuit of "interactive and communicative multiculturality," which is constitutive of the formation of the public sphere. Centered on this analytical axis, interdisciplinary approaches to various issues discussed in these ten chapters are highly complementary with each other and effectively constitute the book as a coherent intellectual project. The book does not directly deal with issues surrounding identity, belonging, and conviviality. However, its key aim has a clear resonance with Hall's argument regarding the multicultural question, and the book offers fresh theoretical and empirical insights into Hall's question, derived from the sociohistorical context of the Asia-Pacific region.

People will become more mobile across borders, and cultural diversity in the Asia-Pacific region will intensify in the years to come. This will exacerbate reactionary movements involving racism and xenophobia, which have already been on the rise in the region. How to advance dialogue between citizens across sociocultural divides will be a key issue for all stakeholders in multicultural societies. Toward this end, further interdisciplinary research is required that critically examines how people live, negotiate, and interact with each other under the neoliberal configurations that administer people's mobility and cultural diversity within nations. *Multicultural Negotiations in Migration, Language and Politics in Asia-Pacific* shows us one such project to be followed.

Koichi Iwabuchi
Monash University

Reference

Hall, S. (2000). Conclusion: The multi-cultural question. In H. Barnor (Ed.), *Un/Settled multiculturalism: Diasporas, entanglements, transruptions* (pp. 209–241). London: Zed Books.

Except where otherwise noted, this work is licensed under a Creative Commons Attribution 3.0 Unported License. To view a copy of this license, visit http://creativecommons.org/licenses/by/3.0/

Acknowledgments

This book is the culmination of a three-year research program of the Afrasian Research Centre, Ryukoku University, Kyoto, funded by the Ministry of Education, Culture, Sports, Science and Technology (MEXT) grant "Project for Strategic Research Base Formation Support at Private Universities" during the years 2011–2013. The theme of the project is "Research into the Possibilities of Establishing Multicultural Societies in the Asia-Pacific Region: Conflict, Negotiation, and Migration." Some of the chapters in this volume were initially published by the Centre in the form of working papers and research articles. Needless to say, all the chapters were substantially revised before this publication.

Completion of this volume would not have been possible without the devoted support of the Centre's staff members. Thus the editors' first thanks goes to the excellent support team of the Afrasian Research Centre, including Masako Otaki, postdoctoral fellow, and research assistants, Shincha Park, Tomoko Matsui, Takumi Honda, and Tomomi Izawa. We also express our gratitude to Yasuhito Okumura, Kyoko Iguchi, and Chiaki Yokoe for their help in administrative issues. In addition, we would also like to thank all the scholars and researchers who supported our research activities in research meetings, workshops, and international symposia in these three years for their stimulating intellectual interventions. In this context, we should specifically mention that we appreciate the personal and intellectual friendship with Prof. Koichi Iwabuchi who kindly agreed to contribute the foreword to this volume.

We would like to thank anonymous reviewers for their suggestive and valuable comments. We should also mention the very valuable help provided by the Palgrave Macmillan publishing team, particularly Christina Brian and Ambra Finotello. They provided us with a very comfortable environment for the publication, and it was our great pleasure to work with them.

Finally, we would like to thank the founding director of the Centre, Nobuko Nagasaki, Professor Emeritus of Ryukoku University whose sincere approach to striving for the truth has been continuously stimulating our intellectual lives. Although we are in no way certain that this volume would satisfy her high standards and scholarly judgment, we would like to dedicate this volume to her without question for her support and inspiration.

Kosuke Shimizu and William S. Bradley

Notes on Contributors

William S. Bradley is Professor in the Faculty of Intercultural Communication, Ryukoku University, and his fields of specialization are education and anthropology. He is the co-editor of *Education and the Risk Society* (with S. Bialostok and R. L. Whitman, eds, 2012) and recently authored a working paper for the Afrasian Research Centre: Studies on Multicultural Societies Series (Vol. 19, 2013), "Is There a Post-Multiculturalism?"

Maria Reinaruth D. Carlos is Professor of the Faculty of Intercultural Communication and Vice-Director of the Afrasian Research Centre at Ryukoku University. Her major field of interest is international migration and/for/in economic development. Currently, she conducts research studies on the stepwise international migration of Filipino nurses, the impact of the 2008 Global Economic Crisis on foreign workers in Japan, and the role of international migrant remittances in Philippine economic development.

Julian Chapple is Associate Professor at Ryukoku University. His major fields of interest are language rights and citizenship and the role of linguists in international politics. Presently he is interested in language policy and its effects on citizens within a nation state. His major publications include: "Exclusive inclusion: Japan's desire for, and difficulty with, diversity," in R. Danisch (ed.), *Citizens of the world: Pluralism, migration and practices of citizenship* (2011), and "Gendai Nihon Shakai no tagentekikyouzon he no kanousei" (The Possibility of multicultural existence and Japanese society), in P. Kent et al. (eds), *Gurobaruka, Chiiki, Bunka* (2010).

Lee Gunderson is Professor and former Head of the Department of Language and Literacy Education at the University of British Columbia, where he teaches both undergraduate and graduate courses in second language reading, language acquisition, literacy acquisition, and teacher education. He received the David Russell Award for Research, the Killam Teaching Prize, and the Kingston Prize for contributions to the National Reading Conference. He has conducted long-term research that explores the achievement of immigrant students. His research formed the basis for a documentary film called "Planet Vancouver."

Takumi Honda was Research Assistant of the Afrasian Research Centre at Ryukoku University. He is also a PhD candidate of the Graduate School of Intercultural Communication at Ryukoku University and currently working on his dissertation that analyzes the relationship between Japanese American concentration camps and national identity construction in the 1940s.

Rieko Karatani is currently Professor of International Relations, Kansai University, Osaka. She has been working on citizenship in the age of mobility, and migration and refugee policies in the UK and EU. Her English publications include *Defining British citizenship: Empire, commonwealth and modern Britain* (2003), "How history separated refugee and migrant regimes: In search of their institutional origins," *International Journal of Refugee Law, 17*(3), 2005, and "A 'responsible' EU, multinational migration regime and the case of ASEM," in H. Mayer & H. Vogt (eds), *A responsible Europe? Ethical foundations of EU external affairs* (2006).

Toshinobu Nagamine is Associate Professor of English teacher education at Kumamoto University, where he teaches English phonetics, research methodologies, and EFL teacher education courses. His research interests include foreign language education policy, language teacher cognition, and EFL teacher education and development. He has been a visiting scholar of the Afrasian Research Centre, Ryukoku University, and served as an editorial board member (a reviewer and an associate production editor) of the Asian EFL Journal.

Shincha Park is PhD student of Sociology at Binghamton University-SUNY. He was affiliated with the Afrasian Research Centre, Ryukoku University (2011–2013) and is also a pre-doctoral fellow at the Academy of Korean Studies (2014).

Kosuke Shimizu is Professor of international relations and Director of the Afrasian Research Centre, Ryukoku University. He is currently working on critical theories, non-Western IRT, and philosophy of the Kyoto School. His recent English publications include "Nishida Kitaro and Japan's interwar foreign policy: War involvement and culturalist political discourse," *International Relations of the Asia-Pacific, 11*(1), 2011, and "Materialising the 'Non-Western': Two stories of Japanese philosophers on culture and politics in the inter-war period," *Cambridge Review of International Affairs*, 2014 forthcoming.

Mitsunori Takakuwa is Professor at Meiji Gakuin University. Trained as an applied linguist, his scholarship focuses on bilingualism, bilingual education, and research methods. His current research interests focus on understanding the role of language education policy in language learning and teaching. His publications include "Lessons from a paradoxical hypothesis: A methodological critique of the threshold hypothesis," J. Cohen et al. (eds), *Proceedings of the 4th International Symposium on Bilingualism* (2005) and "What's wrong with the concept of cognitive development in studies of bilingualism?" (2000).

OPEN

1
Introduction

Kosuke Shimizu and William S. Bradley

This book is the culmination of research carried out at the Afrasian Research Centre at Ryukoku University in Kyoto, the ancient capital of Japan. Ryukoku University was established in 1639 as a Buddhist educational institution by the Nishihongwanji Temple, the head temple of Shin Buddhism, later becoming a university, and is known as one of the oldest tertiary educational institutions in Japan. The Centre was established in 2005 in conjunction with the Ministry of Education, Culture, Sports, Science and Technology of Japan (MEXT) to facilitate a cooperative research body to explore theoretical and pragmatic inquiries into a wide variety of conflicts and confrontations in the Asia-Pacific region. The Centre aims to provide analysis and suggestions for possibilities of conflict resolutions. Research meetings and international symposia were held each year for the past three years to discuss and exchange information about ongoing conflicts caused by the radical changes and expeditious transformations in an increasingly globalizing world. What became ever more clear through our meetings and symposia was the speed of the changes and transitions in the world and the power of liberal discourses of globalization, which eventually resulted in the alteration to the focus of inquiry. The Centre subsequently shifted its focus more to conflict reconciliation and critical engagement with specific attention to the current policies, discourses, issues, and lived experiences of multiculturalism.

Any conflicts in the contemporary era of globalization, whether micro-level conflicts or macro-level confrontations, are intertwined with the concepts of difference viewed through the prisms of the overarching concepts of culture and civilization. These terms have been utilized in many fields in the past several decades. While we can only offer a brief overview of two of the fields with which the editors are most knowledgeable (cultural anthropology and international relations), we can claim without too much controversy that culture and civilization, joined as they are historically, have been threading their way into discussions of difference, appearing at crucial junctures to create seemingly unbridgeable chasms between peoples. This is increasingly evident both in media and in everyday use, as well as in social science analyses, like some unfinished business of the past returning to remind one, almost in a melancholy manner, of the excesses of past misdeeds (Gilroy, 2005). Anthropological discussions that blossomed out of the problem of *"Writing Culture"* (Clifford & Marcus, 1986), and the predicament that culture presents for ethnographers and others (Clifford, 1988) exposed the dilemma of trying to pigeonhole entire peoples under a single unifying term, especially when those doing so were the prominent outsider insiders (i.e. anthropologists themselves). However, the complexity of what to do about the grand scheme of difference remains. Arguments for writing "against culture" (Abu-Lughod, 1991) and suggestions to "forget culture" (Brightman, 1995) meant that anthropologists have in the last two decades been extremely wary of an overarching culture concept unified by the "heroic" narratives derived from hard-earned research in the field. While some have suggested that culture can still be retained as a reasonable mode of analysis, especially if care is taken to avoid overgeneralizing (Brumann, 1999), the penchant for thinking against culture as a certifiable category for more than convenience is assumed by much contemporary anthropological research.

Civilization discourses, bound together with the pathology of 20th century modernity out of control (genocide and racism), have also been similarly viewed with scepticism by many social scientists, including in detailed treatments in anthropology (Patterson, 1997) and global history (Mazlish, 2004). Patterson focused on the (not coincidental) historical overlap of Social Darwinism and the discourses of civilization, industry, and progress, illustrating how these were instrumental in the "invention" of barbarian peoples and the ensuing genocidal actions of colonial powers in the Americas through the slave trade and wars with native peoples. Mazlish traced the first usages of the term "civilization" to Victor Mirabeau in 1756 and its link to European colonial ideology—"a racial interpretretation of civilization in favour of Europe" (Mazlish, 2004, p. 70)—as the 18th century gave way to the 19th century. Nonetheless, despite such critiques, both culture and civilization have steadily found their way back into common parlance, even for some as synonyms of superior models of human development, particularly (but not entirely) through reactions to political events after September 2001. Any attempt to analyze, evaluate, and summarize discussions of multiculturalism in theory and practice must first set out to deflate some of the aspects of the supposedly unifying discourse of cultural commonsense. Then it becomes plausible, taking great care to specify the intervening variables and conditions, to recognize concept(s) of cultural "difference" against the backdrop of a concept of a common human universality of recognition and tolerance based on rules and norms of international conduct, whether or not they are termed public, civil, civilized, or otherwise. It is that conundrum that we attempt to address by using conflict reconciliation in the title of this collection. When we discuss this problem in as large a region as the Asia-Pacific, there are bound to be numerous and unavoidable problems of particularism which threaten to negate any kind of generalizability. Even as earlier work on multiculturalism in Asia (Kymlicka & He, 2005) took care to avoid this kind of overgeneralization by focusing on a thick description of cases in many parts of Asia, it cannot be too surprising to find that Asia is occasionally seen to represent some kind of counter to European and North American models of culture and civilization, here and elsewhere. This may be inevitable, but we hope in this volume that we can move beyond such reductionist thinking, which has typified much of the discussion that revolves around the categories of East and West, to name perhaps the most overused and salient simplifying dichotomy. We are additionally aware that, by including the term Asia-Pacific in the title, we may be eliding a discussion of topics that are mostly focused on Japan with areas far and wide. On the other hand, we wish to draw attention to the multiple chapters that analyze phenomena related to migration, language, and politics in Japan in the Asia-Pacific as well as others that are not primarily focused on Japanese people or categories, even if they may be related to territorial aspects of Japan.

Turning our attention to political science, and international relations in particular, one can say that the overwhelming, one might say excessive, attention paid to Samuel Huntington's "clash of civilizations" thesis has been an archetypal representation of increasing academic concern for the current state of world affairs and its connection to questions of cultural division (Huntington, 1993).

Moreover, as successive publications relating culture and international relations show (Barber, 1996; Fukuyama, 1992; Lebow, 2008; Nye, 2004; Pettman, 2004), the so-called "cultural turn" in the social sciences more generally, and in international relations in particular, has been instrumental in helping to understand conflict, reconciliation, and building understandings between and across diverse populations in localized settings. As a result, a particular way to read multiculturalism as theory and a set of policies and programs to transcend the normative state of affairs of a world in conflict has come to the fore in the academic world.

In the existing literature of migration studies and international relations, culture has been often mistakenly treated as the one of the root causes of conflict. Jihad versus McWorld (Barber, 1996) and the West and the Rest (Scruton, 2002) are cases in point, let alone Huntington's clash of civilizations. Joseph Nye's excessively state-centered concept of "soft power" also provides a good example in which nation-states are destined to endless competition with each other by utilizing the power of culture (Nye, 2004). What permeates these discourses are stereotypically essentialized liberal interpretations of culture and identity with strict demarcating boundaries of selves *vis-à-vis* the other. As is well known, this interpretation is claimed to be the indispensable foundation of contemporary world affairs on the basis of civilizational clash (Huntington, 1993). This is apparently important not only theoretically, but also for its political implications. In fact, many of the discourses of culture and international relations can be read not as academic inquiry *per se* but also as a form of political manifestation of US global hegemony (Jones, 2002, p. 227). In this sense, the old saying is true that culture is political (Brown, 2006, p. 20), and, in the case of international relations, theory is always for someone for some purpose (Cox, 1981).

In order to avoid repeating this naïve approach and concluding that cultures inherently clash with each other through the process of civilizational confrontations, we draw on theoretical perspectives, expanding horizons spread across diverse disciplines and research areas from micro to macro, from regional studies to international relations, from humanities to social sciences, from everyday language to political terminology and theoretical conceptions, and from civil society to power politics. In order to illustrate this more clearly, we may refer here to the Arendtean (following the work of Hannah Arendt) understanding of the public. To Arendt, the differences among individuals and the existence of the public sphere are intimately intertwined and mutually indispensable. Without the public sphere, a society easily falls into the hands of totalitarianism (Arendt, 1973). What we are concerned with in this research project is similar to what Arendt tried to address. This is the way in which we become able to eschew the coercion of politically and culturally specific interpretations of truth and justice of one party onto the others, while at the same time establishing an interactive and communicative public space for reconciliation of conflicts and confrontations in the Asia-Pacific region. This space is characterized by interactive and communicative "multiculturality" (an active and formed-in-process type of multiculturalism) in the case of the present studies. In this manner, it is one that does not stop at cautiously advocating the mere coexistence with those from different cultures, but encourages dialog and negotiation among them.

It is precisely at this moment in the second decade of the 21st century that we have a firm conviction that the public sphere is indispensable in constructing an environment for reconciliation. Yet culture narrowly defined in the essentialized way, mainly formulated in the liberal discourse of multiculturalism, does not automatically (or, in any final sense, authentically) provide a ground for dialog or reconciliation among the parties involved in conflict. Here, the concept of interactive and communicative multiculturality comes to the fore as a form of the public sphere and appears in a way that holds some relevance for transcending the presupposed continuous collision of different cultures. However, even in the framing of multiculturalism, it is argued by some, the essentialized concept of culture still resides robustly in its mainstream discourses (Baumann, 1999; Phillips, 2007).

Accordingly, critical investigation of the widely accepted version of liberal multiculturalism with the essentialized concept of culture becomes particularly imperative. Continuous acceptance of liberal political discourse together with the concomitant interpenetrations of capitalism and globalization has appeared to us as a salient assumption for promoting the doctrine of mutual exchange among individuals with distinctive cultures. Simply put, it claims that we have to be tolerant of those who hold different cultural values and norms. However, culture in this context becomes problematic, as it is implicitly defined in distinctively rigid and inflexible terms. No unitary notion of culture in this context retains the possibility of changes and transformations through encounters and interactions with those who do not possess the same values and norms. Wendy Brown succinctly puts it:

> When ... middle and high schoolers are urged to tolerate one another's race, ethnicity, culture, religion, or sexual orientation, there is no suggestion that the differences at issue, or the identities through which these differences are negotiated, have been socially and historically constituted and are themselves the effect of power and hegemonic norms, or even of certain discourses about race, ethnicity, sexuality, and culture. Rather difference itself is what students learn they must tolerate. (Brown, 2006, p. 16)

As a consequence, the multicultural environment in the present context on the basis of liberal discourses of tolerance, in Japan as in other parts of the world, only constitutes a place in which different cultures merely coexist next to each other. This environment occasionally leads to harsh and hostile confrontations in the name of identity politics, and turns out to be a space which is filled up with the stories of who gets what and how. In its barest and most balkanized version of coexistence, it becomes merely an aggregation of different and isolated identities and cultures. The alleged container of "multi-culture" promotes a display of a fixed collection of different cultures, which totally lacks political orientation to address the conflicts and confrontations between cultures by means of continuous dialog and negotiation.

In the discourse of liberal multiculturalism of tolerance, the widespread inclination of academic discourses to associate each culture with the concept of nation-states has been noted. This is particularly so in the case of studies in international relations. The main agents of interactions and diplomatic relations in contemporary world affairs are, needless to say, nation-states. It is often said that the perception of international relations as a discipline has been formulated on the basis of the assumption of the exclusivity of state sovereignty. As a result, world affairs have been described and articulated with the clear distinction between inside and outside (Walker, 1993). Under the given condition of potential anarchy in the world, where no transcendental political bodies or authorities over nation-states exist, individual states are destined to compete with each other militarily, politically, and economically. This is because all nation-states are assumed to be desperate to maintain their sovereignty. This traditional view of international relations has been severely criticized recently by researchers and scholars of such heterodox approaches to world affairs as post-structuralism, critical theories, gender studies, post-colonialism, and non-Western international relations theories (Acharya & Buzan, 2010; Baylis, Smith, & Owens, 2011, chapters 8, 10, 11, 12, 16; Shilliam, 2010).

Among those critical approaches, non-Western international relations theory is the most recent development. However, despite its initial intention to develop and provide new approaches to world affairs, many works of this emerging literature have shown little change in terms of the concepts and methodologies they employ with regard to nation-states (Chen, 2012). The majority of the non-Western international relations discourse confirms the traditional methodology of social science, in which researchers and scholars pursue the notion of universal truth in contemporary world affairs. Consequently, they focus on the cores and centers of nation-states, and essentialize them with their allegedly distinctive cultures (Shimizu, 2011).

It is here that the concept of culture becomes problematic. While culture itself is very much transformative and unstable by definition, much of the non-Western international relations literature defines culture with pre-given distinctive patterns of thinking and behavior accepted and maintained by the nationals of a given place and which is assumed to be not observable anywhere else. The reason why much of the literature defines culture in such an essentialized manner is its methodological and epistemological modernist orientation of scientific investigation. Modernism has developed with such concepts as ever-continuing progress and civilization, and the development becomes possible only when it is supported by the accurate comprehension of the present (Hamashita, 1994, pp. 2–3). Thus, human progress and civilization have inevitably evolved hand in hand with the positivist scientific epistemology striving for the transcendent and universal truth. Obviously this epistemology assumes the subject/object division, which is inflexible in its ontological quality. The result is the static view towards the object of inquiry as a "thing," and the acceptance of a rigid concept of culture within liberal multiculturalism can be understood according to this line of reasoning.

As this pursuit of the transcendent and universal truth is a distinctive characteristic of modern knowledge construction in general, the analysis of world affairs with a specific focus on the cores and centers of the world mapping, i.e. nation-states, is not confined to international relations. The critique of methodological nationalism with regard to social sciences has been carried forward by a number of scholars in recent years (Chernilo, 2006; Wimmer and Glick-Schiller, 2002). Area Studies, focusing on the East Asian cultural relations, is not an exception either. In the discourse of Asian Area Studies, much attention has been paid to explaining interactions among different parties in the region with such essentialized and immobile concepts as "Chinese," "Japanese," and "Korean" cultures. However, this pre-given analytical framework, based on the concept of nation-state is, we argue, insufficient for fully comprehending, and thus providing a feasible solution for, conflicts and disputes in the Asia Pacific region.

Hamashita (1994) contends in this context that the reason why the contemporary knowledge structures of social sciences and humanities are unable to sufficiently grasp the issues of East Asian politics is due to their ignorance of the margins. Because previous studies have analyzed the region only in terms of nation-states and concomitant cultures, they miss the underlying layers of socio-economic and cultural interactions and negotiations that profoundly influence the perceptions and identities of locals. These margins are not the margins frequently deployed by such contemporary academic discourses as critical international relations, world systems theories, or subaltern studies. While the latter generally assume the center–periphery relations, with the specific concentric circle regularly denoting the West and the rest, Hamashita contends that there are uncountable and ubiquitous concentric circles in the world, and thus a margin has multiple centers against which it is defined. Utilizing such conceptions is an example of a way to enhance approaches to interactive and communicative multiculturality.

Taking into consideration the difference between interactive multiculturalism as a political movement striving to establish a public space in the region (Alagappa, 2004) and traditional liberal multiculturalism as a mere collection of individualized and isolated cultures mainly associated with nation-states, we are obliged to ask the question of which multiculturalism we are referring to, and with what methodology we can formulate an interactive multiculturalism. Accordingly, subsequent questions might include: Who are "we" speaking of in reference to multiculturalism? In what capacity are "we" entitled to speak of "others'" cultures? How does the discourse of multilingualism affect the formation of interactive multicultural environments? How do language education policies make impacts on the processes of establishing the public sphere? Is culture the cause of these myriad types of conflict? What is an alternative interpretation of culture that promotes dialog, negotiations, and reconciliation among different cultures? Are these supposedly different cultures significantly different anyway?

The current volume is a collection of research and investigations on multiculturalism to answer these questions in the search for new and alternative ways of comprehending and analyzing multicultural society in Japan embedded in the Asia-Pacific. Individual parts of the book deal with specific foci on multiculturalism: theories, language, and migration and citizenship. These sections are somewhat separate at a glance, but are deeply intertwined with each other, not only at the theoretical level, but at the everyday level of ordinary individuals.

The concrete themes of individual researchers in this volume are diverse, with the many approaches representative of the multiplicity of disciplines. The methodologies are diverse as well, ranging from traditional methodologies, such as empiricist and positivist, to more contemporary constructivist, critical, and post-structuralist approaches. This diversity reflects our commitment to the idea of the public to represent voices from the margin. In other words, the research program for the Centre itself was established in the public sphere of "interactive multiculturalism," where intense, continuing negotiations take place between communities and individuals. The authors in this volume have a firm conviction, following extended, cooperative research across different disciplines on conflict and reconciliation, that dialog, negotiation, and reconciliation are the keys to achieving an alternative multiculturality. This vision extends to both researchers and ordinary citizens. We thus see the present volume as an important contribution to the existing literature on multiculturalism.

1.1 Focus of the three sections

1.1.1 Theories and identities

The chapters in Part I focus on theories and identities of critical multiculturalism, paying specific attention to the contexts of Asia and Japan. While theories of multiculturalism have been increasingly scrutinized and challenged from a wide range of perspectives, they continue to be used as background and support for understanding policies and programs of diversity in societies, not least, for example, in relation to language and language policies (Part II) and migration and citizenship (Part III). The chapters in Part I focus more generally on society in the larger frame, occasionally starting from a national container perspective (while calling attention to the porous boundaries), but where possible drawing on transnational dimensions. This entails that the various chapters come to some critical understanding of processes that transcend the nation-state, as argued above.

As the chapters in Part I show, the definitions of what counts as multicultural are quite diverse—so much so that another challenge arises in deciding if multiculturalism is the primary object of analysis, a cause, an outcome, or just one of the many intervening elements. In looking at some of the dominant versions of liberal globalization, it had been noted that multiculturalism has often become nothing more than a marketing technique for multinational corporations to show sensitivity in the face of their consumer diversification, or viewed even more critically as a Disneyfication of difference (Gilroy, 2005). The intermingling relationship between nation-states and the global economy makes the issue even more complicated. Even if we try to transcend the prevailing territorial concepts, we often end up with wider geographical areas such as Europe, Asia-Pacific, or the "West." In this case, a version of multiculturalism that is widely accepted is likely to be a multiculturalism of the nation-state based on existing political and economic hegemonies. As a consequence, we subconsciously speak of a multiculturalism of a particular kind initially formulated for someone for a specific purpose, without noticing the embedded bias. Consequently, these chapters attempt to critically investigate the current discourse of multiculturalism and theorize difference in ways that retain sensitivity to important and self-defined differences (by individuals, communities, and wider polities *inter se*). This hopefully ensures the aim of a multiculturalism which addresses the idea of the public, in the Arendtean sense, while avoiding essentialist and retrogressive understandings of ethnic, racial, national, sexual, and class divisions. Thus, what we call for here is multiculturalism without pre-given essentialized culture (Phillips, 2007).

While these contributions in Part I cannot serve as some finalized theory for the types of empirical analyses of "actually existing" multicultural policies, programs, and dynamics in both the international arena and national societies, they attempt to push past the boundaries pre-set by the established discourses of multiculturalism. They explore how critical analysis of the multiple levels of changes of heretofore (at least nominally) nationally self-contained societies in the 21st century can be better formulated. In so doing, they specifically pay attention to phenomena in the interstices of what is termed multicultural and that mediate between the conceptualization and performance of global and local identities.

1.1.2 Language and language policies

Following the theoretical analysis of multiculturalism, the chapters in Part II deal with the role of language, language policies, and language education in constructing a space for negotiation and dialog among those with different cultural backgrounds. The chapters highlight the variety in multiculturalism, which deserves thorough attention in and through analyzing contemporary society and language. Needless to say, languages are regarded as one of the core factors which constitute cultures. But the reason why we pay specific attention to languages is not confined to this aspect. It also includes the fact that one is forced to use language for the expression of whatever arguments one retains and develops. No one can avoid using language as far as he or she tries to express the judgments and thoughts they come up with. Thus, languages are continually formulated and reformulated in power relations. Or, put more bluntly, languages are always products of certain power or power relations (Baumann, 1999). Controlling language not only rules and manipulates the means of expression, but also profoundly influences the way in which the contents of thoughts are formulated and constituted. This is why we place a special focus on the issue of language in comprehending contemporary multiculturalism.

Conflicts focused upon in this section include those from personal-level friction between individuals in daily life through to national-level societal problems of the question of English in world politics. Many conflicts at the personal and national level can be attributed to issues of non-native status in and through language: that is, the fact that immigrants are non-native speakers and learners of the language publicly spoken in the host country. Such problems arise despite the official promotion of immigration policies in the globalized world specifically targeted to provide second language education for immigrants, with the expectation that they will be enabled to become competent and contributing members of the host society. This problem is of particular interest in the context of contemporary discourses of multiculturalism because it becomes impossible for recent immigrants to negotiate with the local community when they are deprived of the means of communication and mutual understanding, let alone the problem that the language (and thus the concepts and categories of negotiation) is by no means set by themselves. The same problem is detectable in the context of world politics, where, as is well known, English has been the main language used in understanding contemporary world affairs. An important dimension of this issue is the establishment of appropriate language policies as a primary prerequisite for the creation of a public space, not only for those who have recently immigrated, but also for those who have the responsibility to include them.

By drawing on their critical analysis questioning the current state of language, the chapters in Part II reveal, in terms of perceptions towards the contemporary world and its relation to language, how language influences our intellectual lives and how language has the potential to reformulate our views of the world. It also reveals, in terms of language education policies, how the results of language education policies in the region, particularly in Japan, are by no means matched to the expected goals. The contributors in Part II ask the following questions, among others. Who are the ideal speakers of the hegemonic language? For what purpose are the language norms formulated? How different are the recently introduced bilingual education policies in Japan from those of multilingualism? What are the consequences of the bilingual education policies? What is the ideal language norm which promotes dialog and negotiations in multicultural environments?

1.1.3 Migration and citizenship

After the theory-oriented analysis of multiculturalism in Part I and the policy-oriented analysis of language in Part II, the chapters in Part III concentrate more on empirical analyses of migration and citizenship. These chapters bring together empirical research studies with a particular focus on the dynamics of formal and informal negotiations in multicultural settings in Asia and Japan. Such negotiations become imperative in light of the intensified movement of people resulting from demographic transformations in host countries as well as increasing economic inequalities between sending and receiving countries. Furthermore, for the migrants themselves, these negotiations are a vital element of their "survival strategies" in the host country.

While Part III focuses on formal negotiations, on which there have been some prior studies, it also depicts the implicit and invisible negotiations that take place as people go through their daily activities. This is particularly important in the case of migrants who have to make social, economic, psychological, mental, and other adjustments and transactions as they struggle to survive in the host country's culture and society. Each analysis in Part III contributes to the discussions on the links between international migration, citizenship, and multiculturalism by directing our attention to existing negotiations.

Culture undeniably plays a key role again in the negotiations between the migrants and the stakeholders in the host society (and sometimes even parties in the sending society like those left behind by the migrants), either as an influencing factor in negotiation or as its consequence. Culture often contributes to the outcome of the negotiation through its influence on the motivations and strategies of the parties involved on the basis of culturally determined notions of language, religion, gender, power, and minority identity. Culture also plays a contextual role as the place where the interactions and negotiation take place. This means that culture can be one of the outcomes. As negotiation progresses and concludes, a new "culture" may take shape, or, in some cases, may be "re"-shaped to accommodate the other's culture, as in a "hybrid" form of culture in which the identities of both sides are subject to reformulation through dialog. In this process, the state of the public, or a type of multiculturality as the space of the negotiation, is achieved in which both sides politically agree on a more convivial relationship through reconciliation. Seen in this way, some contributors to Part III consider the public space as a natural by-product of negotiations arising from the international movement of people.

As the number of people moving beyond geographical boundaries increases and globalization of economy via trade, investment, and information networks, intensifies, the number of negotiations, which are either explicit or implicit, explained or unexplained, and visible or invisible, such as those addressed in this section, is expected to increase. We consider the discussions in this section to be a base for reference in the study of multiculturalism within the context of international migration and citizenship, and our case studies illustrate negotiations that provide the vital links between the phenomena of multiculturalism, migration, and citizenship in the era of globalization.

1.1.4 Issues

Following the introduction, Part I starts with William Bradley's focus on multicultural coexistence in Japan. In Chapter 2, Bradley begins with a discussion of the discourse of multiculturalism and argues that, given that multiculturalism and multicultural policies have been sharply challenged in many parts of the world in the past decade, discussions about what comes after multiculturalism have become more salient. In Japan, debates about multiculturalism (*tabunka kyōsei*) and policies for its implementation have been less vociferous and it could be argued that there is more support than in many other countries (especially Europe), where multiculturalism was at one time more strongly and publicly discussed and supported, at least on some levels. His argument starts by reviewing some examples of multicultural policy in several urban and rural localities in Japan and then moves to a more general discussion of the challenges and necessity for immigration policy and recognition of diversity in Japanese society.

In Chapter 3 Takumi Honda outlines the discourses of multiculturalism in the US regarding immigrants from Japan during the Second World War. Honda focuses on the history of Japanese Americans during that period and shows that this history constitutes part of the wider context of multiculturalism in the US. However, this is not the end of the story. There are Japanese Americans who were disregarded in the story of multiculturalism in the US because they did not fit into the story of what were thought to be good Americans. Honda strives to clarify why they have not been brought into the spotlight, and critically assesses the current discourse of multiculturalism in the US.

In Chapter 4, Lee Gunderson analyzes multiculturalism related to teaching and learning in classrooms that are filled with students who have various linguistic and cultural backgrounds. The purpose here is to develop a multicultural model that can be argued, contested, discussed, and possibly observed and tested in classrooms and schools in Asia. Most countries in Asia are experiencing an increase in school-age immigrants enrolled in their schools. However, the immigrant enrollment varies widely from country to country, area to area, and school to school. The potential for inclusion can be estimated by comparing the cultural features that immigrants bring to a school with the cultural features of the enrolling school (and teachers). Gunderson argues that, overall, the absolute percentages of immigrant students in a classroom can be hypothesized to roughly predict inclusion/exclusion, along with other factors, so that neither a small number nor a very high number of immigrants will likely be easily included in a classroom.

Part II begins with Chapter 5, by Kosuke Shimizu, which specifically targets the relationship between the English language and international relations as an academic discipline. Shimizu starts his argument by claiming that the issue of language has received insufficient attention in contemporary academic circles, partly because of the uncritical assumption that language is a transparent device conveying the meanings in the mind of the subject. Shimizu criticizes the widely accepted claim that using English is a contradiction in the narratives of the Post-Western political theories, because they mistakenly regard English as a Western language. Against these prevailing notions of language and politics, he conducts a thorough investigation that reveals some hidden and unquestioned assumptions underlying the claims, particularly relating to subjectivity. Shimizu strives to criticize this immature acceptance of a naive equation of English with the West, and argues that English can no longer be seen as a Western-owned language, and politics and international relations must be prepared for negotiations with hitherto undreamt of grammatical transformations of English in order to become more multicultural and more literally an international discipline.

In Chapter 6, Toshinobu Nagamine takes up the MEXT's announcement of a new policy in 2009 to mandate that senior high school English teachers conduct all classes in English. He contends that there is no doubt that the new policy is adding to the pressure on both preservice and inservice teachers. The level of associated anxiety, in addition to the level of pressure, might vary among teachers, possibly due to differing language abilities, school settings, employment status, teaching beliefs, and/or the way teachers perceive realities. Nevertheless, dialog by which critical stakeholders (i.e. teachers) can engage with their questions and challenges is lacking in the current discourse regarding the development and enactment of the new policy. Therefore, a qualitative case study was designed and conducted to explore and investigate English teachers' perceptions of the new policy. The study revealed contextualization of realities and issues uniquely recognized and perceived by the participants (preservice and inservice EFL teachers). Some implications were proposed for policy-makers, administrators, and teacher educators to develop and implement language education policy successfully in Asian EFL contexts in general and Japanese EFL contexts in particular.

In Chapter 7, Mitsunori Takakuwa contends that in compulsory education in Japanese public schools, English education is the *de facto* foreign language education. However, the majority of Japanese people can live their daily lives without using English. Rather, there are slightly greater chances for them to use other foreign languages, given that Japanese society is becoming more diversified with "internal internationalization." This is especially the case with teachers at schools in which foreign children who do not have knowledge of the Japanese language are enrolled. In line with the diversification of Japanese society, more effective foreign language education should be implemented, in contrast to MEXT's current policy of bilingualism, through the teaching not only of English but also other foreign languages that Japanese people may have a chance to use in Japan, and this may lead Japan to become more multicultural.

Part III begins with Chapter 8, in which Rieko Karatani focuses on female overseas workers in Britain. She argues that regional regimes such as the EU and global regimes such as the UN superficially appear to offer hope for female overseas domestic workers (FODWs), yet are favorable only to a limited group of women who are willing to accept the current dominant "power geometry." As a result, the lives of FODWs, who often end up finding themselves at the bottom of the society of their host countries, are fixed and controlled by the two transnational regimes in addition to the nation-state. Thus, Karatani argues that the benefits of "global householding" in the developed countries are reaped at the expense of damage by "global de-householding" in the developing countries. In this sense, multicultural environments in the developed countries in fact become possible at the cost of stable lives in the developing world.

In Chapter 9, Maria Reinaruth D. Carlos takes up the issue of contemporary migration. She argues that the movement of Filipino nurses is profoundly affected by various factors in the host and intermediary countries, of which one of the most important factors is multiculturalism in the host countries as they consider and migrate to various locations in what she terms "stepwise migration." Carlos examines the state of multiculturalism in such host countries as Singapore, the UK, Ireland, Australia, and the US, and investigates the extent to which policies based on multiculturalism in these places influence the selection of the final destination by immigrants. She clarifies the difficulties of host countries in providing stable environments for immigrants, which is particularly important for countries facing a shortage of nurses and an aging society. She further analyzes attempts to deliver possible alternative policies for these new circumstances by paying specific attention to multiculturalism.

In Chapter 10, Shincha Park examines the issue of dual nationality in the Asia-Pacific region, with particular attention to South Korea. In an age of increasing interaction and migration, the issue of nationality is attracting more attention than ever. The issue of dual nationality has traditionally been regarded as a problem of and threat to national sovereignty, but his analysis reveals that recent policies in the region are based on rather different perceptions of dual nationality. In some cases, central governments, explicitly or implicitly, promote dual nationality. What purpose lies behind the policies? What are the consequences of the promotion of dual nationality policies? Who is benefiting from the promotion of dual nationality? By answering these questions, Park analyzes the different attitudes among countries in the region towards the issue of dual nationality, and strives to provide a way to achieve the communicative space in the international arena for migrants.

In Chapter 11, Julian Chapple introduces Japan's "*global jinzai*" (global human resources) policy enthusiastically put forward by MEXT. This is an attempt to promote changes in Japanese society to make it become more outward-looking. This is because stated goals, such as economic development and domestic growth, require Japan to interact on a greater scale internationally. However, the *global jinzai* policy is not free from the nationalistic orientation MEXT has been pursuing in the past 150 years. Sometimes more explicitly, other times less so, such an orientation currently resides in the core of this policy, and never fully commits to an opening towards cosmopolitan multiculturalism, instead favoring a clearly instrumental form. If Japanese society is to embrace multiculturalism, Chapple argues, *global jinzai* offers the potential for and possibilities of creating a required social and mental framework for cosmopolitan vision. However, in order to achieve this goal, it should be emphasized that the policy would need to foster global citizens who are empowered by a strong sense of social responsibility from an unbiased global perspective.

1.2 Concluding remarks

As noted at the beginning of this introduction, this volume covers a collection of diverse disciplines and research areas on multiculturalism in the Asia-Pacific. The research fields range from migration to language and politics. The research methodology also varies according to the discipline with which the contributors are familiar and their focus on more empirical or theoretical discussion. However, what permeates these diverse chapters is the firm conviction that dialog and negotiation are the key to providing a reconciliation process for the conflicts and confrontations resulting from co-mingling of those with various cultural and historical backgrounds. In order to provide a space in which the dialog and negotiation take place, mere tolerance towards other peoples with diverse cultures is not enough. Critical insight directed toward the concept of culture itself, which is often mistakenly assumed to be rigid and inflexible, is additionally required. It is questioning the assumption of stable cultural bases that enables us to propose what multiculturalism in the 21st century might mean not only to those who formulate migration and language policies, but also to those who reside in the Asia-Pacific region negotiating between conflict and coexistence in the circumstances of an increasingly globalizing world.

References

Abu-Lughod, L. (1991). Writing against culture. In R. G. Fox (Ed.), *Recapturing anthropology: Working in the present* (pp. 137–162). Santa Fé: School of American Research Press.
Acharya, A. & Buzan, B. (Eds) (2010). *Non-Western international relations theory: Perspectives on and beyond Asia.* London: Routledge.
Alagappa, M. (Ed.) (2004). *Civil society and political change in Asia: Expanding and contracting democratic space.* Stanford: Stanford University Press.
Arendt, H. (1973). *The origins of the totalitarianism.* San Diego: Harcourt.
Barber, B. R. (1996). *Jihad vs. McWorld.* New York: Ballantine Books.
Baumann, G. (1999). *The multicultural riddle: Rethinking national, ethnic, and religious identities.* New York: Routledge.
Baylis, J., Smith, S., & Owens, P. (Eds) (2011). *The globalization of world politics: An introduction to international relations* (5th edn). New York: Oxford University Press.
Brightman, R. (1995). Forget culture: Replacement, transcendence, re-lexification. *Cultural Anthropology* 10(4), 509–546.
Brown, W. (2006). *Regulating aversion: Tolerance in the age of identity and empire.* Princeton: Princeton University Press.
Brumann, C. (1999). Writing for culture: Why a successful concept should not be discarded. *Current Anthropology, 40,* Supplement, 1–27.
Chen, C. C. (2012). The Im/possibility of building indigenous theories in a hegemonic discipline: The case of Japanese international relations, *Asian Perspectives, 36,* 463–492.
Chernilo, D. (2006). Social theory's methodological nationalism: Myth and reality. *European Journal of Social Theory, 9*(1), 5–22.

Clifford, J. (1988). *The predicament of culture: Twentieth century ethnography, literature and art*. Cambridge: Harvard University Press.
Clifford, J. & Marcus, G. E. (1986). *Writing culture: The poetics and politics of ethnography*. Berkeley: University of California Press.
Cox, R. (1981). Social forces, states and world orders: Beyond international relations theory. *Millennium, 10*(2), 126–155.
Fukuyama, F. (1992). *The end of history and the last man*. London and New York: Penguin Books.
Gilroy, P. (2005). *Post-colonial melancholia*. New York: Columbia University Press.
Hamashita, T. (1994). Shuhenkarano Ajiashi [The Asian history from periphery]. In Y. Mizoguchi, T. Hamashita, N. Hiraish, & H. Miyazaki (Eds), *Shuhenkarano Rekishi* [The History from Periphery] (pp. 1–14). Tokyo: Tokyo University Press.
Huntington, S. (1993). Clash of civilizations. *Foreign Affairs, 72*(3), 22–49.
Jones, C. S. (2002). If not a clash, then what? Huntington, Nishida Kitaro and the politics of civilizations. *International Relations of Asia Pacific, 2*(2), 223–243.
Kymlicka, W. & He, B. (Eds) (2005). *Multiculturalism in Asia*. Oxford: Oxford University Press.
Lebow, R. N. (2008). *A cultural theory of international relations*. Cambridge: Cambridge University Press.
Mazlish, B. (2004). *Civilization and its contents*. Stanford: Stanford University Press.
Nye, J. (2004). *Soft power: The means to success in world politics*. New York: Public Affairs.
Patterson, T. C. (1997). *Inventing Western civilization*. New York: Monthly Review Press.
Pettman, R. (2004). *Reason, culture, religion: Metaphysics of world politics*. London: Palgrave.
Phillips, A. (2007). *Multiculturalism without culture*. Princeton: Princeton University Press.
Scruton, R. (2002). *The west and the rest: Globalization and terrorist threat*. Wilmington: ISI Books.
Shilliam, R. (2010). *International relations and non-Western thought: Imperialism, colonialism and investigations of global modernity*. London: Routledge.
Shimizu, K. (2011). Nishida Kitaro and Japan's interwar foreign policy: War involvement and culturalist political discourse. *International Relations of the Asia-Pacific, 11*(1), 157–183.
Walker, R. B. J. (1993). *Inside/Outside: International relations as political theory*. Cambridge: Cambridge University Press.
Wimmer, A. and Glick-Schiller, N. (2002). Methodological nationalism and beyond: Nation-state building, migration, and the social sciences. *Global Networks, 2*(4): 301–334.

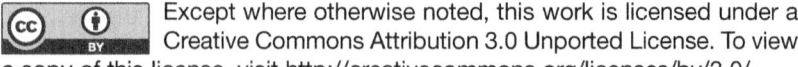 Except where otherwise noted, this work is licensed under a Creative Commons Attribution 3.0 Unported License. To view a copy of this license, visit http://creativecommons.org/licenses/by/3.0/

Part I
Theories and Identities

OPEN

2
Multicultural Coexistence in Japan: Follower, Innovator, or Reluctant Late Adopter?

William S. Bradley

2.1 Introduction

Despite the reasoned claims and detailed research of many social scientists that much of humanity lives in an increasingly multicultural world, the ever-present threat of a set of partitions between "us" and "them" transnationally (but also within countries), seems certain to linger for some years forward. While there is no final answer to the question, "Can't we all just get along?," so seemingly simplified by Rodney King in the aftermath of his beating by Los Angeles police in 1991 and subsequent riots (which led to the deaths of more than 50 people three months later in 1992, when those officers who had brutalized him were acquitted of crimes of excessive force (National Public Radio, 2008)), the incommensurability on multiple levels of such a plea still haunts the supposed naïve proposal of tolerance and respect for difference, let alone celebration of diversity, embedded in a normative liberal multiculturalism.

In this chapter, I discuss the development of multiculturalism in Japan against the background of global retrenchments over and to multiculturalism, visible as a fragile project. Such a project is set against a background of global events that can make theorizing about the future of tolerance and respect for difference appear to be embedded in a hopelessly optimistic utopian dream at any moment, when periodic renewed calls for retribution against the perpetrators of terror attacks, to name just one instantiation of a globalized political event that recurs in the contemporary post 9/11 world, unfolding at a rapid pace, highlighted by targeted drone strikes and invisible communications monitoring, and channeled by media spectacularization of cultural difference as the prominent causal agent of conflict.

The focus of this chapter is multiculturalism in Japan and Asia more generally. This is not because Japan is the best or most dynamic example of a multicultural society in Asia or even that there are relatively straightforward connections between other Asian countries and Japan directly linked to multiculturalism. At the conclusion of the chapter, I will briefly review a case that has been made that Japan, South Korea, and Taiwan share similar trajectories in multicultural policies and trends, despite rather distinct histories and resident groups of minorities. More specifically, however, in connection with the global future of multiculturalism as a vision of 21st century society, the case of Japan offers some corrective to the prominent mainstream discussions of multiculturalism which are taking place currently in Europe, North America, Australia, and New Zealand. Is Japan belatedly following immigration trends seen earlier in other places, or is there something new about Japan's contribution to multicultural policies and multicultural nation-building? Or is Japan simply a late adopter of policies, under duress of demographic pressures, which are increasingly under attack elsewhere?

In the first part of the chapter, I place the discussion of multiculturalism's end firmly as a hegemonic Eurocentric discourse. In the second part, I turn to a discussion of multiculturalism in Japan. Certainly this is an expansive topic, so I will simply point to some exemplary trends in Japanese society that suggest that multiculturalism is not moribund, if not exactly thriving, requiring a discussion of the need for many kinds of qualifications and criticisms: political, economic, and otherwise. In terms of sheer numbers, Japan cannot be considered particularly diverse by the standards of large immigrant countries such as Canada and Australia. Moreover, the diversity that does exist is masked in many ways by the presence of large minorities of phenotypically similar ethnicities, in particular Chinese and Koreans and indigenous peoples. I argue that the Japanese case provides a well-balanced, if tenuous, example by which to track the development of multicultural coexistence (in the Japanese phrase *tabunka kyōsei*) in a large economically advanced democratic society of the 21st century. This phrase for the understanding of Japanese multicultural society, more widely circulated in the aftermath of the Hanshin-Awaji earthquake of 1995 and the cooperation that developed between ethnic communities in Kobe (Okano & Tsuneyoshi, 2011; Takezawa, 2008), who came quickly to the understanding borne of necessity that mutual aid and cooperation would hasten their survival and recovery efforts, is not without its detractors and drawbacks, as I will note below. However, it offers an alternative view to where we, as a human community, find ourselves in the 21st century, learning to get along with each other in the world.[1] Japan's version of multiculturalism, I will argue, has something to suggest not about the end of multiculturalism, but a possible new direction for multicultural understanding or post-multicultural coexistence.

2.2 The end of multiculturalism

The idea of the end of multiculturalism has been much discussed in recent years, particularly in Europe, where dissatisfaction with the integration of Muslim minorities has led to a significant backlash against open-ended immigration and tolerance (Alexander, 2013).[2] Despite this generalized reaction to the negative aspects of 30–40 years of multicultural policies, there is little agreement as to what should come after it. As Kymlicka (2010, p. 97) puts it, "there is a surprising consensus that we are indeed in a post-multicultural era," with near uniform disdain for the reductionism of multiculturalism parodied as the "panoply of customs, traditions, music, and cuisine" (also known as the three Cs: customs, celebrations and cuisine, or the four Fs: folklore, food, fashion, and festivals). I give a further definition of multiculturalism below, but it is important to point out from the outset that there are numerous "multiculturalisms," from conservative to liberal to critical, with the versions parodied above by the pithy reduction to identifiable characteristic material aspects of foods and clothes serving as a shorthand for symbolic multiculti.[3]

Mishra (2012), writing about why what he calls the "crisis" of liberal multiculturalism signals that multiculturalism is a problem itself that needs to be continuously redefined, suggests that a key question is the incommensurability of the universality of rights clashing with the problems of what he and others refer to as the politics of redistribution. In other words, there is an inherent insolubility to the problem of recognition versus the political and economic policies that can be promoted to facilitate and enhance justice for minorities, especially newcomers who more often than not come to a society with little capital—economic or social. Either recognition is seen by the politicians, majorities, and ordinary citizens of a given community as sufficient in itself, in place of solving other pressing problems, or even worse, it leads to a backlash among the majority and other communities (including minorities themselves) who do not feel they gain (or in some cases fear that they will lose their own jobs and positions) from such a form of politics, tied as it often is to demands for equal opportunities.

Within four months of each other at the end of 2010 and the beginning of 2011, the prime ministers and president of Europe's three most powerful countries declared multiculturalism a failure. Angela Merkel stated that multiculturalism in Germany had "failed utterly," David Cameron argued that in Britain "the doctrine of state multiculturalism" had failed to give "a vision of society," and Nikolas Sarkozy said that France had been "too concerned with the identity of the person arriving and not enough with the identity of the country receiving" them. Multiculturalism as a state policy (or set of policies) has been judged by many, including these conservative leaders, as a finished affair, and the time was ripe for new ways to deal with minorities, who are, it is argued, not cooperative enough in adjusting to the society in which they seek to live, either temporarily or for the long term. Such blaming of the "other" for not fitting in has a long trajectory in conservative European politics, intersecting with and growing out of seminal mediated "events" such as the Danish cartoon crisis of 2005 and *l'affaire du foulard*: bans on schoolgirls wearing head scarves in France and other countries.[4]

Multiculturalism has been increasingly attacked by liberal and radical critics as well (Kundnani, 2012; Murphy, 2012). It goes without saying that a comprehensive term such as multiculturalism has been easily critiqued from all corners as it can serve as a proxy for whatever is ailing 21st century societies and causing lack of solidarity among citizens who find themselves less and less able to appeal to so-called common identifiable values. Kivisto (2012, p. 853) writes of the claims of conservative multiculturalism critics, "that diversity inevitably undermines a more universalistic form of solidarity—that the solidarities of particular groups impede or undermine national solidarity." This implies a zero sum game in which people must choose one or the other identity (the particular or the national/cosmopolitan/universal), not both, and that there cannot be a collective identity that embraces both. But in order to examine this question we first need a working definition of multiculturalism.

2.3 Defining multiculturalism

While there are many versions of multiculturalism, from liberal to critical,[5] a prime distinction needs to be made between multiculturalism as philosophy and policy (Murphy, 2012, p. 4). Reducing philosophies to more concrete foci, Murphy (2012, p. 62) lists the following seven types of multicultural arguments: (1) liberal multiculturalism; (2) tolerationist multiculturalism; (3) the value of cultural diversity; (4) the politics of inclusion; (5) deliberative multiculturalism; (6) democratic multiculturalism; and

(7) the politics of recognition. Many of these nuanced differences revolve around the "classic" liberal question of freedom versus the prevention of harm and address central political questions such as equality, accommodation of minorities, and social cohesion (Murphy, 2012, pp. 7–9). A critique of this type of distinction could be made that that the particular policy framework and the philosophy on which it is based are not always identifiable in a singular fashion. In other words, policies can be derived from many sources, problems, ideals, and everything between.

Perhaps a single definition is impossible, but Vertovec (2010) lists the many areas of "institutional objectives" that have come to define multicultural policies. These included providing opportunities for group representation to local and national government authorities; restructuring institutions towards pluralistic public service provision; putting in place measures to promote equality, respect, or tolerance, particularly among the dominant population towards minorities; and providing resources to support continuity of traditions and identities among immigrant groups (as opposed to assimilation) (Vertovec, 2010, p. 84).

Another distinction is made by Kymlicka (2010), who argues that three patterns related to multiculturalism have emerged in Western democracies: (1) new forms of empowerment for indigenous peoples; (2) new forms of autonomy for sub-state national groups; and (3) new forms of citizenship for immigrants. One repeated question is whether these groups with different histories, different aspirations for belonging to the mainstream society, and different motivations for seeking recognition should be considered together by policy makers or separately. For example, some authors argue that the inclusion of "voluntary" immigrants with other groups involves diluting the focus of multiculturalism (Joppke, 2004), leading to hostility and disorder. The rights and benefits in many societies obtained by indigenous and sub-state national groups have been much greater than those of immigrants, partly due to recognition of their "blood sacrifice" in the face of the historical hegemony of the dominant national group, as well as international recognition received from the United Nations (UN) and other organizations (Mishra, 2012, pp. 53–54). With regard to Japan, indigenous groups have applicability as a category (Zainichi Koreans,[6] Ainu, and Okinawans) as do immigrants.

Critiques of multiculturalism have often asserted contradictions through conflations in theorizing about who and what is multicultural. Modood (2007, p. 119) points out five levels of what he refers to as "multi family resemblances." Differences that affect specific policies in specific spatial domains (place and time) are: (1) differences between groups (as alluded to above); (2) labeling based on different types of attributes (such as race or religion); (3) groups not acting the same; (4) groups having different priorities; and (5) individuals within groups differing.

Another key argument used against multiculturalism is to look for the most extreme case of minorities' failure to integrate or even criminal misbehavior and suggest that it is sanctioned by multiculturalism itself in its emphasis on freedom based on cultural rights, in effect conflating ideas advocated by some multicultural theories of epistemological anti-foundationalism with radical relativism, which is advocated by relatively few (Murphy, 2012, p. 24).

Despite the negative reception for multiculturalism recently in academic and popular discourses, there is an irony in the widespread success of multicultural policies (Kymlicka, 2010; Modood, 2012; Vertovec, 2010). Thus, even as the leaders and mainstream media of many countries deem multicultural policies a failure, the policies, plans, implementation, and acceptance of multiculturalism in everyday life continues more or less as it did at its high point in the 1990s.

In a different way, multiculturalism has been boosted by the simple fact of increased levels of diversity in many countries that have accepted immigrants. Not only is immigration increasing,[7] but the types of immigration and routes are changing, and there is more frequent and short-term movement, instead of permanent migration. In addition, families with multiple ethnicities, and individuals with multiple and hyphenated identities, are also increasing. Vertovec (2010) has proposed the term "super-diversity" to describe these developments.

The best that one can conclude at the current juncture about multiculturalism is to suggest that it is in a crisis moment. This is inherent in recent analysis, using terminology such as "panicked multiculturalism" (Noble, 2013) and "ambivalent multiculturalism" (Bygnes, 2012). While the immigrant countries of Western Europe and North America (as well as Australia and New Zealand) seek to contain their overdone stresses to the social fabric and resultant distress over policies that were beneficial to their economies at one time, but now require more attention (both economic and political), it is not surprising that interest in diversity, migration, and multiculturalism would have spread to new places. In the next section, I turn to a discussion of Japanese multiculturalism.

2.4 Japan as an exemplar

Japan's history of accepting immigrants is a long and varied one.[8] As Oguma (2002) has shown in his well-cited study of the flexibility of inclusivity of "Japanese-ness", which extended to Taiwanese and Korean peoples in the Japanese colonial period, a much more porous image of what was a "Japanese" was prevalent than the one that has dominated in contemporary Japan as "one nation, one civilization, one language, one culture and one race" (*Japan Times*, 2005) until recently.[9] Similar research by Morris-Suzuki (1997, 2006) and others shows the deep interconnections with and movements of peoples between the Korean peninsula and Japan both over historically long periods of time and in the modern era in the periods before and after the Second World War. In particular, much of the assumption of a period of little or no immigration during the 35 years after the Second World War (until roughly 1980) can be challenged as masking what she calls the "invisibility" of illegal immigration, along with the growing institutional architecture of detention facilities and courts for deportation (Morris-Suzuki, 2006).

The rise of *tabunka shugi* (multiculturalism) or *tabunka kyōsei shakai* (multicultural existence society)[10] can be said to have commenced in the 1990s as the total number of foreign residents topped one million.[11] This is not to suggest that activism over the human rights of foreign residents (Koreans in particular) in Japan had not existed before this period,[12] but that a level of consciousness in the wider society was attained following the pattern of increased numbers and increased diversity among minorities (including foreigners) in Japan in the 1990s. Several years after this, in approximately 1995, the number of Japanese residents of Korean nationality dropped for the first time since the end of the war to less than half of the total foreign resident population (Tsuneyoshi, 2011, p. 128), and has continued to descend to its current total of 530,048, or 26.1% of the total number of foreign residents as of 2012, falling behind the number of Chinese, who have occupied the top position of total numbers of residents in Japan (by nationality) since 2007. This is explained by a continuous rate of naturalization of long-term Korean residents since the mid-1980s, when Japanese law was changed (roughly 10,000 per year), as well as the increasing numbers of new immigrants from China (and elsewhere). For the past four years the overall number of foreign residents has been decreasing to a total in 2012 of 2,033,658, approximately 1.7% of the total population in Japan.[13] Much of this decline can be attributed to that of a single nationality, Brazilians (the third highest national group until 2012, when Filipinos surpassed Brazilians for the first time), many of whom lost employment opportunities in the economic downturn since 2008, while other groups (with the small continuous decline in Korean numbers as noted above) have either declined or risen only slightly. The number of Chinese residents continued to rise even after

2008, reaching a high or 678,391 in 2010, but then declined slightly in the subsequent two years. The number of Filipino residents, as of 2012 registering 202,974, third after Koreans, has risen every year (except 2004) until 2012, when there was a small decrease. The number of Vietnamese has also risen almost every year and even further in 2012 to attain the position of the fifth highest at a total of 52,364. Of the top 11 foreign resident nationalities, eight of them are Asian (the exceptions being Brazil, Peru at number six, and the USA at number seven).

From this brief and necessarily cursory statistical overview, one can state two things. First the range and degree of diversity has been increasing steadily, illustrating, albeit on a somewhat limited scale, the proposition of superdiversity noted above. Notwithstanding the drops in overall numbers, the countries involved each have different patterns of increases and drops that correspond to historical, economic, and social issues that affect ethnic groups differently. This is even more apparent when the rates of different prefectures are examined, a discussion which I will bracket due to space limitations. However, the pattern of immigration throughout Japan shows a great deal of variation, with the percentage of Chinese immigrants largest in Tokyo, Koreans largest in Osaka, and Brazilians largest in Aichi. Second, the use of numbers of immigrants statistics is deceptive in that if one considers only these numbers, much of the growing diversity in Japan in the past two decades will be overlooked. There are, for example, sizeable populations of indigenous minorities, Okinawans and Ainu, as well as increasing numbers of individuals who have two ethnicities—for example mixed Japanese heritage or hyphenated Japanese.[14]

While it is also true that some have argued that, phenotypically, the majority of non-Japanese in Japan (also including the indigenous minority populations) closely resemble Japanese and are often indistinguishable, there is surely an increase in the awareness of Japan as a multicultural society. Important edited volumes in English on multiculturalism in Japan have been published in succession in recent years (Graburn, Ertl, & Tierney, 2008; Tsuneyoshi, 2011; Willis & Murphy-Shigematsu, 2008; the latter calling its field transnationalism as opposed to multiculturalism), each utilizing a wide range of case studies to make the case for an increase in multiculturalism as an indisputable reality, while reaching varying conclusions about its greater acceptance. Certainly there will be a great divergence in this acceptance across Japan, as variation will exist with almost no sign of diversity in many rural prefectures (but see below for a counter example), and much higher diversity in some urbanized areas (up to 20% minority populations in some parts of Shinjuku Ward in Tokyo). This has led at least one critic to maintain that the positive recognition and conceptualization of multiculturalism as a "new" reality, albeit based on a policy discourse regime that has roots in government initiatives, is a reaction by (mostly) foreign scholars to the persistent discourses of *Nihonjinron* in the 1980s and later into the 1990s (Burgess, 2007).[15] Many other critics have agreed that at the national policy level there is little in the way of aggressive support or legislation for multicultural society,[16] while at the local level there exists, in some places, a growing movement for expansion of rights and inclusion of minorities and a concomitant flow of policy influence from the local to the national (Flowers, 2012; Green, 2013; Lovell, 2010; Nakamatsu, 2013). I discuss these trends at greater length below.

Other edited publications in Japanese have also been published recently foregrounding the concept of *tabunka kyōsei* (Fujimaki, 2012; Kagami, 2013; Satake, 2011), documenting the diversity that exists primarily in prefectures in urban areas with the largest concentrations of non-Japanese (in absolute numbers and percentage of the total of foreign residents, the order is Tokyo, Osaka, Aichi, Kanagawa, Saitama, Chiba, Hyogo, and Shizuoka, each with large cities except for Shizuoka, which does not have a city larger than one million people).[17] Earlier publications had used the term *tabunka shakai* (Ishii & Yamauchi, 1999; Komai, 2003). Whether there is now a consistent agreement in the past decade on the preferential use of *tabunka kyōsei* is beyond the scope of analysis here. However, Graburn and Ertl (2008, p. 8), point out, as have others, that the concept of *kyōsei*, or coexistence, tends to allow differences to remain as unsettled and not melded.[18] In researching this topic, clearly there are valuable studies on many individual minority groups, relating their struggles for recognition and equal rights to the theme of a multicultural Japan, which due to space limitations I will not review. In analyzing the problem of multiculturalism from a holistic and comparative perspective, there is a danger that the important details that separate different groups are left unstated and underanalyzed. Multiculturalism, through its terminology, draws analysis away from the specific to the general and categorical. To cite just two compelling recent studies, Cotterill (2011) writing about the Ainu[19] notes a government survey of 23,782 self-acknowledged Ainu in Hokkaido. However, the actual numbers are far greater, with many having intermarried with other Japanese, many living in metropolitan areas such as Tokyo, and a large number becoming more interested in reclaiming some part of their long submerged identity, but not necessarily "coming out" to their neighbors, and even in some cases family members. In a similar manner, Hankins (2012) in doing research on Buraku[20] minorities, suggests a new interest in "authenticity" of identity. One of the strategies used is the display of suffering, which exists in a dialectic fashion, i.e. by displaying marginalization, one has more authentically "suffered" discrimination, which serves to increase pride in self-identification for those who are part of the group, but also among affirming groups in Japanese society such as progressives, social activists, and others who take interest in multiculturalism.

However, persistent doubts remain about the extent to which Japan can be considered multicultural in any recognizable sense at all, and similar to other countries, mediatized events can produce understandings that conflict harshly with the idea of Japan as multicultural. Perhaps it is not surprising given the aforementioned politicians' comments on Japan as one nation that the perception exists among some internationally of Japan as a "monoethnic" enclave. After Norwegian far-right extremist Anders Breivik was arrested for killing 77 people in Norway in July 2011, his manifesto of more than 1,500 pages, which he had uploaded to the Internet shortly before he carried out his massacre, was examined, and numerous references praising both Japan and South Korea as "monocultural" and for having rejected or avoided multiculturalism were discovered (Japan Probe, 2011; Reuters, 2011).[21]

On a more serious level are critiques such as Kashiwazaki's analysis that immigrants are incorporated into Japan first and foremost as "foreigners," and not as "ethnic minorities," or "hyphenated Japanese" (2013, p. 32). Given the movement towards greater recognition of Japanese national minorities noted above, albeit incremental and still in the face of hardships and discrimination, a question that is inevitable is whether, as in Kymlicka's inclusive definition above, progressive thinking about multiculturalism benefits from more generalized inclusion of all minorities (including, but not limited to, sexual minorities, victims of environmental disasters, atomic bomb victims, and people with disabilities) as opposed to strategic focus that may allow for some coalitions, but not one that includes everyone on all issues. It is clear, whichever way this question is answered (and it is unlikely that a single answer will be appropriate for every context; in other words, multiple types of coalitions between minorities are likely to emerge in different regions and over different issues), the observation of Htun (2012, p. 19) that focus on "diversity and agency within minority groups" means less demand and interest for displays of suffering. The younger members of minority groups, especially, in contrast to previous generations, feel more entitled to be open about their identity both as minorities and as members of a Japanese society moving towards the future, not dwelling on past injustices.

At the same time, however, discussion of the lived reality of multicultural consciousness in Japan reveals problematic lacunae that require critical attention. First, what is the understanding that the mass of average Japanese citizens have about Japanese society being multicultural? Numerous scholars have suggested that even if a plurality of Japanese citizens accept Japan as multicultural, there is still little understanding or acceptance of diversity beyond a division between Japanese and foreigners, leading to models of "coexistence" (read as assimilation) in the simplest form, between the "Japanese" and the "others" (Graburn & Ertl, 2008, p. 4; Ishiwata, 2011; Kashiwazaki, 2013; Nagayoshi, 2011; Nagy, 2012; Okano & Tsuneyoshi, 2011, p. 2; Yamamoto, 2012), sometimes as a homogenous group of non-Japanese and sometimes as their own ethnic group. In other words, the acceptance of a multicultural Japan (i.e. a Japan with a small percentage of resident foreigners), entails a reinforcement of the uniform identity of Japanese-ness, which in turn serves to exclude foreigners and other minorities as (not more than) residents, and not as part of a project for a dynamic and changing multicultural Japanese identity and society of the 21st century.

In an example of empirical work to investigate such a claim, Nagayoshi conducted research utilizing public opinion polls and verified that acceptance of a Japanese homogeneity coincides with support for "endorsement of multiculturalism." This positive affirmation of diversity, however, is coupled with the conclusion that "Japanese people regard minorities as just 'exceptions' within a culturally homogenous society" (2011, p. 574). The question remains, however, what people think they are endorsing when they conceptualize multiculturalism, operationalized here as government assistance to minorities to "preserve their customs and traditions." Some critics argue pessimistically that this leads to a vision of Japanese society that Morris-Suzuki (2002, cited in Nakamatsu, 2013, p. 3) has termed "cosmetic multiculturalism," a discourse that "allows expression of cultural diversity only under strict conditions ... mak[ing] no demands for changes in the existing structure." Or to follow this binary logic to its concluding point, "the positioning of the 'other' is always in relation to and as a means of further discovering what is Japanese" (Yamamoto, 2012, p. 437). Such arguments recall the problem raised by Mishra, at the outset in this chapter, that multiculturalism was (and is) always a problem in need of redefinition. "'Multiculturalism' as theory comes as a challenge to an earlier definition of it as an empirical fact," in short "cultures were part of the nation, without the nation itself sensing the need to theorize itself in terms of multiplicity of cultures" (Mishra, 2012, p. 23). The degree that this challenge to a prior *status quo* is now taking place in Japan then is open for debate.

Nonetheless, such a critique may underestimate the potential for change in consciousness that is occurring among the majority of Japanese, particularly young people, not only in their recognition of documentation and representations of otherness in Japan, but in relation to issues of education, political representation, and discriminatory practices (elaborated on below). Each of these offers only a starting point for discussion and can be framed as much as problems as they are hopes for the future. A point that is made clear, however, is that they are problems that are mostly dealt with on the local level.

There has been quite a lot of forward movement regarding local policy initiatives connected to multiculturalism in Japan, though not all of it is readily visible to the ordinary citizen. One reason is that the diversity in Japan is localized in some areas and relatively invisible (or much less) in other places, mostly (but not only) rural regions. However, from the central government's side, the 2006 Ministry of Internal Affairs and Communications (MIC) report, "Research Group concerning the Promotion of Multicultural Coexistence," also triggered discussion about implementation at the local society level (*chīki shakai*). A number of researchers have looked at the effect of this national governmental policy on local policies. Shortly after the national policy report was produced, a letter was sent to local authorities asking them to investigate "guidelines and plans for the promotion of multicultural coexistence in keeping with the circumstances of their respective regions" (MIC letter cited in Aiden, 2011, p. 215). Thereafter (and shortly beforehand in some cases) a number of prefectures, cities, and wards made such plans (for example, Shinjuku Ward in 2005, Kawasaki City in 2005, Hiroshima City in 2006, and many more; see also Nagy, 2012). The original policy document from the central government divided the type of help that could be provided into four areas: (1) communication (language); (2) lifestyle (housing and employment); (3) coexistence systems in local communities (exchange and organizations); and (4) a more general coexistence promotion system (linkages with business, government and other agencies).

Nagy (2012, p. 5) has described this system critically as a "social integration system," an attempt to fill in "gaps" rather than fostering respect for diversity, promotion of cultural pride, or encouraging steps towards citizenship. Aiden's (2011) analysis of 22 local "multicultural coexistence plans" (MCPs) on the other hand is slightly more optimistic, citing the effect of the MIC document on local governments, urging them to utilize cooperation with NGOs, NPOs, and International Exchange Associations to further the goals of multicultural policies. Lovell's (2010) research on Nagata Ward (with an estimated 10% minority population) in Kobe argues that, indeed, the use of policy drivers (*kokusaika* or internationalization, and *tabunka kyōsei*) has been important in moving the discussion forward and creating policy documentation to address the varying needs of oldcomer and newcomer minority populations. But other research suggests that both local staff and NGO workers have relatively low impressions of *tabunka kyōsei* policies and their implementation from the top down (Nakamatsu, 2013). They questioned both the lack of ideological support and detailed concrete measures. "The government's sudden adoption of a multicultural framework and of the categorization of their work as part of this official discourse" was deemed opportunistic and not an attempt to "bring about cultural, social and political equality," exemplified by the unfamiliar naming involved in the term *kyōsei* coupled with the more understandable *tabunka* (Nakamatsu, 2013, p. 11).

Case studies of local area implementation fill in some of the gaps in understanding what may (or may not) be taking place with regard to action at the local level in various locations in Japan. Flowers' (2012) study of Shinjuku Ward, in particular the town of Ōkubo, which contains up to 20% of non-Japanese residents (many of them Korean) and has been renamed an "ethnic town" by the local government, illustrates both the active aspects of multicultural policy making on the ground and the risks that are concomitant. She describes Ethnic Town Ōkubo as "an entertainment destination" for the consumption of culture, e.g. food and other ethnic goods.

While urban areas are rightly the predominant focus of multicultural activities, in Japan, as elsewhere, the rising number of foreign female spouses in rural areas due to the inability of farming household males to be able to find marriageable Japanese women as partners has led to *tabunka kyōsei* centers and support services in prefectures such as Yamagata. In addition to language education, the centers provide various information about health services, employment, and visas, and serve as spaces for socialization for the women, many from the Philippines, China, and other Asian countries (Kwak, 2009).

2.5 Three areas of contestation

While there are many other areas worth mentioning in regard to multiculturalism and multicultural policy in Japan, including the connection between integration and employment (Kibe, 2011), immigration reform (Yamamoto, 2012), the relatively "extensive usage" of the term "foreigner" as opposed to other terms such as "citizen," "immigrant," "ethnic," or "minority," with the implication of there being impoverished models of citizenship opportunity structures (Kashiwazaki, 2013), I turn in this section to three critical areas of implementation and contestation that will have strong effects on the long-term success (or lack thereof) of multiculturalism in Japan. These are (1) education; (2) local political participation; and (3) anti-discrimination legal frameworks.

Education and multiculturalism is a well-researched topic and many frameworks for understanding different and varied developments have been advanced. If one includes the pioneering efforts in both Korean and Burakumin communities to promote education for human rights, multicultural education can be considered to have a long history in Japan. Tai (2007) documents the many nuances of Korean ethnic education connected to civil rights, particularly in Osaka City, home to the largest number of Koreans in Japan. Koreans' campaign for ethnic classes (which include language, music, history, and other topics) in mainstream schools was partly inspired by the notions of "liberation education" that had been developed previously by Buraku activists (Tai, 2007, p. 8). While placing great emphasis on human rights and the struggles that have achieved them to date, such education is also somewhat limited by its separation into the majority/minority communities (Tsuneyoshi, 2011; see also Okano, 2006).

In contrast, a framework of internationalization for education is used for newcomer education (as well as Japanese returnees from abroad). Much of this education focuses on Japanese language learning. In public schools there is no special budget for teachers who can teach in students' native languages. Research on Brazilian and Peruvian schoolchildren (many Nikkei[22] and some with mixed ethnicity) shows some of the problems of education in a multicultural Japan. Moorehead's (2013) examination of the "Amigos Room" at an elementary school in central Japan shows that teachers are sometimes unenthusiastic (they are not specialized, but chosen to staff the room in rotation) and the room is not well supplied and serves not as a place for supplementary Japanese language instruction so much as a space for students to overcome their feelings of isolation by being with immigrants like themselves.

Next, I turn to local political participation. Kawasaki City in Kanagawa Prefecture became the first city in Japan to establish an assembly for foreign residents in 1996. This was followed by other cities: Tokyo (1997), Kyoto (1998), Mitaka (1999), Atsugi (2002) and others (Green, 2013). Kawasaki also became the first city in Japan to abolish the requirement of Japanese citizenship to work for the municipal government. In 2009, Kawasaki passed a resolution to allow foreign residents to vote in local elections and referenda. Both Kwak (2009) and Green (2013) make a strong case for the effect that local policy initiatives have made on the larger national policy perspective. "The significance of the foreigners' assembly may be trivialized because of a lack of political power. In reality, however, the activities of the assembly have a meaningful influence on decision making through propositions" (Kwak, 2009, p. 173). Even in the absence of central government leadership, cities like Kawasaki "found it in their interest to try and incorporate their immigrant populations into the decision making process. What began as a means of dialogue with foreign residents in Kawasaki gradually spread throughout the country, eventually turning into codified local voting rights for a variety of cities" (Green, 2013).

Finally, regarding anti-discrimination and legal frameworks, numerous authors have pointed out the lack of such protections in Japan. In 2006, the United Nations Commission on Human Rights Special Rapporteur on Contemporary Forms of Racism, Racial Discrimination, Xenophobia and Related Intolerance filed a report on his Mission to Japan in which he criticized discrimination of both a social-economic and political nature. He also "note[d] with concern that there is no national legislation that outlaws racial discrimination and provides a judicial remedy for the victims" (Diène, 2006). This report was followed up in 2010 by another, the United Nations Commission on Human Rights Special Report of the Special Rapporteur on the Human Rights of Migrants (Bustamante, 2010), reiterating the lack of legislation to "address the persistence of racial discrimination," especially as related to migrants and their difficulties in securing education. Most notable as well was the declaration that there was an "overall lack of a comprehensive immigration policy that respects the human rights of migrants and ensures their integration into the Japanese society." This illustrates the distance that is still necessary to be traversed toward ensuring durable structures that will protect foreign residents not only in good situations but bad situations as well. Space precludes lengthy discussion of examples of recent discriminatory acts directed at minorities, but hate speech directed at Korean schools has been slowly increasing (Japan Times, 2013). A recent court ruling declared that such rallies were not protected by constitutional free speech statutes. Whether the ruling will lead to parliamentary action is not clear, but such changes in the law outlawing discrimination could certainly do much to address some of the concerns of the UN reports cited above.

On reviewing these three areas of contestation, the conclusion is that there are both positive and negative evaluations of the sustained commitment to multiculturalism by the national government and down to local levels. As with the previous discussion, which showed that movement in local areas is at the moment more expeditious than in national policy areas, these three foci—education, political participation, and anti-discrimination legislation—show the most dynamism at the local level (particularly with the case of political participation). However, here too the story is mixed, since educational opportunities are also quite variable depending on the locality.

2.6 East Asian multicultural societies

Comparative work done to assess the level of multicultural policy making across national contexts in Asia has shown that Japan has some affinities with other East Asian countries, South Korea and Taiwan in particular. Both Nagy (2013) and Kim and Oh (2011) found commonalities across these three countries, with low fertility rates, increasing but selective immigration, and "passive multiculturalism" policies. In contrast to the low evaluation for educational policies and anti-discrimination legislation, Kim and Oh argue that the mass media representations of foreignness vary between assimilationist and some activism in all three countries (2011, p. 1575). Watson (2012, p. 99) states about South Korean multiculturalism, similar to the critiques regarding homogeneity in Japan above, that the core identity of Korean society is maintained along ethnic lines, with foreigners simultaneously excluded, but representing the diversity of global progress: a "global Korea," as such.

A more nuanced discussion of the convergences as well as divergences of ethnic immigrants (Korea accepting Chinese and Korean-Chinese, while Taiwan accepted larger numbers of Indonesians, Vietnamese and Thais) would suggest that regional effects of multicultural policy making are not insignificant. However, it is clear that multicultural policies in East Asia should be examined further in the near future with respect to regional policy comparative analysis to break down the obsession with borders that hinders the development of more dynamic multicultural models.

Miller (2011, p. 808) has written that the "gradations of inclusion and exclusion are far more subtle and varied in Asia" and "the boundaries between formal and informal rights are often blurred" based on less legalistic conceptions. He and Kymlicka (2005, p. 2) wrote about Asian multiculturalism that "appeals to international human rights instruments and Western policies of multiculturalism are interspersed with appeals to local traditions, national mythologies, regional practices, and religious practices." Each of these dimensions would benefit from more research, but it is certainly true that just as provincialized as Asia is in this statement, so too is the backlash of multiculturalism now visible in the so-called West: fierce in certain European contexts, while not so apparent in others, like North America. Whether it is really Western multiculturalism or Japanese *tabunka kyōsei* that is being appealed to, the point remains that the universality of human rights and the local, regional, and national issues that affect their acceptance and valorization are contentious, no matter the context. Learning from those who have made some contributions to creating communities that broaden participation to those beyond only the majority in any context is useful for application in other contexts. In any case, it can be argued, in the case of these three East Asian countries, that there is significant overlap in societal diversification, and while there is no universality of multicultural policy, there is at least a set of commonalities. At the same time we can note, as above, that much of the leeway that has been afforded with regard to local policy making has taken place in the absence of robust policy making at the national level.

2.7 Conclusion

Do the cases presented by East Asian countries, Japan in particular, as have been examined here, lead us to be more optimistic about the possibility of multiculturalism first of all here in Japan and Asia, but also in relation to the rest of the world? Probably that depends on what work one expects to be done in the name of multicultural policy and to what degree multiculturalism can be removed from limitations of its idealistic liberal usage and reduction to tolerance of diversity. Tolerance is no doubt a quality with much to offer, but it does little to solve the problems of mutual understanding and cooperation that are necessary in communities in many places in Japan. More attention to the dimensions of education, political participation and representation, and anti-discrimination frameworks and laws are necessary to improve the basic conditions of a society for and of *tabunka kyōsei*. This chapter offers no final answer to the question of whether Japan is leading the way forward or struggling on its own terms. If anything, I would argue that is doing both, and that Japan, never having been definitively multicultural, can possibly offer a vision of the post-multicultural, but only by squarely facing the problems that it is confronting from increased diversity in localized pockets across Japan.

Notes

1. I acknowledge that recourse to a "common" humanity is always problematic, especially from the perspective of epistemology and that here it is necessary to acknowledge one's own privilege and position. Mine, in this case, is as a Caucasian North American who holds a tenured position in a Japanese university. My view of humanity and its struggles is no doubt different from those who have suffered multiple and repeated instances of discrimination, to problematize the standpoint in just one way.
2. The contents of the following two sections are derived in part and rewritten from a longer version of the argument I have made elsewhere (Bradley, 2013). See Alexander (2013) for extended examples of the attacks made on multiculturalism by both politicians and academics in Europe in the past decade.
3. Also spelled multikulti, the term was popularized especially in Germany and was referenced in Angela Merkel's 2010 speech regarding the failure of multicultural integrationist policies in Germany. It has been used in English to imply a sarcastic stance towards multicultural policies and events.
4. In France, wearing headscarves resulted in the school expulsions of three girls in 1989 and 23 girls in 1996.
5. According to May and Sleeter (2010, p. 3), critical multiculturalism differs from the liberal varieties by systematically accounting for "structural inequalities, such as racism, institutionalized poverty and discrimination" in contrast to emphasizing liberal multiculturalism's "politically muted discourses" of "culture and cultural recognition."
6. Zainichi refers to "residents," and has been used often for "oldcomer" Koreans (but also some Chinese and others) whose families have been in Japan for three to five (or even six) generations.
7. Modood (2012, p. 19) estimates that in most of the largest cities in northwest Europe the population is 20–35 percent non-European; many cities in North America have large percentages of immigrant populations, with Toronto and Miami, for example, both around or exceeding 50%.
8. The terminology of "oldcomers," consisting mostly of Koreans, and "newcomers," consisting of many other nationalities, is not uniform. I use "foreign resident" and "immigrant" interchangeably in this chapter, using the former to emphasize long-term status (particularly of Koreans, many of whom are long-term residents and non-citizens in Japan) and the latter to emphasize the evolving and changing nature of many foreigners' stays in Japan from temporary to settled and finally permanent.
9. This quote is attributed to former Prime Minister Aso Taro, at a time when he served as Minister of Internal Affairs in Prime Minister Junichiro Koizumi's cabinet and gave a speech at the opening of the Kyushu National Museum in Daizufu, Fukuoka. This is but one of a series of similar comments in the last several decades by cabinet ministers regarding the homogeneity of Japanese ethnicity.
10. I discuss these terms at length below.

Multicultural Coexistence in Japan 39

11. Statistics in this section are derived from the Japanese Ministry of Justice homepage statistics; Ministry of Justice 2013 and previous years).
12. A notable example was the decade long resistance against fingerprinting begun in 1980 and ended in 1991. For some of the history of Korean human rights movements, especially in relation to Korean ethnic education, see Okano (2006) and Tai (2007).
13. An exact percentage is hard to derive, given the discrepancies in counting who is foreign or not. See also footnote 8.
14. Japanese law does not allow dual citizenship, so there are many Japanese (exact numbers unknown) who might be considered as having multicultural backgrounds due to a parent of non-Japanese nationality. The term *haafu* is sometimes used for such individuals, but is controversial for several reasons. First, it is used mostly for those of half European and half Japanese ethnicity, and second because some suggest that it implies a less than whole identity.
15. *Nihonjinron* are theories of Japan and Japaneseness and have been critiqued by many for their cultural exclusivity.
16. This claim is sometimes made, policy documents notwithstanding, such as the 2006 Ministry of Internal Affairs and Communications (MIC) report, "Research Group concerning the Promotion of Multicultural Coexistence," detailed below.
17. Shizuoka has large concentrations of Brazilians who emigrated to jobs in the auto industries and factories in smaller cities such as Hamamatsu; the only city of more than a million residents in a prefecture not in this list is Sapporo in Hokkaido (Ministry of Justice, 2013). See also Hirasawa (2009).
18. The term *tabunka kyōsei* is widely attributed to origins in discussions of biological phenomena in phrases like *shizen to kyōsei*: coexistence with the environment. According to Lovell (2010, p. 5) some have translated it as "multicultural symbiosis" or "symbiotic multiculturalism," maintaining the biological roots. He also writes of the phrase *tomo ni ikiru* (living together) which was used from 1965 onwards by the Japanese government in commitments to improving civil rights for resident Koreans. Chapman (2006, pp. 98–99) also describes the use of *tabunka kyōsei* for disparate groups such as children with disabilities and to address gender inequities. According to Hirasawa (2009, p. 165) the term *tabunka kyōsei* was used by a policy document in Kawasaki City in 1993 for the first time. Nakamatsu (2013, p. 5) also cites 1993 as the first newspaper mention but in relation to development education. Some have argued that *tabunka shakai* is a more sociological and inclusive term.
19. Ainu people, whose origin was in northern Japan and Hokkaido, were acknowledged as an indigenous people by the Japanese government in 2008 (unlike Okinawans who have not been formally recognized). They have also used the name *Utari* to refer to themselves.
20. Buraku, or more formally Hisabetsu Burakumin (people of the hamlet subject to discrimination; a discrimination based on ancestry, dating from the Edo Period, 1603–1868, in which a caste system was prevalent in Japan, which is now illegal) are non-identifiable by names or physical characteristics. They number from 2 to 3 million, and similar to the previous discussion of Ainu, it is difficult to arrive at an exact figure due to stigma of self-identification and intermarriage. However in recent years, a number of well-known politicians and public figures have made their Buraku background open.

21. In preparing this chapter, I was able to find Breivik's manifesto online. I deliberately chose not to cite it, so as not to give further publicity to a racist polemic. However, it is instructive in that he clearly believes that the East Asian countries (Japan, South Korea, and Taiwan) have achieved their successes through maintaining traditional societal patterns of monoethnicity and patriarchal relations.
22. Nikkei refer to people with Japanese ethnic heritage who have settled predominantly in North and South America, a number of whom returned to Japan in the last 20 years. A number of them were forced to leave after the economic downturn of 2008, in some cases receiving money from the Japanese government for repatriation, stipulating that they would not return to Japan for a minimum of three years.

References

Aiden, H. S. (2011). Creating the "multicultural coexistence" society: Central and local government policies towards foreign residents in Japan. *Social Science Japan Journal, 14*(2), 213–231.

Alexander, J. C. (2013). Struggling over the mode of incorporation: Backlash against multiculturalism in Europe. *Ethnic and Racial Studies, 36*(4), 531–556.

Bradley, W. S. (2013). Is there a post-multiculturalism? *Afrasia working paper series: Studies on multicultural societies, 19*. Shiga: Afrasian Research Centre, Ryukoku University.

Burgess, C. (2007). Multicultural Japan? Discourse and the "myth" of homogeneity. *The Asia-Pacific Journal: Japan Focus*. Retrieved from http://japanfocus.org/-Chris-Burgess/2389.

Bustamante, J. (2010). *Report of the special rapporteur on the human rights of migrants, Jorge Bustamante: Enjoyment of the rights to health and adequate housing by migrants* (A/HRC/14/30). New York: United Nations Human Rights Council.

Bygnes, S. (2012). Ambivalent multiculturalism. *Sociology, 47*(1), 126–141.

Chapman, D. (2006). Discourses of multicultural coexistence (tabunka kyōsei) and the "old-comer" Korean residents of Japan. *Asian Ethnicity, 7*(1), 89–102.

Cotterill, S. (2011). Documenting urban indigeneity: Tokyo Ainu and the 2011 survey on the living conditions of Ainu outside Hokkaido. *The Asia-Pacific Journal: Japan Focus* (Vol. 9, Issue 45, 2). Retrieved from http://japanfocus.org/-Simon-Cotterill/3642.

Diène, D. (2006). *Racism, racial discrimination, xenophobia and all forms of discrimination* (E/CN.4/2006/16). New York: United Nations Commission of Human Rights.

Flowers, P. (2012). From *Kokusaika* to *tabunka kyōsei*: Global norms, discourses of difference, and multiculturalism in Japan. *Critical Asian Studies, 44*(4), 515–542.

Fujimaki, H. (Ed.) (2012). *Imin retto Nippon: Tabunka kyōsei* [Immigration Japan: Multicultural co-existence]. Tokyo: Fujiwara Shoten.

Graburn, N. H. H. & Ertl, J. (2008). Introduction: Internal boundaries and models of multiculturalism in contemporary Japan. In N. H. H. Graburn, J. Ertl, & R. K. Tierney (Eds), *Multiculturalism in the new Japan* (pp. 1–31). New York: Berghahn Books.

Graburn, N. H. H., Ertl, J., & Tierney, R. K. (Eds) (2008). *Multiculturalism in the new Japan*. New York: Berghahn Books.

Green, D. (2013). Local foreign suffrage in Kawasaki city: The changing state of voting rights in Japan. *Electronic Journal of Contemporary Japanese Studies, 13*(1). Retrieved from http://www.japanesestudies.org.uk/ejcjs/vol13/iss1/green.html.
Hankins, J. D. (2012). Maneuvers of multiculturalism: International representations of minority politics in Japan. *Japanese Studies, 32*(1), 1–19.
He, B. & Kymlicka, W. (2005). Introduction. In W. Kymlicka, & B. He (Eds), *Multiculturalism in Asia* (pp. 1–21). Oxford: Oxford University Press.
Hirasawa, Y. (2009). Multicultural education in Japan. In J. A. Banks (Ed.), *The Routledge international companion to multicultural education* (pp. 159–169). New York: Routledge.
Htun, T. T. (2012). Social identities of minority others in Japan: Listening to the narratives of Ainu, Buraku and Zainichi Koreans. *Japan Forum, 24*(1), 1–22.
Ishii, Y. & Yamauchi, M. (1999). *Nihonjin to tabunka shugi* [The Japanese and multiculturalism]. Tokyo: Kokusai Bunka Kōryū Shuisin Kyōkai.
Ishiwata, E. (2011). "Probably impossible": Multiculturalism and pluralisation in present-day Japan. *Journal of Ethnic and Migration Studies, 37*(10), 1605–1626.
Japan Probe (2011). Norway shooter admired "monocultural" Japan. Retrieved from http://www.japanprobe.com/2011/07/25/norway-shooter-admired-mono cultural-japan/.
Japan Times (2005, October 18). Aso says Japan is nation of one race. Retrieved from http://www.japantimes.co.jp/news/2005/10/18/national/ aso-says-japan-is-nation-of-one-race/.
Japan Times (2013, October 7). Court bans rightists' hate speech, rallies. Retrieved from http://www.japantimes.co.jp/news/2013/10/07/national/ court-bans-rightists-hate-speech-rallies/.
Joppke, C. (2004). The retreat of multiculturalism in the liberal state: Theory and policy. *The British Journal of Sociology, 55*(2), 237–257.
Kagami, T. (Ed.) (2013). *Tabunka kyōsei ron: Taiyōsei rikai no tame hinto to lesson* [Multicultural existence theory: Hints and lessons for understanding diversity]. Tokyo: Akashi Shoten.
Kashiwazaki, C. (2013). Incorporating immigrants as foreigners: Multicultural politics in Japan. *Citizenship Studies, 17*(1), 31–47.
Kibe, T. (2011). Immigration and integration policies in Japan: At the crossroads of the welfare state and the labour market. In G. Vogt & G. S. Roberts (Eds), *Migration and integration: Japan in comparative perspective* (pp. 58–71). Munich: Iudicum.
Kim, H.-R. & Oh, I. (2011). Migration and multicultural contention in East Asia. *Journal of Ethnic and Migration Studies, 37*(10), 1563–1581.
Kivisto, P. (2012). Migration, national identity, and solidarity. *Ethnicities, 12*(6), 849–854.
Komai, H. (Ed.) (2003). *Tabunka shakai e no michi* [The road to multicultural coexistence]. Tokyo: Akashi Shoten.
Kundnani, A. (2012). Multiculturalism and its discontents: Left, right, and liberal. *European Journal of Cultural Studies 15*, 155–166.
Kwak, J. H. (2009). Coexistence without principle: Reconsidering multicultural policies in Japan. *Pacific Focus, 24*(2), 161–186.
Kymlicka, W. (2010). The rise and fall of multiculturalism: New debates on inclusion and accommodation in diverse societies. *International Social Science Journal, 199*, 97–112.

Lovell, S. (2010, July). *Local-level multiculturalism in Japan: Kobe municipal government and the Takatori community centre.* Paper presented at the 18th Biennial Conference of Asian Studies Association of Australia, Adelaide.
May, S. & Sleeter, C. E. (2010). *Critical multiculturalism: Theory and praxis.* New York: Routledge.
Miller, M. A. (2011). Why scholars of minority rights in Asia should recognize the limits of Western models. *Ethnic and Racial Studies, 34*(5), 799–813.
Ministry of Justice (2013). Heisei 24 nen matsu genzai ni okeru zairyu gaikokujinsu nitsuite (Kaku Tei Chi). Retrieved from http://www.moj.go.jp/nyuukokukanri/kouhou/nyuukokukanri04_00034.html.
Mishra, V. (2012). *What was multiculturalism? A critical retrospective.* Melbourne: Melbourne University Press.
Modood, T. (2007). *Multiculturalism: A civic idea.* Cambridge: Polity Press.
Modood, T. (2012). *Post-immigration "difference" and integration: The case of Muslims in Western Europe.* London: The British Academy.
Moorhead, R. (2013). Separate and unequal: The remedial Japanese classroom as an ethnic project. *The Asia-Pacific Journal: Japan focus, 11*(32), No. 3. Retrieved from http://japanfocus.org/-Robert-Moorehead/3980.
Morris-Suzuki, T. (1997). *Reinventing Japan: Time space nation (Japan in the modern world).* Armonk, NY: M. E. Sharpe.
Morris-Suzuki, T. (2006). Invisible immigrants: Undocumented migration and border controls in early postwar Japan. *The Asia-Pacific Journal: Japan focus.* Retrieved from http://japanfocus.org/-Tessa-Morris_Suzuki/2210.
Murphy, M. (2012). *Multiculturalism: A critical introduction.* Abingdon, Oxon: Routledge.
Nagayoshi, K. (2011). Support of multiculturalism, but for whom? Effects of ethno-national identity on the endorsement of multiculturalism in Japan. *Journal of Ethnic and Migration Studies, 37*(4), 561–578.
Nagy, S. R. (2012). Japanese-style multiculturalism? A comparative examination of Japanese multicultural existence. *JALT Journal of Multilingualism and Multiculturalism, 18*(1), 1–18.
Nagy, S. R. (2013). Politics of multiculturalism in East Asia: Reinterpreting multiculturalism. *Ethnicities,* DOI: 10.1177/1468796813498078.
Nakamatsu, T. (2013). Under the multicultural flag: Japan's ambiguous multicultural framework and its local evaluations and practices. *Journal of Ethnic and Migration Studies,* DOI: 10.1080/1369183X.2013.830498.
National Public Radio (2008, November 28). Like Rodney said, "can't we all just get along?" [Transcript]. Retrieved from http://www.npr.org/templates/transcript/transcript.php?storyId=97490927.
Noble, G. (2013). Cosmopolitan habits: The capacities and habitats of intercultural conviviality. *Body and Society, 19*(2/3), 162–185.
Oguma, E. (2002). *A genealogy of "Japanese" self-images* (D. Askew, Trans.). Melbourne: Trans Pacific Press.
Okano, K. H. (2006). The global-local interface in multicultural education policies in Japan. *Comparative Education, 42*(4), 473–491.
Okano, K. H. & Tsuneyoshi, R. (2011). Introduction: An interactive perspective for understanding minorities and education in Japan. In R. Tsuneyoshi, K. H. Okano, & S. S. Boocock (Eds), *Minorities and education in multicultural Japan* (pp. 1–26). London: Routledge.

Reuters. (2011). Norway attack: Killer praises Japan as a model country. Retrieved from http://in.reuters.com/article/2011/07/26/idINIndia-58454720110726.
Satake, M. (Ed.) (2011). *Zainichi gaikokujin to tabunka kyōsei* [Foreign residents and multicultural existence]. Tokyo: Akashi Shoten.
Takezawa, Y. (2008). The great Hanshin-Awaji earthquake and town-making toward multiculturalism. In N. H. H. Graburn, J. Ertl, & R. Kenji Tierney (Eds), *Multiculturalism in the new Japan* (pp. 32–42). New York: Berghahn Books.
Tai, E. (2007). Multicultural education in Japan. *The Asia-Pacific Journal: Japan Focus*. Retrieved from http://japanfocus.org/-Eika-TAI/2618.
Tsuneyoshi, R. (2011). Three frameworks on multicultural Japan: Towards a more inclusive understanding. *Multicultural Education Review, 3*(2), 125–156.
Vertovec, S. (2010). Towards post-multiculturalism? Changing communities, conditions and contexts of diversity. *International Social Science Journal, 199*, 83–95.
Watson, I. (2012). Changing policy in South Korea: Reinforcing homogeneity and cosmetic difference? *Journal of Asian Public Policy, 5*(1), 97–116.
Willis, D. B. & Murphy-Shigematsu, S. (Eds) (2008). *Transcultural Japan: At the borderlands of race, gender, and identity*. London: Routledge.
Yamamoto, B. (2012). From structured invisibility to visibility: Is Japan really going to accept multiethnic, multicultural identities? *Identities, 19*(4), 428–439.

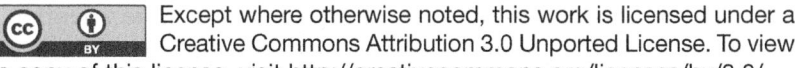 Except where otherwise noted, this work is licensed under a Creative Commons Attribution 3.0 Unported License. To view a copy of this license, visit http://creativecommons.org/licenses/by/3.0/

OPEN

3
A Critical Analysis of Multiculturalism and Deviant Identities: Untold Stories of Japanese Americans without Nations

Takumi Honda

3.1 Introduction

What part have Japanese immigrants played in multiculturalism in America? How have such immigrants been described in the prevailing multicultural discourse? In recent years, discussions of multiculturalism and Japanese immigrants are increasingly attracting more attention. In fact, Japanese immigrants are now regularly mentioned in American history textbooks as representative "good Americans." This suggests that Japanese immigrants have become an integral part of multicultural education in the US. However, the history and identity of Japanese immigrants described in these discussions and textbooks do not completely cover the stories of Japanese immigrants in America, especially those who were marginalized and forced to struggle to maintain their distinctive identities. Those aspects of Japanese immigrants depicted in the established discourse of history and identity present only one model for Japanese immigrants. When the immigrants crossed national borders, they encountered complicated struggles over their own identities. How should such a struggle be understood? What does this understanding mean to the contemporary literature of multiculturalism?

In order to address these questions, this chapter starts by focusing on how Japanese immigrants have been described in conventional discourses of American multiculturalism. Second, I will pay specific attention to people who have been heretofore barely described in the traditional history of Japanese immigrants. Third, I will examine the significant influence that conventional multiculturalism discourses have exerted on the omission of particular types of Japanese immigrants, with a focus on the concepts of "tolerance" and "integration." This will be followed by brief concluding remarks.

3.2 Mainstream discourses regarding multiculturalism and Japanese immigrants in America today

The issue of migration is, needless to say, important for understanding modern society. The global flow of people is obviously a major concern of policy makers as well as scholars of international affairs. In America, after 9/11, multiculturalism, which is deeply tied to the image of "tolerance" in the minds of Americans, is actually spurring disputes in the international community. While many of the discourses of multiculturalism straightforwardly promote tolerance and acceptance of other cultures, some argue that such discourses only result in concealing the violence that certainly continues to this day (Yoneyama, 2003, p. 223). This is also the case in the context of Japanese immigrants in the US. What has been described as the history of Japanese immigrants continues to exclude and marginalize particular identities from the legitimate history. Behind a series of such descriptions of Japanese immigrants has always been a politics habitually controlled by the majority. The repetition of such a description in classrooms and everyday conversations leads to the continuous exclusion of those do not fit the ideal immigrant figure of multicultural discourse. Multiculturalism in this sense has performed its function of absorbing Japanese Americans and other ethnic groups into the "multiculturalism" framework by establishing certain models of "good Americans," and often ended up by homogenizing them into the unified idea of patriotic citizens (Grant & Sleeter, 2009).

In America in the latter half of the 1980s, a new concept of "diversity" began to be widely referenced, and the concept of "multiculturalism" subsequently began to be discussed intensively. The word "multiculturalism," with a concomitant concept of tolerance, was derived from America's efforts to promote a change in the majority's conventional public awareness of minorities (Inoue, 1999, p. 88). It has often been said that this type of multiculturalism was the result of identity politics primarily developed by African Americans and Asian Americans in order to protest discriminatory structures in the US (Tai, 1999, p. 38). Initially, multicultural movements strived to create a multicultural society by embracing all minority ethnic groups and cultures. However, multiculturalism is said to have begun performing the role of concealing the political and economic gap between minority groups and cultural diversity within a minority group (Gordon & Newfield, 1996). Subsequently, it was often said that the discourse of multiculturalism only functions to integrate such people into the framework of the pre-given "multi-cultural," creating an impression of tolerance presumably residing in the minds of the majority. In this way, multiculturalism began to be used as a theory of national integration (Yui & Endo, 1999).[1]

In the 1990s, multiculturalism became even more visible. This concept continues to be welcomed widely in the US even now. Discussion of multiculturalism is particularly active at educational institutions, higher educational institutions in particular, where ethnic groups with different roots are actively featured in classrooms as a part of the history of multicultural America. Multiculturalism is, therefore, still believed to represent an imperative and indispensable aspect of America that comprises a wide variety of cultures (Hollinger, 1995, p. 150).

The cases where Japanese immigrants are utilized by mainstream multicultural discourse in America often emphasize the collapse of their identity resulting from compulsory confinement during the Second World War, and regularly refer to the reconstruction of their identity as Japanese American with the victory of the compensation movement in the post-war period. Although textbooks feature Japanese immigrants as a part of the success of multiculturalist policies in the US, they ignore the complicated, multi-layered, and diverse experiences of Japanese immigrants. In fact, multicultural education often fails to focus on the identity of Japanese immigrants during the period from their first arrival in the US to their compulsory confinement (Petersen, 1971). In order to clarify this point, it is necessary to review the academic research previously conducted on Japanese immigrants, and compare this with the narratives of those who were marginalized and the movements continuously protesting against the established social structure.

The period from Japanese immigrants' first arrival in the US until their confinement in the camps was essentially characterized by the discriminatory sentiment they encountered. In the receiving society, the government and the majority usually strive to integrate minorities into the established rules and norms of the society, as well as maintain and expand their social merits and privileges. If the majority in the receiving society finds no difference between themselves and immigrants, and if the majority shares a mutual interest with them, the immigrants are easily accepted into the society. This type of integration is often related to the interest not only of the receiving society, but also of those who are accepted (Muller, 2001, pp. 17–40).

However, the first generation of Japanese immigrants had a different story and experienced many difficulties. It is impossible to explain these difficulties with only the simple understanding of multiculturalism that insists that they were eventually able to reclaim their identity as Americans because of the success of the compensation movement (Okamoto, 2005, p. 74). Their struggle largely emanated from the "shaking" of their identity, especially from the time of their arrival in the US in 1900 until 1945. Although they are "accepted" in multicultural American society today, it is impossible for them to erase their complicated experiences and memories from that period.

Sakaguchi (2001) contends that the period during which the identity of Japanese immigrants was transformed can be divided into three periods: (1) from the 1900s, when they first migrated, to the 1920s, when they "did not care that they were Japanese"; (2) from the 1920s to the 1930s, when they were "half-Japanese"; and (3) the period after the 1930s, when they had to identify themselves as either Japanese or American. In this way, Japanese immigrants continually sought an identity that could bridge the two conflicting nations for approximately 45 years (Sakaguchi, 2001, pp. 17–42).

The selection of a nation, Japan or the US, that Japanese immigrants in America were forced to identify themselves with successfully led some of them to reside in harmony with fellow Americans, but left others with an unbearable contradiction and unforgettable experiences. This was partly because, regardless of the result of their selection, the structure of the society of Japanese immigrants was profoundly, sometime uncontrollably, influenced by the national interests of the US and Japan, and thus influenced by their diplomatic relations. One of America's true goals was securing its national interests. It might be natural that when a national interest is tied to the loyalty of immigrants, the immigrants are induced to transform their identities into something that confirms the prevailing order of their living environment and demonstrates their loyalty to the receiving country. In reality, an uncountable number of Japanese immigrants followed this path toward acceptance in America (Muller, 2007, pp. 73–82). However, the influence of the diplomatic relationship between Japan and the US became particularly salient for Japanese immigrants when it deteriorated before and during the Second World War. At that time, neither government showed any interest in the immigrants' decisions about the nation to which they demonstrated their loyalty. Even if the immigrants demonstrated their loyalty to Japan, with a firm belief that they were Japanese, the Japanese government did not make any real efforts to improve the living conditions of Japanese Americans isolated in the US. Similarly, when they demonstrated their loyalty to America, the US government did not try to respectfully accommodate them or improve their living environment either. Consequently, Japanese immigrants had no choice other than being held in concentration camps from the beginning of the war between Japan and the US (Hayashi, 2004, pp. 76–81).

This analysis of Japanese immigrants' history in the US varies significantly from what has been told in the context of contemporary American multiculturalism. The history of Japanese immigrants in the widely accepted discourse of multiculturalism usually concentrates on their successful identity transformation during the period from their compulsory confinement to the compensation movement, and scarcely mentions the fact that American society during those 45 years was characterized by widespread political, economic, and social oppression of Japanese immigrants, of which the compulsory confinement was just an ultimate consequence (Togami, 1986, p. 319). The mainstream discourse of multiculturalism in the US ignores these historical complexities and only emphasizes the compulsory confinement and victorious compensation campaign by Japanese immigrants after the war, which presumably led them to transform their identities successfully. In a way, multiculturalism only touches upon the history of Japanese immigrants in order to recognize and share their story of loyalty and successive contribution to America.

The reason why American multiculturalism discourses deal with the compulsory confinement and the compensation movement, and recognize the loyalty and contribution of some Japanese immigrants, is to promote the integration of minority ethnic groups in America (Morimo, 1999, pp. 175–180). In other words, the compulsory confinement and compensation movement of the Japanese immigrants are described only in the context of "loyalty" and "contribution." What is missing in this context is the exclusion of those who did not fit the ideal figure of the successful immigrant. Those who have not been described in the history are those who did not demonstrate their loyalty to America, who were consequently excluded from the social structures of both America and Japan, and who continuously experienced the "shaking" of their identities even after the success story of Japanese immigrants prevailed.

3.3 Narratives of Japanese immigrants

According to Creswell (2013, p. 13), there are five major research designs that are typically found in a qualitative approach. The first, phenomenological research, is a design of inquiry in which the researcher describes the lived experiences of individuals in relation to a phenomenon and as they are described by the participants. This description culminates with a description of the essence of the experiences for several individuals who have all experienced the phenomena (Giorgi, 2009; Moustakas, 1994). The second, grounded theory, is a design of inquiry from sociology in which the researcher derives a general, abstract theory of a process, action, or interaction grounded in the views of participants (Charmaz, 2006; Corbin & Strauss, 2007). Ethnography, the third type, is a design of inquiry coming from anthropology and sociology in which the researcher studies the shared patterns of behaviors, language, and actions of an intact cultural group in a natural setting over a prolonged period time (Creswell, 2013). The fourth type, case studies, are a design of inquiry found in many fields, especially evaluation, in which the researcher develops an in-depth analysis of a case, often a program, event, or activity, and researchers then collect detailed information using a variety of data collection procedures over a sustained period of time (Stake, 1995; Yin, 2009, 2012). Narrative research, the final design of inquiry, comes from the humanities and features researchers who study the lives of individuals and ask one or more individuals to provide stories about their lives (Riessman, 2008). This information is then often retold and re-storied by the researcher into a narrative chronology. Often, in the end, the narrative combines views from the participant's life with those of the researcher's life in a collaborative narrative (Clandinin & Connelly, 2000).

In order to research the "shaking" of the identities of Japanese immigrants in this thesis, I conducted oral and written interviews using the methodology of qualitative narrative research with 15 second-generation Japanese Americans in January 2009.[2] For this narrative approach, the interviewer sought to examine issues related to the oppression of individuals. To study this, stories were collected of individual oppression using a narrative approach (Creswell, 2013). Interviewees were interviewed at some length to determine how they have personally experienced oppression. Interviewees were selected for whom the interview could increase the opportunity "to identify emerging themes" (Erlandson et al., 1993, p. 82) embedded in the interview's context. Along with this research, recorded data were segmented in consideration of every utterance's meaning and subtle nuance. Thus, in the analysis of the data, the information was so dense and rich that the inquiry needed to "winnow" the data (Guest Macqueen & Namey, 2012), a process of focusing in on some of the data and disregarding other parts of it. Narrative interviews were conducted through an unstructured, open-ended format and the interviewer took notes during the interview.

The interviews focused on events related to conscription during the Second World War, which is often described as a constitutive part of the successful history of multiculturalism policy in America. This history regularly treats Japanese immigrants as a positive, and more or less idealized, model of minority groups, with a particular focus on such events as "compulsory confinement" and "conscription of second-generation Japanese Americans," as well as "the compensation movement," which presumably led to the successful transformation of their identities. With these examples, the discourse of multiculturalism frequently associates stories of "the collapse of the identity," "loyalty to America," and "the reconstruction of the identity," in order to present the image of Japanese immigrants as a model of "good citizens" (Japanese American Citizens League, 1996).

As a consequence of the compensation movement, the US government granted prominent recognition to the excellent performance of the 442nd Regimental Combat Team in Europe.[3] The excellent performance of the combat team was treated as evidence of the Japanese immigrants' loyalty to the US as Americans. Actually, their performance is still widely remembered among Japanese immigrants, and a monument ceremony for the 442nd team in Washington was organized by Japanese immigrant organizations from across the US in 2001 (Befu, 2002, p. 235).

In the context of the mainstream discourse of multiculturalism and the majority of Japanese immigrants, the victory achieved by the compensation movement meant the acceptance of Japanese immigrants. However, it is difficult to tell whether all Japanese immigrants believe that this understanding is reasonable. In fact, Interviewee A, a second-generation Japanese American, has a negative perception of this belief. In addition, Interviewee B, another second-generation Japanese American, indicates that the reason why he served in the military did not stem from loyalty to America but from something else. Why do they have a different interpretation of the history of Japanese immigrants? What lies behind their distinctive comprehension of the compensation movement?

Interviewee A, a second-generation Japanese American, was born in Sacramento, California. He was taken to a concentration camp when he was 14 years old. His parents, first-generation Japanese Americans, did not have American citizenship because of the act concerning "aliens ineligible for citizenship." Based in California, he currently visits various schools and other facilities in America to present materials and talk about what the compulsory confinement really meant to him. Through these actions, he expresses his identity to the public. The reason why he attracts our attention here is that his identity was not exclusively determined by nationality. He was a model for *The No-No Boys*, by Teresa Funke (2008). Although this book is a fictional work, it deals with the actual issue of Japanese Americans' struggle for their identity.

He chose to become one of the "No-No Boys," who demonstrated no loyalty to America and refused to serve in the US armed forces.[4] This choice caused him to be sent to the Tule Lake Camp, which was famous, or infamous, for having the severest surveillance in the US. The Tule Lake camp was a specific facility for those who did not demonstrate their loyalty to America, and for those who were subject to investigation by the FBI. It is said that approximately 18,000 prisoners were held in the Tule Lake Camp, under constant armed surveillance.

Interviewee A talks about the compulsory confinement of Japanese immigrants and their conscription as follows ("[ ]" signifies information added by the researcher):

> In America, many people call where I used to be held a "relocation camp," rather than a "concentration camp." However, based on our understanding, we call it not a relocation camp, but a "jail" or a "concentration camp." We were deprived of our homes, land, stores, jobs, and everything. Nevertheless, it is called a "relocation camp." We feel upset about it. It was a concentration camp without any doubt. Not serving in the military, we had no national identity. We did not know who we were or where we could go. And what was waiting for us, those who did not serve in the military, was detention by the FBI, or repatriation to Japan, or life-long imprisonment at Tule Lake. Meanwhile, I was grateful that I was able to work in the camp as a time-keeper, a cook, a cleaner, and so on. Although the payment was low, it was still good to have a job. Also, I was able to go to school and play sports. That was something to be grateful for, but people around me and I thought that we would be killed if Japan won the war. That kind of anxiety was always with us in the life at the camp. Of course, there was no way of knowing about the progress of the war. We lived our lives at the camp without knowing what was going on. As for the 442nd Team, I, from the perspective of [being a member of] the No-No Boys, have a complicated feeling. Not all the team members who did a good job in the European battlefields demonstrated their loyalty to America. There has always been a political use [of the history of Japanese immigrants].

Interviewee A's comments reveal that second-generation Japanese Americans taken to the camps in those days were given only two choices: (1) become a No-No Boy, which would result in either arrest, repatriation to Japan, or life at the Tule Lake Camp, or (2) serve in the military and achieve great performance on the battlefield, which means in this context the 442nd Team.

Based on his own experience, Interviewee A talks about the compulsory confinement and conscription. Interviewee B, another No-No boy, also touches upon the compulsory confinement and conscription. But he goes further to mention the discrimination and exclusion that he experienced after leaving the camp.

Interviewee B was born in Portland, Oregon. He is a second-generation Japanese American, with American citizenship. Since his mother died when he was young, his father made him go back to Japan, where his grandparents lived, but he returned to the US in 1934. Although in the interview he tried not to provide actual details of the compulsory confinement, he explained the exclusion that he had gone through and his agony toward it as follows:

> I was born in Portland. But since my mother died while I was still young, my grandparents living in Japan educated me. In 1934, when I was a third-grade student at elementary school, I returned to America. That's why I speak Japanese better than I speak English. Due to the economic downturn [in America] in 1929, I had difficulty finding a job. Since there was terrible economic aggravation and a horrific anti-Japanese attitude at companies run by white Americans, I worked for a Japanese trading company called "Furuya Shoten." The pay was very low. I married my wife before we were sent to a concentration camp. I still feel frustrated that even though we had American citizenship, we were held in the concentration camp. When we were in the camp in Portland, we had our first baby. Since ours was the first baby to be delivered in the camp, this was featured in a newspaper. While I was at the camp, I did not join the military. If I demonstrated my loyalty to America and became conscripted, I could have legally left the camp. But I did not do so. When I left the camp, I was only given a small amount for transportation expenses, enough to go to Ontario. I was completely out of money. The only choices that I had were to work as a farmer or to serve in the army. Every day, I carried my child on my back to school. Actually, after the end of the war, I did serve in the army, because I had no money. The anti-Japanese movement was so severe that I could find no work. In daily life, a shop even refused to sell me an ice cream that my child

wanted to eat. At a Denny's restaurant, they wouldn't even come to take our order. After leaving the camp, we had no money or job. We just continued to be exposed to the anti-Japanese movement.

Interviewee B felt resentment that he had been held in a concentration camp, even though he had American citizenship. Also, he stated that he served in the army after the end of the war, but that the choice was not because of loyalty to America but instead the fact that he had no job. Moreover, he emphasized that the discrimination against Japanese immigrants in American society at that time deprived them of opportunities to work.

Interviewee C was held in the Granada Camp. She describes her experience at the concentration camp and her identity as follows:

> I was held in the Granada Camp. I lived in a tiny shack. It was a horrible camp. My parents worked at a vineyard. I had an elder brother. He was drafted as a second-generation Japanese American and went to war in 1944. I spent my years of eighth, ninth, and tenth grades in the camp. Even after leaving the camp, I experienced a lot of difficulties. Since my family had no money, I was taken to my uncle's. I worked at a strawberry farm for low daily wages. My uncle used to tell me that he had actually wanted to go to Tule Lake while he was held in camp. He thought that, if he was taken to Tule Lake, he could leave America for Japan. Meanwhile, even after leaving the camp, I tried not to talk about my experience there. I think that this was because I had something in my mind that could not be classified as American or Japanese. One day, at school, I wrote my American name. It was soon rewritten as my Japanese name by my Japanese teacher. This was an identity problem. I did not understand what my identity was. Japanese Americans like me often use the phrase "facial character." It is something like a surface identity. After the civil rights movement in my living town in 1965, I thought that my name was called for the first time in my life because that was the first time many minorities started to insist their own ethnic identities. For me, it was the identity of a Japanese American. But later, I noticed that I did not fit in it. The 442nd Team as the symbol of the loyalty of Japanese immigrants is irrelevant to me. To make myself fit in it, I had to throw away something. In my case, it can be said that I've thrown away my Japanese identity.

The "shaking" of her complicated identity is clearly expressed in her national name. She spent her childhood without a clear recognition of whether she was Japanese or American.

The evidence from these interviews reveals that second-generation Japanese Americans who were held in concentration camps were deprived of their freedom in American society. In discourses regarding multiculturalism, it is said that Japanese Americans have been merged into the majority in America, and that public acceptance by American society relieved the Japanese Americans from having to struggle to establish their identity. However, the descriptions and insistences by each interviewee show that the compulsory confinement did not seem to contribute to their identity formation. Their powerful statements show that they did not assimilate themselves into America and that they have always been residing at the margin of American society. Actually, interviewees talked about their experiences from their own positions. Their descriptions reveal their insistence that they want the world to know about their experiences and they want to tell the world that they have not belonged to a pre-set identity or group.

3.4 Mainstream discourses of multiculturalism and Japanese immigrants in America

In order to understand multiculturalism in America, it is necessary to concentrate on the question of the nation state. It can be said that maintaining the identity of Americans is one of the most important issues for maintaining the nation. In America, until the 1970s, 60% of white residents had British ancestors, and Anglo-conformity was regarded as an ideal of assimilation. In those days, the prevailing socio-cultural understanding was that European culture was central to America. Actually, until the 1960s, Japanese and other Asian immigrants, as well as Mexican immigrants, were not granted rights equal to those of white citizens (Tai, 1999, p. 39).

Homi K. Bhabha analyzes the country's integration process and the issue of ethnic-cultural thought. Emphasizing that identity is never *a priori*, nor a finished product, Bhabha argues that identity itself is only ever the problematic process of access to an image of totality (Bhabha, 1990, p. 194). In a way, he criticizes the prevailing discourse of diversity that focuses solely on ethnicity. While the integration of ethnic groups into "America" was promoted under the name of multiculturalism, a particular discourse has been accepted as the core narrative of the multicultural environment for American citizens. The implicit assumption held by the majority of the population is that the core of multicultural society needs to be European.

Arthur Schlesinger, Jr. and David A. Hollinger provide typical discussions in this regard. Schlesinger criticized the insistence by African

Americans on protest against American society. He was absolutely against the protest by African Americans and called their protest self-pity and self-ghettoization as follows:

> The ethnicity rage in general and afrocentricity in particular not only divert attention from the real needs but exacerbate the problems. The recent apotheosis of ethnicity, black, brown, red, yellow, white, has revived the dismal prospect that in happy melting-pot days Americans thought the republic was moving safely beyond—that is, a society fragmented into ethnic groups. The cult of ethnicity exaggerates differences, intensifies resentments and antagonisms, drives ever deeper the awful wedges between races and nationalities. The endgame is self-pity and self-ghettoization. (Schlesinger, 1992, p. 102)

He subsequently refers to their protests as separatism. He argues for a core culture in America and suggests that the culture should be based on the superiority of Western culture (Schlesinger, 1992). Similarly, Hollinger strives to promote a discussion that transcends multiculturalism in *Postethnic America* (Hollinger, 1995). Presenting a negative view of cultural identity generated by ethnic culture, a concept emphasized in the discourse of cultural pluralism and multiculturalism, he expects that such an ethnic element will disappear in terms of political culture. In this context, he criticizes Horace Kallen, who developed and promoted cultural pluralism, and even insists that Kallen was too conscious of his own Jewish ethnicity.

Hollinger regards middle-class people of European ancestry as standard Americans, and defines non-white people as those who stuck to their ethnicity. In the end, his assumption originates in a perception that the center of America was comprised of people with a European tradition.

> A truly postethnic America would be one in which the ethno-racial component in identity would loom less large than it now does in politics as well as culture, and in which affiliation by shared descent would be more voluntary than prescribed in every context. Although many middle-class Americans of European descent can now be said to be postethnic in this sense, the United States as a whole is a long way from achieving this ideal. This ideal for the American civic community is, indeed, just that – an ideal, embodying the hope that the United States can be more than a site for a variety of diasporas and of projects in colonization and conquest. (Hollinger, 1995, p. 129)

He argues that non-white people were ethnic groups sticking to their ethnicity. He continues by suggesting that non-whites do not understand the ideal of the American civic community, of which "individuality" is the indispensable basis, but stuck to their race and ethnicity and ultimately weaken the unitary state of culture. Ultimately, the reason why he tries to transcend multiculturalism is that he thinks the insistence of minority ethnic groups in America would disrupt the superiority of the whites (Hollinger, 1995).

In these discussions, multiculturalism is reduced to "the Politics of Recognition" (Taylor, 1994), which is often criticized for using the concept of diversity to protect the narrator's own culture. Using the phrase "the Politics of Recognition," Charles Taylor contends that the contemporary demand for recognition by minorities has been refused. He insists that in the politics of recognition, the demand for equal citizenship and the uniqueness of each individual must be recognized (Taylor, 1994). However, the problem for multiculturalism is that, under the name of the politics of recognition, there is only one-way recognition of "minority cultures" by the "mainstream culture." Not discussing the question of subjectivity, that is, the question of who has the right to "recognize," overlooks the power relations of narration involved in the case of Japanese immigrants in the context of multiculturalism.

Where cultural differences are observed, multiculturalism supposedly recognizes each different culture with the word "diversity," Bhabha argues that multiculturalism was an effort to control a dynamic process of cultural differences (Bhabha, 1990, p. 209). He contends that both cultural pluralism and multiculturalism regularly function to control cultural differences. The ethical recognition by discourses of multiculturalism deadens the floating and hybrid aspects of minority cultures, and makes the minority cultures named and controlled by the dominant multiculturalism through an essentialist understanding of culture. In the case of Japanese immigrants, no history has been provided in the multicultural education regarding those who did not demonstrate their loyalty to America. Those who have not been described in the discourse of multiculturalism are deprived of the words to explain themselves, and are thus often silenced. Bhabha (1994) analyzes this process as the containment of cultural difference.

In discussions of multiculturalism in American society, Ronald Takaki (2008) touches upon the "cultures recognized." Takaki, a second-generation Japanese American intellectual, emphasizes that American history has been very fragmentary and America has been formed by mutual interactions among a wide variety of ethnic groups. With this emphasis, he strives to draw a complicated portrait of America. Stating that all groups contributed to the establishment of America, he aims to redefine American history from multiple perspectives by describing the experiences of each group (Takaki, 2008). The multiculturalism advocated by Takaki can apparently be regarded as multiculturalism because of the diversity among the minority viewpoints. In fact, he insists "we originally came from many different shores, and our diversity has been at the center of the making of America" (Takaki, 2008, p. 438). By indicating this diversity, he seeks to establish a shared past for America. By describing history from multiple perspectives, he attempts to create a unified America with assumed diversity, rather than an America constituted by only one specific group.

However, those who continue to be marginalized in the discourse of multicultural America, such as the "No-No Boys," are under continuous pressure to be incorporated into the pre-given American social structure, even while their identities remain marginalized. In short, the problem here is that the existence of those who have been unremittingly pressured by the discourse of multiculturalism, and tried to escape from it, remains silenced and marginalized. The discussion by Takaki is a typical example of the recognition of Asian Americans in the prevailing context of multiculturalism. It functions to promote social integration and conceal the structure of control by the majority, and has enabled the containment of protest movements against the alleged tolerance of America.

If the main function of contemporary multiculturalism is to ceaselessly control minorities, this suggests an imperialist character. In fact, Edward Said frequently referred to the US as an imperialist country (Said, 1993). Has multiculturalism in America been critical of the nation's culture of imperialism? While strengthening national identity, it seems that a multiculturalism based on cultural control, with the veil of tolerance, has been exempt from self-criticism and self-denial. Likewise, not many Japanese immigrants in the US have had a point of view that would generate criticism of the nation. As explained above, while criticizing the mainstream, Japanese immigrants have not sufficiently criticized the essentialist understanding of culture. In a word, the mainstream multiculturalist discourse in the US has continuously been producing the story of "what it is to be an American" and has constantly depicted the "characteristics of the good Japanese Americans" for Japanese immigrants. This results in the production and isolation of those who have neither "characteristics of Americans" nor "characteristics of the Japanese."

In reality, history textbooks have incessantly produced such "other people" and used them to spread the discourse of a multicultural America. One history textbook, for instance, told the story that some California residents began to be concerned about the increasing number of Japanese immigrants in their state, and that Japanese immigrants worked for very low wages, depriving native-born non-Japanese American workers of their jobs (Brown, Helgeson & George, 1964). While emphasizing that Japanese Americans were industrious workers, the textbook ultimately categorized Japanese immigrants as "other people" who caused a negative impact on American society. The textbook tells us about the different perceptions of work held by whites and Japanese Americans. This difference in work ethic is entwined with racial differences and culturally essentialized. In this way, the textbook implants the essentialist idea of ethnicity, on the basis of a comparison between "native-born Americans" and "Japanese immigrants," in the minds of the readers.

Another interesting example is a story described in a textbook about Japanese Americans along the Pacific coast who were forced to leave their homes and were gathered in camps administered by the army following the attack on Pearl Harbor (Bragdon & McCutchen, 1964). The textbook refers to this violation of compulsory confinement as "the sole significant event." However, the description of the confinement is problematic, because the expression "sole important event" is not correct. This expression conceals the history of compulsory confinement of German Americans and Italian Americans during the same period. Moreover, the textbook implies that the cause of this compulsory confinement was mainly Japan's attack on Pearl Harbor, and this depiction suggests that compulsory confinement would not have been carried out if there was no attack. In other words, the confinement was because of Japan's wrongdoing, and the US's decision on the confinement was inevitable. However, the textbook does not refer at all to the traditional historical aspect described by Japanese immigrants, who say that the compulsory confinement was a mere extension of the exclusion of and discrimination against Japanese immigrants (Okamoto, 2005).

As suggested above, multiculturalism, which was originally supposed to be related to the concept of "diversity," has come to function as an apparatus for controlling minority identity, while still being intertwined with the concept of "integration." The result was the reproduction of a strong American identity. Avery F. Gordon and Christopher Newfield described this as "the control of diversity," and insists that multiculturalism does not question the imbalance generated by race, class, and gender differences in the context of the multicultural situation and instead conceals this problem while providing an effective control (Gordon & Newfield, 1996).

3.5 Conclusion

Through discussing problems regarding Japanese immigrants in the context of multiculturalism, this chapter has striven to indicate the difference between those who were assimilated in multiculturalism and those who were not. In past studies, Japanese immigrants have been understood from a certain fixed perspective, which is a multiculturalism of essentialization and isolation. This results in promoting the isolation of "others" while accepting them with its supposed tolerance. However, this process inevitably produces another form of "others" who appear within the community of the pre-given "others." As the antithesis to such an understanding, this chapter aimed to emphasize the differences among Japanese immigrants. The statements by each interviewee describe the "shaking" of their identity woven through their experiences. In order to promote discussions of multiculturalism in the circumstances surrounding immigrants, it is necessary to pay careful attention to ensure that the discussions are not oriented towards the integration of difference but rather toward the diversification of identities.

Notes

1. Since the process of the historical development and transformation of multiculturalism and multicultural education is more deeply discussed in the third section, I focus here on how Japanese immigrants have been described in the current discourse of multiculturalism.
2. The field research for this thesis was supported by the Graduate Program of Asian and African Studies of Ryukoku University. Further, direct contact and oral or written interviews with second-generation Japanese Americans became possible through the cooperation of Ronald Nakasone (Stanford University).
3. In 1942, General Emmons, in Hawaii, formed a battalion of Japanese Americans—the 100th Battalion. The 100th was called the "Purple Heart Battalion." In June 1943, the 100th Battalion merged with the newly arrived 442nd Regimental Combat Team, composed of Japanese Americans from Hawaii as well as from the concentration camps on the mainland (Takaki, 2008, pp. 348–349).
4. In 1943, the War Relocation Authority administered a loyalty questionnaire to all male and female internees 17 years and older. The crucial questions were No. 27 and No. 28, as follows (Tule Lake Committee, 2000, p. 8):
No. 27: Are you willing to serve in the armed forces of the United States on combat duty, wherever ordered?

No. 28: Will you swear unqualified allegiance to the United States of America and faithfully defend the United States from any or all attack by foreign or domestic forces and forswear any form of allegiance or obedience to the Japanese emperor, to any other foreign government, power or organization?

References

Befu, H. (2002). *Nikkei americajin no ayumi to genzai* [Steps by Japanese Americans and today]. Tokyo: Jinbun Shoin.
Bhabha, H. K. (1990). The third space. In J. Rutherford (Ed.), *Identity: Community, culture, difference* (pp. 207–221). London: Lawrence and Wishart.
Bhabha, H. K. (1994). *The location of culture*. London: Routledge.
Bragdon, H. W. & McCutchen, S. P. (1964). *History of a free people*. New York: The Macmillan.
Brown, R. C., Helgeson, C. A., & George, L. H. (1964). *The United States of America: A history for young citizens*. Morristown, NJ: Silver Burdett.
Charmaz, K. (2006). *Constructing grounded theory*. Thousand Oaks, CA: Sage.
Clandinin, D. J. & Connely, F. M. (2000). *Narrative inquiry: Experience and story in qualitative research*. San Francisco: Jossey-Bass.
Corbin, J. M. & Strauss, A. C. (2007). *Basics of qualitative research: Techniques and procedures for developing grounded theory* (3rd edn). Thousand Oaks, CA: Sage.
Creswell, J. W. (2013). *Research design: Qualitative, quantitative, and mixed methods approaches* (4th edn). Thousand Oaks, CA: Sage.
Erlandson, D. A., Harris, E. L., Skipper, B. L., & Allen S. D. (1993). *Doing naturalistic inquiry: A guide to methods*. Newbury Park, CA: Sage.
Funke, T. (2008). *The no-no boys*. Fort Collins, CO: Victory House Press.
Giorgi, A. (2009). *The descriptive phenomenological method in psychology: A modified Husserlian approach*. Pittsburgh, PA: Duquesne University Press.
Gordon, A. F. & Newfield, C. (Eds) (1996). *Mapping multiculturalism*. Minneapolis: University of Minnesota Press.
Grant, C. A. & Sleeter, C. E. (2009). *Turning on learning: Five approaches for multicultural teaching plans for race, class, gender, and disability* (5th edn). New York: Wiley.
Guest, G., MacQueen, K. M., & Namey, E. E. (2012). *Applied thematic analysis*. Thousand Oaks, CA: Sage.
Hayashi, B. M. (2004). *Democratizing the enemy: The Japanese American internment*. Princeton, NJ: Princeton University Press.
Hollinger, D. A. (1995). *Postethnic America: Beyond multiculturalism*. New York: Basicbooks.
Inoue, T. (1999). Tabunkashugi no seiji tetsugaku: Bunkaseiji no toriade [Political philosophy of multiculturalism: Triade of cultural politics] In D. Yui, & Y. Endo (Eds), *Tabunkashugi no america: Yuragu nashonaru aidentiti* [The US of multiculturalism: Shaken national identity] (pp. 87–114). Tokyo: Tokyo Daigaku Shuppankai.
Japanese American Citizens League, National Education Committee. (1996). *A lesson in American history: The Japanese American experiences, curriculum and resources guide*. San Francisco: JACL.
Morimo, T. (1999). America no rekishikyouiku niokeru kokumintougou to tabunkashugi [Multiculturalism and integration of American history

education]. In D. Yui, & Y. Endo (Eds), *Tabunkashugi no america: Yuragu nashonaru aidentiti* [The US of multiculturalism: Shaken national identity] (pp. 165–186). Tokyo: Tokyo Daigaku Shuppankai.

Moustakas, C. (1994). *Phenomenological research methods*. Thousand Oaks, CA: Sage.

Muller, E. L. (2001). *Free to die for their country: The story of the Japanese American draft resisters in World War II*. Chicago: The University of Chicago Press.

Muller, E. L. (2007). *American inquisition: The hunt for Japanese American disloyalty in World War II*. Chapel Hill, NC: The University of North Carolina Press.

Okamoto, T. (2005). *Rekishi kyoukasho ni miru america* [The America found in history textbooks]. Tokyo: Gakubunsha.

Petersen, W. (1971). *Japanese Americans: Oppression and success*. New York: Random House.

Riessman, C. K. (2008). *Narrative methods for the human sciences*. Thousand Oaks, CA: Sage.

Said, E. W. (1993). *Culture and imperialism*. New York: Alfred A. Knopf.

Sakaguchi, M. (2001). *Nihonjin america iminshi* [History of Japanese American immigrants]. Tokyo: Fuji Shuppan.

Schlesinger Jr., A. M. (1992). *The disuniting of America: Reflections on the multicultural society*. New York: Norton.

Stake, R. E. (1995). *The art of case study research*. Thousand Oaks, CA: Sage.

Tai, E. (1999). *Tabunkashugi to diaspora* [Multiculturalism and diaspora]. Tokyo: Akashi Shoten.

Takaki, R. (2008). *A different mirror: A history of multicultural America*. New York: Little Brown and Company.

Taylor, C. (1994). The politics of recognition. In A. Gutmann (Ed.), *Multiculturalism: Examining the politics of recognition* (pp. 25–73). Princeton, NJ: Princeton University Press.

Togami, S. (1986). *Japanese American: Ijyuu kara jiritu eno ayumi* [Japanese American: Steps of self-reliance from immigration]. Kyoto: Minerva Shobo.

Tule Lake Committee. (2000). *Second kinenhi: Reflections on Tule Lake*. San Francisco: Tule Lake Committee.

Yin, R. K. (2009). *Case study research: Design and methods* (4th edn). Thousand Oaks, CA: Sage.

Yin, R. K. (2012). *Applications of case study research* (3rd edn). Thousand Oaks, CA: Sage.

Yoneyama, R. (2003). *Bouryoku, sensou, ridoresu: Tabunkashugi no politics* [Violence, war, and redress: The politics of multiculturalism]. Tokyo: Iwanami Shoten.

Yui, D. & Endo, Y. (Eds) (1999). *Tabunkashugi no america: Yuragu nashonaru aidentiti* [The US of multiculturalism: Shaken national identity]. Tokyo: Tokyo Daigaku Shuppankai.

 Except where otherwise noted, this work is licensed under a Creative Commons Attribution 3.0 Unported License. To view a copy of this license, visit http://creativecommons.org/licenses/by/3.0/

OPEN

4
Theorizing Multiculturalism: Modeling the Dynamics of Inclusion and Exclusion in School-Based Multicultural Settings

Lee Gunderson

4.1 Introduction

A theoretical review of multiculturalism is incredibly complex. I am aware, for instance, of the complexities and arguments associated with multiculturalism (called multiracialism in Singapore) in many Asian countries. Considering the multiple discourses involved in all of the countries in Asia and the vastness of the topic, I will focus on multiculturalism as it relates to teaching and learning in classrooms that, I am aware, are filled with students with varying cultural backgrounds. This chapter will include some views of individuals I have described in previous reports (Gunderson, 2000, 2007). My purpose is to develop a multicultural model that can be argued, contested, discussed, and possibly observed and tested in classrooms and schools in Asia.

Millions of people around the world are enrolled in classes where they learn a language different from the one they speak at home; they are also immersed in a culture different from their first one (Gunderson, Odo, & D'Silva, 2011). In British Columbia, Canada, for instance, it is not unusual to find classrooms that are filled with students from various cultural backgrounds. Matsumura (2012, personal communication) describes one school in Shiga, Japan, that has a majority of students from Brazil who speak Portuguese but are ethnically Japanese. I have visited many classrooms in Asia with multicultural students. In some cases, students are native-born, but their culture differs from the mainstream culture. In other cases, there are students who are immigrants or come from families that are temporary or work-stay immigrants; they are sometimes called sojourners. But let me first define "culture."

4.2 Culture

About 60 years ago, Kroeber and Kluckhohn (1954) recognized 160 different definitions of culture. Larson and Smalley (1972) proposed that culture represented a map or blueprint which guides the behavior of people in a community and is nurtured in family life. Culture organizes our behavior in groups, makes us sensitive to matters of status, and assists us to know what others expect of us and what will happen if we do not live up to expectations. Culture helps us to know how far we can go as individuals and what our responsibility is to different groups. "Different cultures are the underlying structures which make Round community round and Square community square" (Larson & Smalley, 1972, p. 39).

Condon (1973) proposed that culture "is a system of integrated patterns, most of which remain below the threshold of consciousness, yet all of which govern human behavior just as surely as the manipulated strings of a puppet control its motions" (p. 4). Vontress (1976) concluded that each of us lives in five cultures that intermingle: the universal, ecological, national, regional, and racio-ethnic. Culture is more than the sum of its parts and each of us is more culturally complex than we realize or can describe. Culture allows human beings to survive by providing them the mental constructs to categorize the world. Murdock (1961) describes seven characteristics of cultural patterns: (1) they originate in the human mind; (2) they facilitate human and environmental interaction; (3) they satisfy basic human needs; (4) they are cumulative and adjust to changes in external and internal conditions; (5) they tend to form a consistent structure; (6) they are learned and shared by all the members of a society; and (7) they are transmitted to new generations. Culture can be viewed at two levels: macro—a broad generalization consisting of shared features across a group—and micro—particular features related to an individual or a very small group of individuals.

A discussion of culture often includes descriptions, discussions, and arguments for and against such issues as race, ethnicity, socioeconomic status, economy, gender, religion, and political philosophy. Culture is defined within the parameters of a particular academic perspective. Sociolinguistic definitions differ from anthropological definitions, which differ from ethnolinguistic definitions, and so on. Culture affects the way an individual perceives the world on both macro- and micro-levels. Culture has a direct relationship with one's beliefs about, attitudes toward, expectations for, and views of teaching and learning, and the importance of learning.

When individuals move from one culture to another, there are both micro- and macro-level consequences. According to Schumann (1978a), micro-level features may include such phenomena as culture shock, motivation, and ego permeability. Schumann categorized acculturation relative those who wish to assimilate fully into a culture and those who do not. Schumann (1978a,b, 1986) proposed that two factors affect the degree to which a learner acculturates: social and psychological distance. Variables related to social distance include social dominance, integration pattern, enclosure, cohesiveness, size, cultural congruence, attitude, and intended length of residence. Psychological distance is related to language shock, culture shock, motivation, and ego permeability.

Schumann sees culture shock as one of the most difficult experiences that immigrants encounter. He argues that one who is new to a culture begins to go through acculturation and other processes, during which there are "stages" that represent the degree to which one has become part of or adapted to the new culture.

In acculturation, an individual from one culture must adapt to a new culture. In assimilation, on the other hand, an individual's first culture is submerged in the new one and there is often a loss of values, beliefs, and behavior patterns of the original culture. Acculturation is often associated with an individual's success in learning a new language. Indeed, many have suggested that the failure to acculturate is often associated with the failure to learn a second language (Ellis, 1985).

"Normal" acculturation occurs in four stages: euphoria, culture shock, recovery, and acculturation. "Under normal circumstances, people who become acculturated pass through all the stages at varying rates, though they do not progress smoothly from one stage to the next and may regress to previous stages" (Richard-Amato, 1988, p. 6). There is variation in acculturation, both between and within cultural groups.

A number of factors affect the degree to which individuals become acculturated: nation of origin, reasons for immigrating, age on entry, amount of prior schooling, economic status, difficulties related to travel, extent of disruption and trauma related to war, and a family's immigration status (Gunderson, 2007). Schumann's (1978a) model "seeks to explain differences in learners' rate of development and also in their ultimate level of achievement in terms of the extent to which they adapt to the target-language culture" (Ellis, 1994, p. 230). Acculturation, according to Schumann, means "the social and psychological integration of the learner with the target language (TL) group" (Schumann, 1986, p. 379). However, a number of researchers carry a negative view of acculturation.

Second-language researchers have suggested that acculturation is negative (see, for instance, Duff & Uchida, 1997) because it depicts the second-language learner as one who must give up a first culture. Socialization theorists have a more positive view, though. Duff (2010) notes that "students in classrooms are often socialized into and through discourse of (showing) respect (and self-control, decorum) to teachers, to one another, and to the subject matter itself" (p. 173). Children and other novices learn to function communicatively with members of a community by organizing and reorganizing sociocultural information that is conveyed through the form and content of the actions of others (Schieffelin & Ochs, 1986a,b). Schieffelin & Ochs (1986b) conclude that as children learn to become competent members of their society, they also learn to become competent speakers of their language. Talmy (2012) states that second-language socialization research "is typically longitudinal, ethnographic in design, and favors analytic frameworks that allow for the examination of microgenesis and ontogenesis in (L1 and L2) linguistic and other social practices, as well as how such practices relate to matters of extra-situational, or macro, cultural and social logical significance" (p. 571). Duff and Talmy (2011) note, "Language socialization also differs from cognitivist SLA in its focus on the local social, political, and cultural contexts in which languages are learned and used, on historical aspects of language and culture learning, on contestation in chains across timescales, and on the cultural content of linguistic structures and practices" (p. 96). It is suggested here that the potential for socialization in classroom discourses is associated with a number of cultural features and variables.

4.3 Propaedeutic to a multicultural model

4.3.1 Teaching and learning

Teaching and learning, that is, schooling, are not culture-free. I conclude that "North American educators continue to view education within a 'mainstream' viewpoint, one that focuses on European values and beliefs, even though their school populations grow increasingly multicultural" (Gunderson, 2000). It is clear that immigrant students bring with them complex cultural beliefs about teaching and learning that are, in many respects, different from the views of mainstream teachers and students (Gunderson, 2007).

4.3.2 Significant cultural variables

I believe that culture constitutes the ideas, customs, language, arts, and skills that characterize or reflect a group of individuals in a given period, particularly as they relate to the scholastic learning of the group's members. However, culture is not a singular unitary phenomenon. Indeed, human beings live within the contexts of multiple cultures. In a study of secondary students, Gunderson (2000) notes, "Members of the diasporas in this study were lost in the spaces between various identities: the teenager, the immigrant, the first language speaker, the individual from the first culture, the individual socializing into a second language and culture, the individual in neither a dominant first or second culture but one not of either culture" (p. 702). People exist in multiple intercultures, so that a student who enrolls in a school in a new country brings with her a complex set of beliefs, perceptions, and behaviors related to privacy, cooperation/competition, personal space, eye contact, body movements, and physical contact. In addition, she possesses individual differences that are developed within a culture, which are often referred to as cognitive style. The features include such characteristics as analytic, methodical, reflective, global, relational, and intuitive (Reid, 1987; Scarcella, 1990). Helmer and Eddy (2012) also identify features such as assertiveness/compliance, dominance/submission, and direct/indirect communication styles. Individuals also possess backgrounds that include information about family structure—roles of family members, child-rearing practices, gender roles, adult–child interactions, educational expectations, expression of emotions, conversational rules, child-rearing practices, individual responsibility, and spirituality. The difficulty, of course, lies in the fact that families exist within cultures, and their views and beliefs are formed through interactions with their broader culture, their family's first culture, and their local community's culture, to name a few.

Cultural influences are highly evident in classrooms. But this should not be a surprise, since schools everywhere are designed by persons who represent their cultures. There are variables that represent cultural features—sometimes directly, sometimes indirectly—that can help predict cultural inclusion and exclusion (Gunderson, 2009). Groups of variables can constitute factors.

Cultural differences can affect the degree to which an individual from one culture is included or excluded in the environment of another culture. There would appear to be hundreds of variables that could be identified that are either directly or indirectly related to culture. It would also appear doubtful that a useful model could account for them all. As a consequence, I will attempt to hypothesize factors that impact group dynamics in multicultural classrooms. It is important to note in advance that the proposed factors are neither mutually exclusive nor uniquely different in content.

4.3.2.1 Country of origin

The first factor to consider is a student's country of origin. Where do students come from? This often informs one about the kinds of schools a student has or has not attended. What are the reasons families leave their home countries? Most immigrant families that come to British Columbia (BC) report that their purpose is to get a better education for their children (Gunderson, 2007). Unfortunately, the country of origin often predicts an immigrant's likelihood of success in schools in BC because, in many cases, the country of origin is a marker of other underlying features that are associated with school success or difficulty. The country of origin is likely a factor that impacts school success around the world.

4.3.2.2 Family

The notion of what constitutes a family varies from country to country and, it would seem, within a country as well (Gunderson, 2007). This is one of the most powerful multicultural factors, and probably the most complex as well. Parents and their children have views of teaching and learning that are related to both the views of the first culture and the socioeconomic status.

> *We waste too much time in school. Too much time not working. Teachers are too lazy they don't tell you what to do.* (Male, Cantonese, 15 years old)
> *The labs are better equipped in Canada, but the teachers don't show us what to do with them.* (Female, Cantonese, 16 years old)

Many individuals from higher socioeconomic families generally view learning the way they view business (Gunderson, 2007). From this perspective, the teacher is responsible for supplying the pieces of knowledge, somewhat like products, that are needed to pass a test. The student's responsibility is to memorize (acquire) all of the knowledge the teachers deliver. A measure of success is the number of items the student gets correct in an examination. They have what Freire (1970) called the banking view of teaching. In some cases, the comments clearly differentiated those who were affluent ...

> *There aren't enough parking spaces at school* (male, Mandarin, 18 years old).
> *Canada is really stupid because it builds big beautiful super highways but only lets you go 50 K an hour. That's a waste of money. They waste*

money on immigrants. They give tax money for immigrants to stay in Canada and all they are doing is taking advantage of Canada. It's not good use of tax. Canada people have to get.smart, not waste money on people who don't work. (Female, Cantonese, 16 years old)

... from those who were less affluent:

ESL students work so hard. Even if you do really well you just get an ordinary job. They have no future, that's why so many drop out. Kids have to work to make enough money for comfortable life, no, not even comfortable life. In school there's gangs, there's drugs, oh, it's horrible thing and school's so small, it's unhealthy. I have a few cousins, they all drop out. There's no future so what's the point? You pay extra to go to better class. Money is so important. Most parents can't afford it. (Female, Vietnamese, 17 years old)

Variables related to the family factor are complex. What are the family dynamics? What is the family decision-making structure? Who should be contacted if needed at home? What is the naming system? How are individuals addressed? This is an important issue because the way an individual is addressed or named in some cultures may be considered impolite, insulting, or inappropriate in others. Are there communication patterns associated with different roles, such as those of a parent, child, teacher, or relative?

What are the general attitudes toward school and schooling? Are there strong overall cultural values that might make a difference? Are there views of teaching and learning that might impact students' and parents' views of the instruction occurring in a school? Are there epistemological differences in parental views about what should or should not be the focus of instruction? That is, do the teachers' views of what is valuable for students to learn the same as those of the parents? In some cases, teachers focus on process rather than product (Gunderson, 2000). Differences in views clash and the result is an unfortunate conflict between schools and homes (Li, 2006).

Often, religious orientation has a significant influence on how a family perceives what is being taught in school. What might this mean for teaching–learning relationships? What might this mean for teacher–student, student–student, adult–student, and male-female relationships in school? There are numerous reports of clashes between the views or practices of teachers or the school and the religious views of parents. For instance, parents went to Federal Court in Tennessee (1986, *Mozert v. Hawkins County Public Schools*) because they felt their beliefs were being assaulted by the materials being used in their children's classrooms. DelFattore (1992) wrote this about the trial:

> The protesters, who described themselves as born-again fundamentalist Christians, based their entire understanding of reality on their particular interpretation of the Bible. In their way of looking at life, all decisions should be based solely on the Word of God; using reason or imagination to solve problems is an act of rebellion. Everyone should live in traditional nuclear families structured on stereotyped gender roles. Wives should obey husbands and children their parents, without argument or question. (p. 36)

The reading books used by the teachers were filled with imaginary creatures, fantasy, and fairy tales. Parents were upset about the material, but they were as upset about the notion of asking learners to become critical readers. DelFattore (1992) further notes:

> Imagination, like independent thinking and tolerance for diversity, has no place in the Hawkins County protesters' world view. They alleged that the process of imagination, regardless of the content, distracts people from the Word of God. Once the mind is open to imagination, all kinds of alien thoughts may enter, and the soul may be lost. Moreover, using imagination to solve problems substitutes a human faculty for the absolute reliance on God that is necessary for salvation. (p. 44)

In some cases students are not expected to ask questions of the teachers or of texts, while in other cases, they are. These differences in views are potentially extremely contentious.

4.3.2.3 First and second languages

Language differences can impact student interactions in school. What are some specific language features that might make a difference? Vietnamese speakers, for instance, find it difficult to learn English for various reasons (Honey, 1987). Honey notes, "Because their mother tongue has no inflections, differentiates words by tone, and makes great use of syntax and particles for grammatical purposes, Vietnamese find a language like English, which is so dissimilar to their own, very difficult to learn" (p. 238). There is a relationship between the degree to which one can communicate in the language of instruction and one's inclusion into the culture of the classroom. There is also an overall relationship between L1 and L2 that suggests individuals who speak an L1 that is similar to the L2 may find the latter easier to learn and, as a result, be included into the culture of the classroom. But again, compared to other factors, this relationship is not a major one. Language does make a difference, however.

> The white kids are big and loud like gorillas. You have to get out of the way because they so big. They think they own school because they are born here. They are so, so loud you can't be a friends with them cuz they don't talk, they scream. They are so rude. (Male, Vietnamese, 15 years old)

Perceptions are influenced by L1 backgrounds in complex ways. Language can be a barrier to inclusion:

> I spend two years with no friends, no one. I spend two years not talking, anyone. I go school, I go home, I talk only my mother, my brother. Best friend United States. Cry, all time, cry. Being sick, all time, sick, stomach hurt, head hurt, heart hurt, all time, bad dream, all time, all time. (Female, Kurdish, 16 years old)

4.3.2.4 L1 teaching and learning practices

The methods, procedures, and practices of teaching and learning in an individual's first culture or home country constitute a powerful factor in inclusion/exclusion. I conducted a number of factor analyses to explore English reading as a dependent variable and found that the standard models of L2 reading were not substantiated (Gunderson, 2007). It appears that instructional practice is a variable that may mask underlying differences. Students were taught in systems that used bottom-up teaching styles, and the results revealed bottom-up processing. Immigrants possess a deep-seated view of what constitutes teaching and learning. Many expect to be involved in activities that focus on rote memorization, attention to facts and details, teacher-centered instruction, and a focus on grades. Li (2006), for instance, found that the Chinese parents she studied rejected the teaching and learning going on in their children's school and opted, instead, to rely on activities outside school to give their children the skills they believed to be valuable.

4.3.2.5 Overall numbers and inclusion/exclusion

Schools and school districts in British Columbia vary greatly in the number of immigrant or ESL (English as a second language) students enrolled in them. The range extends from essentially zero immigrants to 100%

(Gunderson, 2007). We designed a study to investigate whether ESL numbers make a difference in reading achievement. Two ESL consultants working in two large school districts were convinced that ESL numbers in a classroom likely affected the English reading achievement of students. They opined that there is probably a critical mass of ESL numbers that would have a negative effect on learning (Eddy, Carrigan, and Gunderson, 2008). We hypothesized that the smaller the ESL number was, the higher their learning would be because more models of the target language would be available to them. The findings were interesting and may say something about inclusion/exclusion.

The study took place in two large urban school districts and included six schools that enrolled students from kindergarten to grade seven. In total, there were 1,013 students in 33 classrooms involved. There were no statistically significant differences in mean income in the six schools. We measured the ratio of native English to ESL speakers; the results for the six schools were A: 87–13%, B: 35–65%, C: 64–36%, D: 39–61%, E: 23–77%, and F: 68–32%. Ratios varied dramatically from classroom to classroom (from 5% to 90% ESL). Reading achievement varied relative to the percentage of ESL students in the classroom. However, the relationship was not linear. Classrooms that had low and high percentages of ESL students scored lower than those that varied from 40% to 60%. The relationship is similar to a bell curve. The results of the interviews suggest that inclusion was also associated with the number of ESL students.

Conversations with the teachers led the research team to conclude that ESL students in low ESL classrooms were, in essence, integrated into the classrooms based on the notion that they would learn English and how to read English simply because their classmates were English speakers and readers, not by making accommodations for their special needs and abilities. This feature is not one of inclusion, but of submersion. In short, these students were excluded unconsciously by being ignored. This finding was corroborated by three independent researchers, who observed and recorded notes over the nine months of the study.

Teachers in high ESL classrooms appeared overwhelmed by the challenges they perceived in the diversity of abilities their students represented. Students were excluded by having teachers ignore their special needs and abilities. Secondary-level students reported that they felt like they were excluded and that it was like being in a ghetto (Gunderson, 2007). Students felt ESL classes were for second-class students—those who had little chance to go on to university. ESL classes made students feel inferior, "like those who are crippled or blind." One 16-year-old male Polish student said, "People make fun of me because I was in ESL." As I argued, "Those who were in ESL classes the longest scored lowest on all of the examinable courses and also had the highest disappearance rate;" also, "parents complained bitterly that ESL classes were roadblocks to students' success and they interfered with the learning of examinable courses."

> *It was hard to make new friends. All my good friends are in Somalia. I don't know anyone in ____ school who is from my country.* (Male, Somali, 16 years old)
> *Too much Chinese. ESL class are fill with Chinese. Teachers no good, not stop Chinese talk. No help Spanish. I not passing nothing.* (Male, Spanish, 14 years old)
> *I'm Kurd, Iraq. No one know (?), no one. Here, many India people, think we being India. Here Chinee people, think India. No one know I not India.* (Male, Kurdish, 14 years old)
> *Too much Chinee talk. Too much Chinee people. No English. Bad class, teacher no good, not stop Chinese talk.* (Male, Kurdish, 14 years old)

So, as a factor, I hypothesize that overall numbers and inclusion/exclusion are complex.

4.3.2.6 Individual differences

Human beings are unique in their ability to cope with elements of their environments. Different authorities and researchers have identified characteristics, such as analytic, methodical, reflective, global, relational, and intuitive, to describe individual differences in the way ESL learners make sense of and cope in the world, especially the classroom (for reviews, see Reid, 1987; Scarcella, 1990). It is unclear what individual differences account for as regards the finding that some students are able to achieve way beyond their apparent capacities in schools where the language of instruction is different from their home languages. These are the resilient students, and some believe resilience can be taught (Roesingh, 2004). Individual differences may account for students' inclusion or exclusion, but it is not clear how strong this factor is or whether teachers can, in fact, reliably and validly measure features associated with variables that make up this factor.

4.3.2.7 The multicultural model

The purpose of this model is to hypothesize variables that are associated with inclusion in multicultural classrooms where the cultural background of the student differs from the culture in the classroom. While there are hundreds or thousands of variables that likely influence the inclusion of a person from one culture into another culture, five factors are proposed here: family, first and second language, overall numbers, individual differences, and first cultural teaching practices. To explore these factors I have used an approach that features focus groups. Several members of a culture (usually no more than 10) are recruited to explore these factors. Practice has shown that the following focus questions are helpful in exploring the five factors (Gunderson, 2009). These questions can also form the basis of an inquiry into the culture of a particular school in order to describe first cultural features.

4.3.3 Focus group questions

(a) Where do students come from?
(b) What is the main religious orientation? (What might this mean for teaching–learning relationships? What might this mean for teacher–student, student–student, adult–student, male–female relationships in school?)
(c) What are the reasons that families leave their home countries?
(d) What is the naming system? (How should people be addressed?)
(e) What are the family dynamics? (What is the family decision-making structure? Who should be contacted if needed at home?)
(f) Are there strong overall cultural values that might make a difference in "our" schools?
(g) What are general attitudes toward school and schooling?
(h) What specific language features might make a difference?
(i) Are there communication patterns associated with different roles, such as parent, child, teachers, authorities, and others?
(J) Are there ways in which the teacher can be sensitive to cultural differences?

4.4 Focus group: An example

Culture is difficult to define, as shown above. It is also difficult to get human beings to agree on what features are common in their own cultures. Gunderson (2009) notes,

> The following observations were made at the University of British Columbia and were developed from a focus group. The reader is cautioned to consider the following as being an extremely limited view developed by five informants who themselves also made it

74 Lee Gunderson

clear that these views were very limited and non-representative. They also concluded and argued strongly that there is no single view that could adequately represent the broad category "Arab." It was noted by one member of the group that there was a great deal of contention and often bitter vituperation related to the inclusion of Egyptians as Arabs. It was noted that many Egyptians have deep respect for their rich cultural and historical roots and view Arabs as being nomadic wanderers without established cultural and historical roots. They often resent being included in the category. The reader is cautioned to remember that the results are dependent on the experience and backgrounds of a local group and they are related to where the individuals came from (Saudi Arabia and the United Arab Emirates).

The task is to compare the knowledge acquired about the first culture, as shown above, with the cultural features of the school to see the matches and mismatches, predict inclusion/exclusion, and identify areas in which the teacher might accommodate students from different cultures. A model is presented in Figure 4.1.

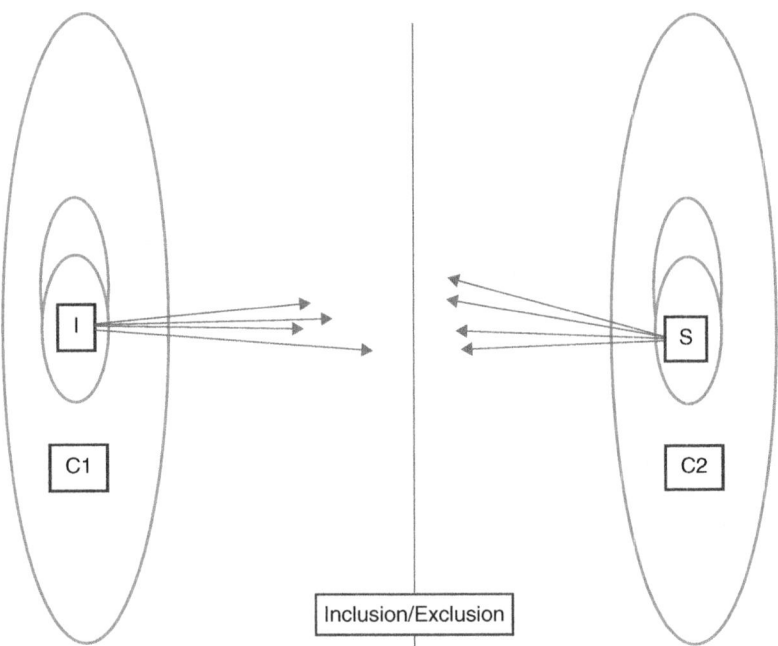

Figure 4.1 First (C1) and second (C2) cultures and inclusion/exclusion
Source: Drawn by author.

A student (I) possesses a complex cultural background that is a composite learned within the overall First Culture (C1). The background includes cultural features associated with family, community, and individual differences. The graphic contains only two intersecting local cultures, although in reality there are many. The second culture (C2) is just as complex. In this case, the school (S) and community cultures overlap within the larger national culture, although the graphic is also considerably less complex than it likely really is. The degree to which a student is included in the C2 is initially related to the match (or mismatch) of C1 and C2 features. The teacher's views are also reflected in the C2. In the case of Arabic speakers, the feature that may be problematic in some schools relates to gender roles. It may be difficult for a young Arabic-speaking immigrant boy to enter a classroom where the teacher is female. This would certainly have a negative effect on his inclusion into the culture of the classroom.

4.5 Conclusion

My purpose was to develop a model of inclusion/exclusion, where students' first cultural features differ from or match those of the classroom. Inclusion and exclusion are complex variables. One feature that is not mentioned has to do with national identities (Pickett & Brewer, 2005). Individuals may not be included because of the way they are perceived relative to a national identity. Esses et al. (2005) conclude that "when national attachment takes the form of nationalism—belief in the superiority of one's nation over others—increased attachment is associated with unfavorable attitudes toward immigrants" (p. 332).

It was proposed that L2 focus groups should be organized within the local school community. Results should be considered local snapshots rather than grand generalizations. A focus group of local L1 individuals should also undertake the same exercise to develop a picture of the same school-related features.

Five factors were hypothesized to be important differentially in the degree to which they are associated with the inclusion of an individual of one culture into a school environment of another culture. As Duff and Talmy (2011) suggest, this approach is one that "addresses the manifold complexities of children or adults with already developed repertoires of linguistic, discursive, and cultural practices as they encounter new ones" (p. 97). As such, it can be described as an L2 socialization view.

Every country in Asia appears to have school-age immigrants enrolled in their schools. It appears that immigrant enrollment varies widely from country to country, area to area, and school to school. The potential for inclusion, theoretically, can be estimated by comparing the cultural features that immigrants bring to a school with the cultural features of the enrolling school (and teachers). Overall, absolute percentages of immigrant students in a classroom are hypothesized to roughly predict inclusion/exclusion, along with other factors. Thus, a small number of immigrants in a classroom will likely not be easily included, nor would students in a class that has a very high number of immigrant students.

At some point, it would be interesting to study the features of this model in classrooms that have varying numbers of immigrant students. At this point, the model is presented here to generate discussion, disagreement, and argument. As a test, one could compare the Arabic cultural features noted above with those in schools in Asia. The question to ask is how do these cultural features compare to the cultural features in my school in Japan, Korea, Taiwan, China, etc.? What potential difficulties might students have and what accommodations might a teacher make to include them?

References

Condon, J. C. Jr. (1973). When people talk with people. In C. David Mortensen (Ed.), *Basic reading in communication theory* (pp. 45–63). New York: Harper and Row.

DelFattore, J. (1992). *What Johnny shouldn't read: Textbook censorship in America*. New Haven, CT: Yale University Press.

Duff, P. A. (2010). Language socialization into academic discourse communities. *Annual Review of Applied Linguistics, 30*, 169–192.

Duff, P. A. & Talmy, S. (2011). Language socialization approaches to second language acquisition: Social, cultural, and linguistic development in additional languages. In D. Atkinson (Ed.), *Alternative approaches to second language acquisition* (pp. 95–116). Oxford: Routledge.

Duff, P. A. & Uchida, Y. (1997). The negotiation of teachers' sociocultural identities and practices in postsecondary EFL classes. *TESOL Quarterly, 31*, 451–486.

Ellis, R. (1985). *Understanding second language acquisition*. Oxford: Oxford University Press.

Ellis, R. (1994). *The study of second language acquisition*. Oxford: Oxford University Press.

Esses, V. M., Dovidio, J. F., Semenya, A. H., & Jackson, L. M. (2005). Attitude toward immigrants and immigration: The role of national and international identity. In D. Abrams, M. A. Hogg, & J. M. Marques (Eds), *The social psychology of inclusion and exclusion* (pp. 317–337). New York: Psychology Press.

Freire, P. (1970). Banking v. problem-solving models of education. *Pedagogy of the oppressed* (pp. 71–86). New York: Continuum.

Gunderson, L. (2000). Voices of the teenage diasporas. *Journal of Adolescent and Adult Literacy, 43,* 692–706.
Gunderson, L. (2007). *English-only instruction and immigrant students in secondary school: A critical examination.* Mahwah, New Jorge: Lawrence Erlbaum Associates.
Gunderson, L. (2009). *ESL (ELL) literacy instruction: A guidebook to theory and practice.* New York: Routledge.
Gunderson, L., Murphy Odo, D., & D'Silva, R. (2011). Second language literacy. In E. Hinkel (Ed.), *Handbook of research in second language teaching and learning* (Vol. II, pp. 472–487). New York: Routledge.
Helmer, S. & Eddy, C. (2012). *Look at me when I talk to you: EAL learners in non-EAL classrooms* (3rd edn). Don Mills, Ontario: Pippin Publishing.
Honey, P. J. (1987). Vietnamese speakers. In M. Swan and B. Smith (Eds), *Learner English: A teacher's guide to interference and other problems* (pp. 238–251). Cambridge: Cambridge University Press.
Kroeber, A. L. & Kluckhohn, C. (1954). *Culture: A critical review of concepts and definitions.* New York: Random House.
Larson, D. N. & Smalley, W. A. (1972). *Becoming bilingual: A guide to language learning.* South Pasadena, California: William Carey Library.
Li, G. (2006). *Culturally contested pedagogy: Battles of literacy and schooling between mainstream teachers and Asian immigrant parents.* Albany: State University of New York Press.
Murdock, G. P. (1961). The common denominator of cultures. In R. Linton (Ed.), *The science of man in the world crisis* (pp. 123–142). New York: Columbia University Press.
Pickett, C. L. & Brewer, M. B. (2005). The role of exclusion in maintaining ingroup inclusion. In D. Abrams, M. A. Hogg, & J. M. Marques (Eds), *The Social psychology of inclusion and exclusion* (pp. 89–111). New York: Psychology Press.
Reid, J. M. (1987). The learning style preferences of ESL students. *TESOL Quarterly, 21*(1), 88–112.
Richard-Amato, P. A. (1988). *Making it happen: Interaction in the second language classroom: From theory to practice.* New York: Longman.
Roesingh, H. (2004). Effective high school ESL programs: A synthesis and meta-analysis. *Canadian Modern Language Review, 60,* 611–636.
Scarcella, R. C. (1990). *Teaching language minority students in the multicultural classroom.* Englewood Cliffs, New Jersey: Prentice-Hall Inc.
Schieffelin, B. B. & Ochs, E. (1986a). Language socialization. *Annual Review of Anthropology, 15,* 163–191.
Schieffelin, B. B., & Ochs, E. (Eds) (1986b). *Language socialization across cultures.* New York: Cambridge University Press.
Schumann, J. (1978a). The acculturation model for second-language acquisition. In R. C. Gingras (Ed.), *Second language acquisition and foreign language teaching* (pp. 27–50). Washington, DC: Center for Applied Linguistics.
Schumann, J. (1978b). Psychological factors in second language acquisition. In J. C. Richards (Ed.), *Understanding second language and foreign language learning* (pp. 163–178). Rowley, Massachusetts: Newbury House Publishers.
Schumann, J. (1986). Research on the acculturalization for second language acquisition. *Journal of Multilingual and Multicultural Development, 7,* 379–392.
Talmy, S. (2012). Second language socialization. In P. Robinson (Ed.), *Routledge encyclopedia of second language acquisition* (pp. 571–575). New York: Routledge.

Vontress, C. E. (1976). Counseling the racial and ethnic minorities. In G. S. Belkin (Ed.), *Counseling: Directions in theory and practice* (pp. 277–290). Dubuque, Iowa: Kendall/Hunt Publishing Company.

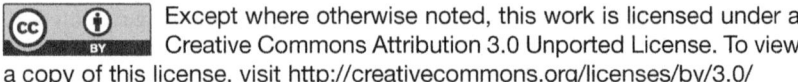 Except where otherwise noted, this work is licensed under a Creative Commons Attribution 3.0 Unported License. To view a copy of this license, visit http://creativecommons.org/licenses/by/3.0/

Part II
Language and Language Policies

OPEN

5
Who Owns Our Tongue? English, Academic Life, and Subjectivity

Kosuke Shimizu

5.1 Introduction

The issue of language as it relates to the disciplines of politics, International Relations (IR) and Asian Studies has received insufficient attention in contemporary academic circles, in part because of the uncritical assumption that language is an unloaded and transparent system of signs that merely conveys the meanings in the mind of the subject. Some scholars argue, however, that using English is a contradiction for the narratives of non-Western political theories and critical Asian Studies because, these critics suggest, English is an exclusively Western language. Nevertheless, the main language in contemporary academia is English, which accounts for a great deal of the publications, particularly in the case of the disciplines noted above. Even though the argument against the use of English in non-Western intellectual activities seems to be reasonable at first glance, a thorough investigation of the language and the disciplines will reveal some hidden and unquestioned assumptions underlying contemporary academic life, particularly relating to subjectivity. This article strives to criticize this immature acceptance of a naive equation of English with the West. Moreover, it argues that English is no longer a Western-owned language and that diversifying the ownership of English will direct us to a more democratic intersubjectivity. However, for this very reason, we must be prepared to accept a hitherto undreamt of grammatical transformation of English.

This grammatical transformation will have a substantial impact on academic circles because it relates to issues of translatability and subjectivity. Translation inevitably involves questions of grammar and pre-determined worldviews. For example, when one moves from the subject-centered ontology of Aristotle to the predicate-centered ontology of Nishida Kitaro (which one can interpret as an abstract form of a world order based on the China-centered tribute system), then the epistemological center of the world—the subject—acquires completely different, sometimes even opposite, forms (Shimizu, 2011). In order to reconcile differences of subjectivity and transcend the problem of incommensurability, contemporary intellectuals need to conduct a thorough investigation of the relationship between academic life and language.

The investigation in this chapter will concentrate on IR as a discipline because of the limited knowledge of the author, but this by no means implies that the argument developed here is inapplicable to other disciplines. Rather, I contend that any academic discipline must take into account the importance of language, particularly in an age of hegemonic domination by English. In order to clarify the points mentioned above, the chapter begins by introducing some arguments about IR and English mainly found in the literature of non-/post-Western International Relations theory (IRT). Second, I will strive to explain the meaning of English's hegemonic domination of IR by referring to Gramsci's theory of hegemony. Next, I will provide an introduction to the theory of World Englishes in order to comprehend the current state of language education and thereby acquire a clearer view of English. Fourth, I will focus on the issue of subjectivity and language by introducing Nishida's theory of the "place of nothingness" and the tribute-cum-trading system of China. I will argue that academic life has to prepare for different approaches towards subjectivity, and hence become an open-ended system of different discourses.

5.2 Practicing IR in English

People have long said that English is the world's *lingua franca*. It is true that the number of people speaking English—either as their first or second language—has been increasing steadily worldwide. According to Kachru, there are three circles of English use. The inner circle includes countries where English functions as the first language, such as the UK, the US, Australia, Canada, and New Zealand. The outer circle includes countries such as India, Nigeria, and Singapore, where English is institutionalized. The expanding circle represents countries such as China, Japan, and Korea, where the diffusion of English has occurred relatively recently, although the social acceptability and social penetration of English is rapidly increasing (Kachru, 2006, p. 453). The fact is that users of English in the outer and expanding circles numerically overwhelm the users in the inner circle. Therefore, the common argument that English is shrinking because the number of English speakers is declining (Huntington, 1996) is misleading. Indeed, one to two billion people worldwide use English, and this means that 18% to 36% of the total global population was using English in 2005 (Kachru, 2006, p. 452).[1]

The situation is the same with IR. Indeed, English seems to be indispensable for understanding contemporary IR, as well as for publishing local knowledge internationally. Chris Brown, in his discussion of British IRT, succinctly summarizes this situation by stating that while Britain's quasi-hegemonic status has disappeared, the "English language remains the language of the discourse of IR" (2011, p. 310). This happened not because of the ease of teaching IR in English, or any recent re-acceptance of the English School by the world audience, but because of American dominance over the discipline (Hoffman, 1977). The English School should be referred to, in this context, as a partial counter-movement to Hoffman's idea of "IR as an American discipline" (Brown, 2011, p. 311), although this confrontation is occurring between two self-identified English-speaking groups.

However, the domination of English over the discipline is found even in the case of non-Western or post-Western IRT literature (Acharya & Buzan, 2007; Chen, 2011; Shani, 2007, 2008; Shilliam, 2010) and one naturally expects the future to see more publications in English in this particular academic area.

Pedagogical practice is one of the most important dimensions of the relationship between IR scholarship and English. As has been observed for a long time, IR is taught mainly in English in the Anglophone world as a Western, or American, discipline. However, even elsewhere, English is gradually becoming the dominant language. In the Asian region, for example, English is becoming the language of IR education. This is caused partly by the lack of appropriate teaching materials for IR in local languages (Hadiwinata, 2009, p. 57), and partly by the gradually increasing recognition in scholarly publications of what "international" means to the concept of subjectivity, which is exclusively based on the assumption of individualistic and self-centered actors in world affairs rather than collective and group-oriented ones (Wæver, 1998, p. 721). How is IR presently taught in Asia? The teaching methods for IR in Asia vary according to region. With respect to Southeast Asia, Chong and Hamilton-Hart (2009) argue that IR course content is sometimes inclined towards certain schools of thought in the region, either because of the influence of national educational policies or because of the educational background of teachers. A good example of the former is Vietnam, where Marxism is treated as the central theory. In the case of the latter reason, realism is mainly taught in some countries in Southeast Asia because the teachers, who were trained in Western institutions, internalize the Western perception of the non-Western world that these countries have unstable regional political relations and insecure governments (Chong & Hamilton-Hart, 2009, pp. 5–6). The latter reason is particularly important for the purpose of the present article. Consequently, the issue of classroom language becomes central in teaching IR to local students. Indeed, teaching is occasionally conducted in English elsewhere, such as in Thailand (Prasirtsuk, 2007, p. 98), while countries such as Indonesia and Malaysia use local language textbooks that are translations from English (Balakrishnan, 2009, p. 117; Hadiwinata, 2009, p. 57). Even in Japan—where it is common knowledge that IR has been taught mainly in the local language with locally written textbooks—teachers started teaching IR in English, using textbooks distributed by Western publishers.

In terms of research, it is worth mentioning that the two leading journals of Asian IR—*The Pacific Review* and *International Relations of the Asia Pacific*—are published in English (Chong & Hamilton-Hart, 2009, p. 2). Further, we find more English-language journals in this field listed in the Social Science Citation Index—e.g. the *Chinese Journal of International Relations, Korean Observer,* and *Asian Perspectives.* The number of Asian scholars producing published works in English shows, in general, an increasing trend, although others do face difficulties, mainly because of the language barrier and heavy workload. In the case of the Japanese Association of International Relations (JAIR), about one hundred members out of roughly two thousand published their books in English, and over three hundred members published articles in English. One expects the number to increase even more if the rate of increase remains the same in the future (Inoguchi, 2007, p. 374). However, some argue that this is an exceptional case. Hadiwinata, for instance, contends that academics and researchers in Indonesia still suffer from a lack of quality research and publications that meet international standards, despite the encouraging development of IR as an academic subject receiving a growing appreciation in many universities (Hadiwinata, 2007, p. 57). The situation is essentially the same in other Asian regions. In China, despite the country's growing presence as a political power in the international arena, related to its successful economic development, scholars seem to be reluctant to reach an international scholarly audience. David Shambaugh contends, "Chinese scholars have little voice or impact on the international IR studies community" because, besides linguistic barriers, they make "no effort whatsoever to publish in English or other foreign language journals and newspapers abroad" (2011, p. 366). In addition, the international output of Chinese scholarship is so tightly controlled and regulated by the government that a relatively small handful of China's IR scholars have received government approval to attend international meetings (Shambaugh, 2011, p. 366).

In the case of Asian IR, English is certainly an impediment. Acharya and Buzan write:

> For those having to work in English as a second or third language, they may feel like it is a barrier, both because of the additional work necessary to put one's thoughts into a foreign language and because of the high rejection rates in the leading English-language IR journals. (2007, p. 296)

These factors certainly keep those working in the "rest of the world" away from engaging in IR in English. This results in relatively low rates of attempts to publish one's writing in a foreign language. This phenomenon is, in a sense, international. The prevalent reluctance to publish one's work in English is not confined to Asia. Indeed, there are some reports that similar trends can be found in the case of IR in non-Anglophone European countries (Friedrich, 2004; Wæver, 1998).

Is English really an impediment for IR scholars in non-Anglophone regions? Should we give up any attempt to announce to a global audience that there are different, and in some cases more convincing, interpretations of IR in these regions? Although the number of scholars engaging in IR research and teaching in English in these areas is still limited, this engagement contains the possibility of an immense impact on IR literature itself when we further investigate the relationship between English and politics.

5.3 What does it mean to study IR in English? Cultural hegemony

As the development of IR is mainly confined to specific areas—the UK and the US—the widespread recognition that English is a *lingua franca* leads us to focus on the issue of politico-cultural hegemony in the Gramscian sense. Because IR as an academic subject is mainly organized in English, it is clear that academic work and publications cannot affect the international audience unless they are written in the dominant language or are translated into it. However, editorial boards and publishers determine and tightly control what is deemed to meet the "international standard," and proficiency and fluency in English are indispensable determinants in international publications and conferences. Scholars publishing articles and books in English receive large numbers of emails every day from companies providing translation and proofreading services.

The ascendance of English in the field of IR leads us to an argument of cultural hegemony, in the (Gramscian) sense that "the use of any language privileges a certain pattern of thought, a specific culture, and particular way of constructing truth" (Friedrich, 2004, p. 8). In other words, the achievement of worldwide recognition in the IR community requires a profound understanding of a certain pattern of thought inherited from a specific geographical area, of a specific cultural background and of the influence of the language on truth constructions. Therefore, to understand IR, we naturally feel the need to internalize not only the language structure but also its historical and cultural background. This, of course, shapes our language pattern and the logical arrangement of knowledge production. Thus, when we write our ideas in English, the arguments we make often result in subconsciously representing, or at least partially representing, the culture and history shared by English-speaking societies.

This leads us to suggest that there is indeed a hegemony of Anglophone IR theories—of the US in particular—in the contemporary academic discipline of IR.

This situation regarding the language and the hegemony of Anglophone IR stays the same if the current mutually reinforcing relationship remains. However, this narrative does not seem to be inevitable if we take into account the recent development of "World Englishes" theory in the study of second language acquisition. The term "World Englishes" here refers to an academic sub-field that accepts localized indigenous English as a legitimate language and encourages the diversification of English, ranging from dialect to creole and pidgin. This theory was initially developed in the late 1980s and the early 1990s, and now seems to have been increasingly accepted in the field of applied linguistics. The term "World Englishes" is often mistakenly assumed to be interchangeable with "World English," but the two terms have very different meanings. The latter refers to English as the *lingua franca* in business, diplomacy, and other forms of global activity, while the former refers to English in a variety of localized forms, including hybrids and creoles.

The arguments that support World Englishes theory inevitably involve focusing on the former British colonies, where English is still used on a regular basis. Theorists of World Englishes often concentrate on the power relationship between the former colonizers and the colonized. Thus, the arguments are highly political and some scholars working on this new development often cite postcolonial critiques in explaining the power relations embedded in language use (Dhillon, 2006).

From the beginning, as seen in Edward Said's *Orientalism*, postcolonial critique has been profoundly influenced by Gramsci's theory of hegemony, as well as Michel Foucault's use of "genealogy." By citing these philosophical works, Said dramatically revealed that the Western political powers constructed both the representation of the "Orient" and the identity of the "Occident" (Said, 1978). The critique of Orientalism intersects with the broad intellectual movements contesting the homogeneity and essentialism that Enlightenment humanist values were said to assume, and the wide-ranging acceptance of Said's *Orientalism* represents a manifestation of the crisis of Western humanism in both its Enlightenment and modernist forms. Said argues that, as a discourse of power, Orientalism constrained and shaped the ways in which the object of its vision, the non-Western other, was perceived and represented (Dhillon, 2006, p. 531). This critical project involved two distinct operations. The first was Foucault's *re-visioning* of Enlightenment science as that which generated a series of "othering" discourses and was thus deeply involved with the project of control. The second program involved revealing the supremacist implications of the Enlightenment idea of progress (Dhillon, 2006, pp. 531–532). This, in turn, transformed the intellectual field of Oriental Studies and Colonial Studies by pitching the discussion in a new way (Spivak, 1988). By bringing this theory into the discussion of language and IR, we inevitably become aware of the power relationship between the "self" and "other."

However, it is often said that Said's theory of Orientalism is based upon a perception that assumes a rigid dichotomy between the West and the Orient. His explanation, therefore, repeatedly renders an image of the world with inelastic boundaries and continuous confrontations over these boundaries. However, culture is not rigid or inflexible. Indeed, it often changes through encounters with other cultures and this generates the dynamism of cultural politics.

5.4 World Englishes and the politics of language

When we focus on the World Englishes literature more thoroughly, the dichotomy of the Occident and Orient becomes less sharp. One of the main architects of this theory is Braj Kachru, who, as I mentioned earlier, explains contemporary English by using three concentric circles, and his concept is the key to overcoming the dichotomy. In Kachru's three circles model, the inner circle consists of Anglophone countries like the UK, US, Australia, Canada, and New Zealand, where societies developed on the socio-linguistic foundation of English and English has been the first language. The outer circle refers to areas that have adopted English and used it as the first or second language because of their colonial past. These areas include India, Pakistan, Malaysia, the Philippines, and Singapore. The expanding circle involves Japan, China, Russia, and the non-Anglophone portion of the EU (Kachru et al., 2006).

These categories are closely related to four types of diaspora. Kachru and Smith (2008) write:

> The first (diaspora) was to Ireland, Scotland and Wales, where local languages were supplanted by English; the second was to regions of North America, Australia, and New Zealand; the third to places such as India, Nigeria, Singapore, and the Philippines; and the fourth to countries such as China, Japan, Korea, Brazil, Germany, and Saudi Arabia, to name only a few in this category. (p. 5)

In this way, the inner circle was mainly constructed by the first and second diasporas, while the outer circle was constructed by the third and the expanding circle by the fourth. The existence of diasporas as mediators means that these three circles are in constant transformation. As different people intermingled with each other, so did the languages they used.

More interestingly, Kachru assigned different functions to each circle. He saw the inner circle as "norm-providing," which means that these countries provide what is regarded as Standard English. The outer circle is defined as the "norm-developing" zone, which develops its own local and endocentric variant of English norms. The third circle consists of "norm-dependent" countries that are seen to rely on the set of standards of English initially developed by the norm-providing countries (Kachru, 1992).

Although there has been a considerable amount of criticism of Kachru's three circles model (Higgins, 2003; Jenkins, 2003; Modiano, 2006; Pennycook, 2003; Seidlhofer, 2001), the model has played the vital role of questioning the existence of a uniform and inflexible English. Questioning the universality and uniformity of English leads us to the next question, namely, that of the diachronic evolution of language. Underlying this approach is the notion that any given language has never been and never will be static (Chew, 2010, p. 46). It is always in the process of transformation. The ever-changing nature of language, in turn, directs us to focus on the way in which a language is ceaselessly reformulated by socio-political forces.

> The impact of the English language as an instrument of intellectual hegemony should not be overstated: it is possible to make good use of English without being over-conditioned by the linguistic medium. More than any other language, English has become neutralised with regard to the specific culture and/or patterns of thought in the mother country, so much so that one may even speculate whether, in addition to British and American English, a new branch of global and/or European English is in the making. (Friedrich, 2004, p. 9)

In a sense, English is probably one of the languages most influenced by the political and economic state of world affairs. Kachru, for instance, suggests that "English has not colonized us but we have colonized the language," quoting Philippine writer Francisco Sionil Jose, and argues that there is a "new revival, and a fresh awakening, about the use of a liberated English in the Philippines" (2006, p. 454).

In this sense, Kachru's statement that "the sun has already set on the Empire but does not set on the users of English" (2006, p. 452) certainly seems true, and this raises another question about the relationship between English and English-speaking societies in the norm-providing nation-states. Indeed, some argue that the separation of English as a language from English as a cultural representation is essential in teaching English. Asmah Haji Omar (1996) argues that English should be looked at "as an entity which can be separated from English culture," and she therefore advises those who are learning English "to learn English but not to ape the Western culture" (p. 532). If culture and language are distinguishable from each other, as Omar claims, then English is by no means the exclusive property of those living in the norm-providing areas and whose lives are embedded in English culture.

In this way, the theory of World Englishes provides contemporary English with a moment of disjuncture between culture and language, and this has major political implications for IR. First, the Westphalia system, which has long been regarded as a political arrangement based on the "Western" method of power distribution, can be revisited as the abstract form of an inter-state system because we can see that nation-states have been applied to and adopted by those areas that do not subscribe to the alleged "Western" political norms. Rather than perceive all nation-states, regardless of their geographical location, as standardized and homogenized in the way that the Westphalian norms prescribe, hybrid forms of nation and state are far more likely in reality. In fact, many writers from the outer circle, such as Salman Rushdie, Rohinton Mistry, Shashi Tharoor, Amitav Ghosh, and Arundhati Roy, employ hybrid forms of English and question the monolithic image of nationhood. Dissanayake contends:

> These writers are seeking to gain entrance to their multifaceted subjectivities by "decolonizing" the English language and the sedimented consciousness that goes with it. Many of them regard the English language as the repressive instrument of the hegemonic colonial discourse. They wish to emancipate themselves from its clutches by probing deeper and deeper into their historical pasts, cultural heritages, and the intricacies of the present moment. Through these means, they seek to confront their protean selfhoods. What is interesting is that these writers are striving to accomplish this liberation through the very language that has in the past shackled them to what can be characterized as an ambiguous colonial legacy. (2006, p. 557)

In the stories of these writers, we can locate the counter-narratives of nation and the passionate endeavor to destabilize the political maneuvers through which imagined communities with essentialist identities become possible. This pluralized English here becomes the strategic means by which the given identity of the nation-state is questioned. We can say here that English is no longer the exclusive property of those residing in the core, but is owned by the entire population, who use it every day as a device for communication.

Second, if the theory of World Englishes not only transfers our focus onto a new awareness of the subjectivity of the periphery, it also questions the subjectivity of contemporary world affairs in general. As the above quotation reveals, the theory of World Englishes, in the age of postcoloniality, dismantles a fundamental notion. Identity is seen as neither rigid nor robust; rather, it is often protean and amalgam-like. This protean self often strategically takes an identity in one place and substitutes it with another identity in a different context.

> These writers are constantly crossing and recrossing boundaries both topographical and linguistic so as to capture the complex dynamics of the present historical conjuncture and cultural moment. Some of them move back and forth between home and exile, at times

interchanging their ontologies. They are exiled from home but at home in the language that over-determines the exilic experience, and their identities are shaped in the tensional interstices of two cultures. This liminality, in-betweenness, appears to be vital maker of postcolonial spaces. (Dissanayake, 2006, p. 558)

Those who hold different identities at different points in time and space move through and cross over the pre-set boundaries of cultures. They continuously generate the space of encounters, conflicts, and amalgams for various cultures and traditions. Therefore, cultures, like languages, undergo social construction and are subject to continuous transformation.

The idea of ever-transforming cultures and languages has an immense impact not only on the periphery of the concentric circles but also at the very core. In fact, harsh reactions have erupted from the core against the idea of transformative cultures and languages. Samuel Huntington, for instance, argues that the English spoken in certain areas is "unintelligible" (1996, p. 62). Quirk calls for "universally recognized standards" of English so that the language retains its "reliability" (2003, pp. 13–14). This reaction also involves economic interests. Kachru (2006) rightly talks about "English as a commodity, with immense value in the international language market." Those who "own" the commodity demand the right to "safeguard it and preserve it in terms of pounds and dollars" (Kachru, 2006, p. 463). In such cases, ideas about "standard" and "normative" English are a part of the production of economic profit.

The problem here is that safeguarding the boundaries of English conflicts with the hybridity of English that we can see around the world. What we should focus more on is instead *creativity*, which the pluralization of English brings into being; this focus in turn forces us to reorient our perception towards "what constitutes a harmonious, cohesive, integrated, and motivated speech community" (Kachru, 2006, p. 463).

5.5 From confrontation to relationality

The controversy over World Englishes is characterized by the rigidity of the contestants, both those who strive to protect the privileged status of norm-providing cultures and those who shake the pre-given structure of domination through the means of language as explained above. Both sides have their own justifications and rationalizations. Those trying to protect the dominant regime of English argue that the concept of varieties of English leads to unintelligibility and incommensurability among the users, while those attempting to portray the hybrid nature of identities through their defense of localized English contend that the idea of varieties of English is essential in constituting democracy in the newly emerging cosmopolitan culture.

What permeates both positions, however, is a subjectivity constructed prior to the confrontational encounter between the two sides of the World Englishes dispute, and the subjectivity that each side focuses on is presumably constructed by socio-political factors and elements elsewhere. Some may argue against the statement that the hybrid forms of identities are not set *a priori*, in the sense that their subjectivities are constituted through the practice of crossing over cultural boundaries. This is correct, and this is precisely the reason why I contend that their identities are pre-set. Their subjectivities are assumed to exist *before* the dispute. What is missing in this argument is the awareness that subjectivity is constituted and discovered *through* the World Englishes dispute over who owns the language. In other words, the presumed dialectical relationship between the core and periphery misses the point of the construction of subjectivity through the investigation of relationality. It is not local history, heritage, and the experience of crossing over boundaries that perform an essential role in the construction of subjectivity. Rather, one can say that those engaged in the dispute in search of these elements discover these subjectivities, which account for their peculiar identities that then must be distinguished from the "other."

In this sense, the concept of World Englishes clarifies a system of relationality, which includes the subjectivity of the disputants in the World Englishes dispute, where the emergence of relationships constructs the subjects. Therefore, the important issues here are how relationships shape and engender the subject, and how this process of subjectivity production ensures the emergence of an inclusive public domain in world affairs.

The idea of relationality, which constitutes subjectivity, is relatively visible and is often understood as common sense in the peripheries of the contemporary hegemony. Perhaps one of the archetypal examples in this context is Nishida Kitaro's philosophical concept of the "place of nothingness." Nishida, one of the most prominent Japanese philosophers, claimed that individuals do not exist prior to experience, but, rather, experiences construct individuals (Nishida, 1947, p. 4). Thus, individual identity relies entirely on its experiences. In society, the experiences that produce individual identities are, by definition, social, and therefore relational. This means that the relationality of subjects becomes the central focus of inquiry into socio-politics.

How, then, do socio-political relations constitute the subject? Here, probably, it is important to distinguish self-image from self-identity. Shih (2012) contends that self-identity is about drawing boundaries between the self and others in order to distinguish between them (p. 25). Identity construction is therefore intended to discover something different from the character of everyone else. This becomes a cause of violence, whether physical or discursive. In sum, identity making is a practice of violent "othering." Imamura (2008) goes even further, arguing that violence is caused by what he calls the "original division," and this original division resides in the use of the "I" that draws a boundary between "I" and "You." This original division is inherently violent in the sense that it engenders a distance between entities, and this distance is stabilized and institutionalized through the universalization of specific subjects through a standardized vocabulary (Imamura, 2008, p. 73).

Image, by contrast, is about the "evaluation" of others. In this context, the subject "performs in accordance with a certain consensually agreed upon role, explicitly as well as implicitly, between one and other who presumably evaluate" (Shih, 2012, pp. 25–26). Because others are the mirror that reflects the image of the subject, the latter is inevitably involved in relationships with others. While identity is rigid in the sense that it is presumably an *a priori* construction existing before the formation of relationships, image is, by definition, context-sensitive and, therefore, flexible with respect to the relationship (Shih, 2012, p. 26).

In this system of relationality, the subject is always changing and so is the system. Thus, "order" means the continuous transformation of subjectivity and relationality. There is no pre-given order or norms, but instead an interminable flow of relations. A reification of this system in IR is China's tributary trading system.

Hamashita (1990) defines the tributary system as an always-changing system based on trade relations, which is inclusive of different elements. This inclusivity emanated from the core of the system, which actually had a relatively weak centripetal force (Hamashita, 1990, pp. 32–33). All relationships among member countries were bilateral rather than multilateral, so that no member faced exclusion as a result of the violation of universal norms and regulations, simply because there was no such thing. Rather, all bilateral relationships were dealt with on a case-by-case basis (Shih, 2013) and this resulted in constant systemic transformations. Since this system was not constructed on a foundation of strong centripetal power, unlike the hegemony generally familiar to the contemporary IR audience, all members in the tribute system were allowed to have their own "centres" (Hamashita, 2003, p. 20).

What becomes the central theme in comprehending this complex system is the "periphery," as in the case of World Englishes. By focusing on the periphery of the system, it becomes clear that "inclusiveness," "mediation," and "differentiation" are the essential characteristics of a tribute structure of multiple centers (Hamashita, 1994, p. 3). According to Hamashita, what characterized the indispensable functions that those peripheries performed in the tributary system was the spontaneous relationship among ports. The intricate network was composed of a web of maritime trading routes between the center and the peripheries, and between one periphery and another, in each case on a bilateral basis. Unlike the general perception that prevails in the contemporary geographical understanding of oceans, which sees them as obstacles and impediments to trading, the perception presented by Hamashita (2003) is one in which the oceans shaped a public sphere in Asia before the sudden arrival of Western modernity and civilization.

The region's socio-political and socio-economic dynamism was mainly generated at the peripheral areas instead of at the center. This is because there were multiple centers in the system; the entire structure of tribute-cum-trading was constructed on the premise of multiple circles overlapping with the major system (of concentric circles) and with each other. The peripheries thus occurred at the intersection of the various circles, and were characterized by mixed cultures.

The above analysis reveals the blurred core of the tribute system, and resembles the concept of diffuse centers of World Englishes. The World Englishes theory suggests that the dynamism of English is mainly generated in the "outer circle." Similarly, the primary functioning part of the tribute-cum-trading system was the periphery. This in turn reveals the inflexible perception of the hegemony of contemporary IR, and raises serious doubts about the unquestioned superiority of the subjectivity residing at the core of the system of IR.

How could we theorize the blurred subjectivity evident in both the theory of World Englishes and the tribute-cum-trading system? This vague image of the subject is completely opposed to that assumed by traditional Western philosophy—an autonomous and sovereign subject with strictly demarcated boundaries. In order to find a possible answer to this question, we have to go back to what Nishida Kitaro calls the "place of nothingness." Nishida argues that the subject is not autonomous or independent. The subject in the ordinary sense is always to open to society and depends on relationality for its construction. However, at the same time, this subject encompasses all the relationality that appears to the subject. Therefore, the subject is constructed by interactions with others while also providing the space for such interactions. This space is, in a sense, not a subject, however, because it only accepts and permits these interactions to take place. Therefore, it is a place (Nishida, 1949).

This is, in a sense, a double subjectivity, which consists of a constructed and an encompassing subject. These two are contradictory, but are integrated simultaneously. This contradiction is absolute rather than relative, because this contradiction involves the self's opposition to itself. There is nothing in this place prior to the interactions, and thus Nishida sometimes describes it as the "place of absolute nothingness," which is in sharp contrast to "relative nothingness," which is indeed antonymous to "being." In this sense, a place of nothingness is based on the concept of the absolute nothingness, and in fact Nishida later used a different concept to refer to the same idea, namely, "absolute contradictory self-identity" (Nishida, 1965).

It is possible to say that Nishida's concept of the "place of nothingness" is the key to understanding the political meaning of World Englishes and the tribute system of China. Both are inclusive towards others and have a blurred center. Nevertheless, they function as systems with coherence and continuity. They transform themselves into something new in a continuous manner. In this sense, using Englishes as a communicative device for comprehending contemporary world affairs is equivalent to saying that IR is a place that is inclusive towards different narratives and the discourses of others.

Introducing the concept of the "place of nothingness" and the tribute system of China into our intellectual activities is more of a thought experiment than the provision of a concrete policy program. It is suggestive, however, in considering the future paradigm of research methodology. In order to transform IR into a more diverse and democratic discipline, we have to ready ourselves for the forthcoming changes that will presumably take place at the peripheries. Rather than turn down arguments and theories of non-Western traditions mainly because of their "imperfect" English quality or logical inconsistency, we have to focus more on elements, whether intentional or coincidental, generated by new and unfamiliar forms of representation. IR will otherwise become one of those means of unification and standardization at the world scale that, according to Hannah Arendt, are a typical feature of the disappearance of the public and totalitarianism. Thus, we can conclude here that it is not others who need to be transformed into something new, but those who are working on contemporary world affairs.

5.6 Conclusion

In this chapter, I have tried to explain how language easily becomes a device for the totalizing and unifying power of modern politics, while nevertheless also containing the potential for transformation and diversification of our perception of the contemporary world. I also strived to clarify that the transformative elements often appear not in the center of the world, but in the relationship with peripheries. It is in this relationship between the core and peripheries that diversification processes initially take place. The diversification of perception is of particular importance in the context of contemporary multiculturality in the region in the sense that it presumably creates a more democratic sphere for intersubjectivity. Without the democratic intersubjective space, conflicts and confrontations in the substantive world would seem to be more likely.

However, this diversification is by no means an easy task, because language is often associated with and controlled by nation-states with established subjectivities. When we focus on Japanese, for instance, it automatically gives us the impression that we are to deal with Japan as a nation-state, Japanese culture as maintained by Japanese nationals, and Japanese history as something continuous and linear. This is the conceptual power of the nation-state that severely controls our intellectual lives. In this sense, conducting critical investigations into language— and subsequent critical analysis of subjectivity—must inevitably involve a critical inquiry specifically into the concept of the nation-state. Therefore, the next questions to address in this context include the following: Why does the concept of the nation-state hold such a strong power over human thinking? Why is it extremely difficult to think of the world without the concept of the nation-state? What sort of world could we imagine if we consciously avoided the use of the concept? These questions obviously pose a serious challenge to researchers, but I firmly believe that they are worth trying to answer.

Note

1. The population estimates are from 2004.

References

Acharya, A. & Buzan, B. (2007). Why is there no non-Western international relations theory? An introduction. *International Relations of the Asia-Pacific, 7*(3), 287–312.
Balakrishnan, K. S. (2009). International relations in Malaysia: Theories, history, memory, perception and context. *International Relations of the Asia-Pacific, 9*(1), 107–130.

Brown, C. (2011). Development of international relations theory in the UK: Traditions, contemporary perspectives, and trajectories. *International Relations of the Asia-Pacific, 11*(2), 309–330.
Chen, C. C. (2011). The absence of non-Western IR theory in Asia reconsidered. *International Relations of the Asia-Pacific, 11*(1), 1–23.
Chew, P. G. L. (2010). From chaos to order: Language change, lingua francas and world Englishes. In M. Saxena, & T. Omoniyi (Eds), *Contending with globalization in world Englishes* (pp. 45–71). Bristol: Multilingual Matters.
Chong, A. & Hamilton-Hart, N. (2009). Teaching international relations in Southeast Asia: Historical memory, academic context, and politics—An introduction. *International Relations of the Asia-Pacific, 9*(1), 1–18.
Dhillon, P. (2006). Colonial/postcolonial critique: The challenge from world Englishes. In B. B. Kachru, Y. Kachru, & C. L. Nelson (Eds), *The handbook of world Englishes* (pp. 529–544). Oxford: Blackwell.
Dissanayake, W. (2006). Cultural studies and discursive construction of world Englishes. In B. B. Kachru, Y. Kachru, & C. L. Nelson (Eds), *The handbook of world Englishes* (pp. 545–566). Oxford: Blackwell.
Friedrich, J. (2004). *European approaches to international relations theory: A house with many mansions.* London: Routledge.
Hadiwinata, B. S. (2009). International relations in Indonesia: Historical legacy, political intrusion, and commercialization *International Relations of the Asia-Pacific, 9*(1), 55–81.
Hamashita, T. (1990). *Kindai chugoku no kokusaiteki keiki* [The international turning point of modern China]. Tokyo: Tokyo University Press.
Hamashita, T. (1994). Shuhenkarano ajiashi [The Asian history from periphery]. In Y. Mizoguchi, T. Hamashita, N. Hiraishi, & H. Miyazaki (Eds), *Shuhenkarano rekishi* [The history from periphery] (pp. 1–14). Tokyo: Tokyo University Press.
Hamashita, T. (2003). Tribute and treaties: Maritime Asia and treaty port networks in the era of negotiation, 1880–1900. In G. Arrighi, T. Hamashita, & M. Selden (Eds), *The resurgence of East Asia: 500, 150 and 50 year perspective* (pp. 1–16). London: Routledge.
Higgins, C. (2003). Ownership of English in the outer circle: An alternative to the NS-NNS dichotomy. *TESOL Quarterly, 37*(4), 615–644.
Hoffman, S. (1977). An American social science: International relations. *Daedalus, 106*(3), 41–60.
Huntington, S. P. (1996). *The clash of civilizations and the remaking of world order.* New York: Simon and Schuster.
Imamura, H. (2008). Boryokuizen no chikara, boryoku no kongen [The power prior to violence, the origin of violence]. In T. Tani (Ed.), *Boryoku to ningen sonzai* [Violence and human existence] (pp. 70–86). Tokyo: Chikumashobo.
Inoguchi, T. (2007). Are there any theories of international relations in Japan? *International Relations of the Asia-Pacific, 7*(3), 369–390.
Jenkins, J. (2003). *World Englishes: A resource book for students.* London: Routledge.
Kachru, B. B. (1992), *The other tongue: English across cultures.* Urabana: University of Illinois Press.
Kachru, B. B. (2006). World Englishes and culture wars. In B. B. Kachru, Y. Kachru, & C. L. Nelson (Eds), *The handbook of world Englishes* (pp. 446–471). Oxford: Blackwell.
Kachru, B. B., Kachru, Y., & Nelson, C. L. (Eds) (2006). *The handbook of world Englishes.* Oxford: Blackwell.

Kachru, Y., & Smith, L. E. (Eds) (2008). *Cultures, contexts and world Englishes*. New York: Routledge.
Modiano, M. (2006). Euro-Englishes. In B. B. Kachru, Y. Kachru, & C. L. Nelson (Eds), *The handbook of world Englishes* (pp. 223–239). Oxford: Blackwell.
Nishida, K. (1947). *Zen no Kenkyu* [An inquiry into the good]. In *Nishida Kitaro zenshu* [Collected works of Nishida Kitaro] (Vol. 1, pp. 3–200). Tokyo: Iwanami.
Nishida, K. (1949). *Basho* [The place]. In *Nishida Kitaro zenshu* [Collected works of Nishida Kitaro] (Vol. 4, pp. 208–289). Tokyo: Iwanami.
Nishida, K. (1965). *Zettai mujunteki jiko doitsu* [The absolute contradictory self-identity]. In *Nishida Kitaro zenshu* [Collected works of Nishida Kitaro] (Vol. 4, pp. 147–222). Tokyo: Iwanami.
Omar, A. H. (1996). Imperial English in Malaysia. In J. A. Fishman, A. W. Conrad, & A. Rubal-Lopez (Eds), *Post-Imperial English: Status change in former British and American colonies 1940–1990* (pp. 513–533). Berlin: Mouton de Gruyter.
Pennycook, A. (2003). Global Englishes, rip slyme, and performativity. *Journal of Sociolinguistics, 7*(4), 513–515.
Prasirtsuk, K. (2007). Teaching international relations in Thailand: Status and prospects. *International Relations of the Asia-Pacific, 9*(1), 83–105.
Quirk, R. (2003). From Latin to English. *The Use of English, 55*(1), 7–15.
Said, E. (1978). *Orientalism*, New York: Vintage.
Seidlhofer, B. (2001). Closing a conceptual gap: The case for a description of English as a lingua franca. *International Journal of Applied Linguistics, 11*(2), 133–156.
Shambaugh, D. (2011). International relations studies in China: History, trends, and prospects. *International Relations of the Asia-Pacific, 11*(3), 339–372.
Shani, G. (2007). "Provincializing" critical theory: Islam, Sikhism and international relations theory. *Cambridge Review of International Affairs, 20*, 417–433.
Shani, G. (2008). Towards a post-Western IR: The *Umma, Khalsa Panth*, and critical international relations theory. *International Studies Review, 10*, 722–734.
Shih, C. Y. (2012). *Civilization, nation and modernity in East Asia*. London: Routledge.
Shih, C. Y. (2013, March). *Balance of relationships: A Confucian route for international relations system*. Paper presented at the International Symposium on English School. Ritsumeikan University, Kyoto.
Shilliam, R. (2010). *International relations and non-Western thought: Imperialism, colonialism and investigations of global modernity*. London: Routledge.
Shimizu, K. (2011). Nishida Kitaro and Japan's inter-war foreign policy: War involvement and culturalist political discourse. *International Relations of the Asia-Pacific, 11*(1), 157–183.
Spivak, G. C. (1988). Can the subaltern speak? In C. Nelson & L. Grossberg (Eds), *Marxism and the interpretation of culture* (pp. 271–313). Urbana: University of Illinois Press.
Wæver, O. (1998). Sociology of a not so international discipline: American and European developments in international relations. *International Organization, 52*(4), 687–727.

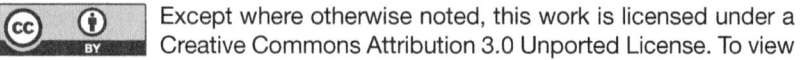
Except where otherwise noted, this work is licensed under a Creative Commons Attribution 3.0 Unported License. To view a copy of this license, visit http://creativecommons.org/licenses/by/3.0/

OPEN

6
Preservice and Inservice English as a Foreign Language Teachers' Perceptions of the New Language Education Policy Regarding the Teaching of Classes in English at Japanese Senior High Schools

Toshinobu Nagamine

6.1 Introduction

To date, Japan has attempted to create national-level standardization so as to consolidate the quality of education. One reason for this is an awareness of "global competitiveness" (Hargreaves, 1994, p. 5). Knowledge of science and technology is assumed to promote Japan's productivity and prosperity and to stabilize its national position in international affairs. Thus, the government, especially after the Second World War, carried out a series of education reforms in order to institutionalize "scientific disciplines after Western models" (Figal, 1999, p. 77). As a result, national conformity in the quality of education has made it possible for Japan to claim excellence in basic education founded on the rigid compulsory education system (see Lucien, 2001).

It cannot be denied, however, that such educational conformity has generated some negative repercussions. For instance, scientific knowledge and mathematical certainty are excessively valued and actively sought in the education system, while humanistic aspects of education are undervalued, particularly in the area of the liberal arts (McCarty, 1995; cf. Toulmin, 1990). Furthermore, since the quality of teachers was for a long time left unquestioned, what the Japanese call *shishitsu* (i.e. the quality of teachers) has recently been called into question. This issue has become a crucial theme in today's educational debates in Japan (e.g. Grossman, 2004). This fact, among others, clearly indicates that the top-down approach to education reforms should be replaced with a bottom-up approach (Nagamine, 2008).

The new version of *The Course of Study* (national curriculum guidelines) was announced by the Ministry of Education, Culture, Sports, Science, and Technology (MEXT) in March 2009 (MEXT, 2009). The new version includes measures to improve students' communicative competence in English in Japanese senior high schools. One of the measures is to mandate that senior high school English as a Foreign Language (EFL) teachers conduct all classes in English. Chapter 3, provision 4 of the common content for all subjects in the new *Course of Study* states the following:

> When taking into consideration the characteristics of each English subject, classes, in principle, should be conducted in English in order to enhance the opportunities for students to be exposed to English, transforming classes into real communication scenes. Consideration should be given to use English in accordance with the students' level of comprehension. (MEXT, 2011)

This new language education policy has been implemented since the 2013 academic year. Even before the enactment, however, it had already generated repercussions among preservice and inservice EFL teachers and teacher educators in Japan (Yamada & Hristoskova, 2011).

Many scholars and researchers alike asserted that the new policy was developed and introduced abruptly by MEXT in a top-down fashion and that it does not reflect the reality facing EFL teachers in local school settings. Glasgow (2012), for instance, highlighted native English-speaking teachers' and Japanese EFL teachers' uncertainty about their roles in implementing the policy, and implied the possibility of an unsuccessful policy implementation. It was also argued that the quality of English education would likely decline as a result of the policy enforcement (cf. Shin, 2012). This argument appears to be based primarily on the presupposition that the use of students' mother tongue or first language in class (i.e. teachers' and students' use of Japanese in Japanese EFL contexts) plays a crucial role in developing Cognitive Academic Language Proficiency (CALP); thus, the new language education policy was criticized as merely forcing teachers to emphasize the development of Basic Interpersonal Communicative Skills (BICS) (see Cummins, 1979, 1984).

As Yamada and Hristoskova (2011) mention, MEXT's new language education policy has indeed become the subject of heated debates in the field of English education. What is missing in the nationwide debates, however, is in-depth, constructive discussions not only on how inservice EFL teachers perceive the new language education policy, but also on how preservice EFL teachers perceive it in teacher education settings. The new language education policy certainly requires EFL teachers to change their beliefs regarding English learning and teaching, as well as their pedagogical approaches and teaching practices. Nevertheless, while the voices of policy makers and academics (people who hold more power) can be heard, the voices of critical stakeholders, such as preservice and inservice EFL teachers (people who hold less power), are rarely heard. In other words, a dialogue in which the critical stakeholders can engage each other is lacking.

This observation is crucial because, as Freire (1993, pp. 92–93) asserts, "[w]ithout dialogue there is no communication, and without communication there can be no true education." Another remark by Freire (1993, p. 90) may be pivotal to cite here: "How can I dialogue if I am closed to—and even offended by—the contribution of others? How can I dialogue if I am afraid of being displaced, the mere possibility causing me torment and weakness?" It can therefore be argued that the voices of critical stakeholders should receive greater attention, and that these voices need to be taken into consideration and reflected in the process of policy making and implementation (cf. Mâṭă, 2012; Mahboob & Tilakaratna, 2012).

Gorsuch (2000) claims that conditions in schools and classroom settings tend to affect teachers' perceptions of pedagogical approaches. Unless such context-bound, socioeducational, and often political factors are taken into account, our arguments for and against the new language education policy may ultimately prove fruitless. Or, even worse, English teachers (both preservice and inservice teachers) will most likely end up as the main barrier to educational change (cf. Shin, 2012; Pan & Block, 2011). Therefore, a qualitative case study was designed and conducted to explore and investigate preservice as well as inservice EFL teachers' perceptions of the new language education policy.

This chapter discusses the major research findings of the study. Primary data were gleaned from multiple sessions of semi-structured, in-depth interviews with four participants: two preservice teachers (one male and one female) and two inservice teachers (one male and one female). The collected data were analyzed employing the grounded theory approach (GTA) (Strauss & Corbin, 1994, 1998). In what follows, the research design and its rationales are explained, and the major research findings presented. Based on the research findings, some implications are also proposed for policy makers, administrators, and teacher educators to develop and implement language education policies successfully in Asian EFL contexts in general and Japanese EFL contexts in particular.

6.2 Research methodology

6.2.1 Qualitative research design and case-study approach

According to Maxwell (1996), five major research purposes typically appear in qualitative research: (a) to understand meaning(s); (b) to understand a particular context; (c) to identify unanticipated phenomena and influences; (d) to understand processes; (e) to develop causal explanations. Considering such purposes and the nature of the present study (i.e. descriptive, particularistic, and heuristic), a qualitative research design was employed. In addition, a case-study approach was applied by regarding "case" as "a thing, a single entity, a unit around which there [were] boundaries" (Merriam, 2001, p. 27). The present study aimed to provide an "in-depth insight into complicated situated and social issues" (Mann & Tang, 2012, p. 477) involved in enacting the new language education policy in Japanese EFL contexts.

Since four participants were investigated, the present study may be categorized as a collective case study (Stake, 2005) allowing the researcher to examine "both the uniqueness and similarity" (Mann & Tang, 2012, p. 477) of the participants. This study was a small-scale study that incorporated four cases. Hence the primary goal was not "generalization in a statistical sense" (Merriam, 2001, p. 61) (cf. Maxwell, 2002), but instead, the particularization of observed and interpreted phenomena (cases) was considered the main goal (see Davis, 1995).

6.2.2 Participants

As noted earlier, the participants comprised four EFL teachers; two preservice EFL teachers (one male and one female) and two inservice EFL teachers (one male and one female). All participants were selected in such a way that the researcher could increase the opportunity "to identify emerging themes" (Erlandson, Harris, Skipper, & Allen, 1993, p. 82) embedded in the context, choose "information-rich cases" (Patton, 2002, p. 230), and achieve typicality or representativeness of Japanese EFL contexts and EFL teachers (both preservice and inservice teachers). Rather than using probability sampling or random sampling, purposeful sampling was used to select the participants (see Creswell, 1998; Eisenhardt, 2002; Maxwell, 1996; Merriam, 2001). Their biographical information is presented in Table 6.1, in which pseudonyms are used to protect the identity of the participants.

6.2.3 Data collection and analysis

Primary data were collected through multiple sessions of individual in-depth interviews. Each in-depth interview had a semi-structured format and was conducted in Japanese. All interview sessions were recorded using an Integrated Circuit (IC) recorder. Recorded data were then transcribed for later data analysis. The data analysis was conducted following GTA procedures (see Strauss & Corbin, 1994, 1998). Prior to the implementation of the present study, there were no hypotheses or theories on which this study could be based due to a lack of research on preservice EFL teachers' perceptions regarding the new language education policy. In other words, there was no *a priori* theory on which any hypothesis could be deductively formulated for testing (Eisenhardt, 2002). Thus, a deductive, hypothesis-testing

Table 6.1 Participants' biographical information

	Sayaka	Yuji	Tomoko	Makoto
Age	28	36	24	23
Gender	Female	Male	Female	Male
Employment Status	Inservice (temporary teacher)	Inservice (full-time teacher)	Preservice (graduate student)	Preservice (graduate student)
Education	Bachelor's degree	Bachelor's degree	Bachelor's degree, Master's degree (in progress)	Bachelor's degree, Master's degree (in progress)
Teaching Experience	3-week teaching practicum at a junior high school, 5 years at a public senior high school	2-week teaching practicum, 13 years at public senior high schools	3-week teaching practicum at a junior high school	2-week teaching practicum at a senior high school, 1 year as a private tutor
Studying/ Traveling Abroad Experience	None	None	None	Enrolled in an English as a Second Language program in Canada for 1 month
Teacher Employment Exam	Not yet passed	Passed	Passed	Not yet passed

Source: Primary data collected by the author.

research design was speculated to be inappropriate. Accordingly, the present study aimed at "theory building."

The researcher of this study made an attempt to construct a grounded theory consisting of essentially conceptual categories. Strauss and Corbin (1998, p. 12) describe the rationale as follows: "[t]heory derived from data is more likely to resemble the 'reality' than is theory derived by putting together a series of concepts based on experience or solely through speculation (how one thinks things ought to work)." Suddaby (2006, p. 634) adds that it is appropriate to use GTA when the researcher wants "to make knowledge claims about how individuals [social actors] interpret reality." Therefore, the study focused on the interpretive process of the collected data by analyzing "the actual production of meanings and concepts used by social actors in real settings" (Gephart, 2004, p. 457).

All transcribed interview data were segmented in consideration of every utterance's meaning and subtle nuances (translation from Japanese to English was carried out in this stage). Open coding was then performed. Open coding is the part of data analysis concerned with identifying, naming, categorizing, and describing phenomena found in the transcribed interview data. Open coding is usually done based on identified features of the phenomena under investigation (the properties and dimensions of all segmented data) (see Table A6.1). Referring to the identified properties and dimensions of the data, axial coding was performed to verify the relationships/connections among the categorized data (i.e. sub-categories and core categories). After the axial coding, selective coding was carried out. In the process of selective coding, core categories were selected, identified, and systematically related to other categories. During this stage, the relationships among targeted phenomena (which included sub-categories and core categories connected by common properties and dimensions) were verified and validated to construct a theory.

During the data coding, a concept map (category diagram) was developed (see Figure A6.1). The concept map underwent several revisions, mainly due to some modifications of labels and categories. The researcher's interpretations of the obtained data were checked for accuracy by consulting the participants throughout the term of the investigation (member checking). Finally, story lines were developed taking into consideration the three aspects of the analyzed data, namely condition, action/interaction, and consequence. According to Strauss and Corbin (1998), these three aspects collectively constitute a "paradigm" (the paradigm model).

6.2.4 Research questions

Prior to the investigation, the following three research questions were formulated:

(a) How do participants perceive the development process of the new language education policy of conducting EFL classes in English at Japanese senior high schools?
(b) How do participants perceive the implementation of this new policy?
(c) How do participants perceive school and classroom conditions, particularly in relation to the enactment of the new policy?

6.3 Major research findings

Salient, recurring themes that represent "information-rich cases" (Patton, 2002, p. 230) are presented in this section. Among multiple meta-themes that emerged in the present study, the following three were chosen: (a) native speakerism; (b) resistance to change; and (c) teachers' practical knowledge and lack of information-sharing. For each meta-theme, the research findings are described and documented in the form of story lines. Pseudonyms are used to refer to the participants (see Table 6.1). As will be seen, each theme shows the uniqueness of individual participants' cases: the uniqueness of the participants' perceptions of the new language education policy, which were deeply rooted in context. Moreover, it is evident that the participants' perceptions were greatly influenced by socioeducational and political factors.

6.3.1 Native speakerism

When asked how they felt about the development of the new language education policy, Sayaka, Yuji, Tomoko, and Makoto all expressed various levels of pressure as well as anxiety regarding their teaching practices. One of the themes that emerged in the participants' data was their perception of the position of non-native English teachers. It was evident that they had started to regard their position as disadvantageous and inferior to that of native English speakers in conducting all classes in English. Sayaka, for instance, mentioned as follows:

> There are many weaknesses that I can find in being a non-native speaker [of English]. The level of my speaking proficiency is not high enough. If MEXT can allow native English speakers to teach all English classes in [senior high] school, I would appreciate that! If there is a role that a Japanese English teacher can play ... maybe

the role of providing instruction on test-taking techniques for entrance exams. That's all.[1]

It was reported that in the field of teaching English to speakers of other languages, non-native teachers tend to perceive and identify themselves and native English-speaking teachers more or less in the same fashion (see Gebhard & Nagamine, 2005; Moussu & Llurda, 2008). As Sayaka implied, this tendency might have been intensified by the introduction of the new language education policy. What should be noted here is that Sayaka, Yuji, Tomoko, and Makoto commonly perceived the development of the new policy as a "critical incident" (Farrell, 2008). Critical incidents in professional experience are known to trigger teachers' awareness of professional identities (cf. Sakui & Gaies, 2002; Vavrus, 2002) and prompt them to become more concerned about who they are as persons and teachers than about what they know (knowledge and skills) (Connelly & Clandinin, 1999). In addition, the awareness of professional identities determines teachers' motivation to stay in the profession. Accordingly, it is a legitimate action to change the way teachers (both preservice and inservice) are supported in terms of their professional identity formation (Nagamine, 2012).

As the above quote from Sayaka exemplifies, all participants showed a similar tendency to limit their teaching role to a specific area of instruction, such as grammar and entrance-exam preparation. It was also found that Sayaka and Yuji (the inservice teachers) emphasized non-native EFL teachers' superior role in classroom management and disciplining students. By (re-)conceptualizing their role in comparison to that of native English speakers, Sayaka and Yuji possibly tried to maintain their self-esteem and avoid losing face.

When asked what level of English proficiency would be required to teach EFL classes in English, Makoto answered, "Ideally, a native speaker level," without hesitation. He continued as follows:

> People may say, 'You're a Japanese teacher! It's definitely OK if your English is not as good as native [English] speakers!' There is no way I would ever accept that idea. So, I think Japanese English teachers must improve their English skills ... I don't think it's possible to become like a native [English] speaker. No matter how hard I study ... If there are native [English] speakers who have learned very well about English education in Japan, we [referring to a prefectural board of education] should employ them as senior high school English teachers. I think it's the best [idea].

Tomoko commented on the same issue, alluding to her belief that MEXT has the ultimate intention of laying off Japanese senior high school English teachers whose English proficiency is not up to the level of native English-speaking teachers.

Any educational change thus necessitates that teachers change because an individual teacher is "the acting subject of change" (Carson, 2005, p. 6). Such transformative change implicates teachers' professional identity formation (Carson, 2005). The observed perceptual characteristics (particularly, perceiving and identifying non-native speaker teachers' position in a specific manner) indicate that teachers' self-images, as well as their self-esteem, might be at stake due to the new policy implementation.

6.3.2 Resistance to change

Sayaka and Yuji, in particular, expressed a strong feeling of dislike toward MEXT and the new language education policy. Yuji, for example, stated that MEXT does not fully understand local school situations and the variety of problems that inservice teachers face on a daily basis (e.g. parents' and students' expectations and needs, class size, dealing with students' different levels, lack of cooperation with junior high school teachers) and that the realities as perceived by inservice teachers are not taken into consideration in the process of policy making. All participants implied that they felt a sense of distance from MEXT, especially when they learned about the new language education policy. Yuji criticized MEXT for starting a teacher-certificate renewal system in 2009:

> The Democratic Party [of Japan] promised the abolishment [of the teacher-certificate renewal] system. But, it never happened. I trusted politicians then ... Our burden has already increased since then [April 2009]. And, now we have the new policy.

The coalition government of the Liberal Democratic Party and the New Komeito Party decided to start the teacher-certificate renewal system. The government then experienced a governmental change in 2009, when the Democratic Party began a new administration. As Yuji asserted, the Democratic Party publicly announced prior to its administration that the teacher-certificate renewal system would be abolished, and that alternative measures would be undertaken to ensure preservice and inservice teacher quality (*shishitsu*). The aforementioned remark by Yuji implies that teachers' expectations of the government were effectively violated and that they may have been demotivated to seek positive changes in the field of education.

Sayaka, Tomoko, and Makoto argued that teaching all EFL classes in English would only be effective in helping students to improve their listening skills, and that the policy implementation would likely lower the quality of English education. Such negative attitudes toward the policy implementation were possibly born out of teachers' negative feelings (i.e. disappointment and frustration) about the descrepancy between what was pledged and what was done by the politicians.

Furthermore, Tomoko stated:

> I didn't tell you this last time [in the previous interview session]. I took a teacher employment exam this year, and I passed it ... My dream was to become a senior high school [English] teacher. I think I told you that. But, I took an exam for [prospective] junior high school [English] teachers ... That's right! I gave up!

Even though Tomoko's initial intention was to become a senior high school English teacher, she changed her mind because of the new policy: "I couldn't imagine myself using English fluently to teach [English] classes, so I intentionally avoided aiming for a senior high school position." Yet another type of resistance was observed. Sayaka, for instance, reported that she made a firm decision to continue using Japanese in her EFL classes. Sayaka also confessed that she had never even thought about using English to teach EFL classes, and that the percentage of time spent using her spoken English in class was "probably close to zero."

6.3.3 Teachers' practical knowledge and lack of information-sharing

Sayaka, Yuji, Tomoko, and Makoto demonstrated, though in different ways, their perception of the necessity to change their pedagogical approaches and teaching practices in senior high school settings. What they did not demonstrate was a consistent explanation of MEXT's expectations for change. The need to incorporate communicative activities into EFL classes is clearly mentioned in the recent versions of *The Course of Study*, and the necessity to enrich the quality of communicative activities is similarly articulated in the latest version. Moreover, it is clear that MEXT is trying to generate a shift from traditional approaches (e.g. the teacher-centered, textbook-based grammar translation method) to student-centered, communicative approaches (cf. Stewart, 2009). As Nishino (2012) argues, this attempt appears to conflict with teachers' familiar teaching practices and beliefs about English learning and teaching. Tomoko mentioned as follows:

> It's just extremely difficult [for me] to plan a lesson in which I use English to teach ... Perhaps, I'm thinking that ... I will need to apply the grammar translation method at the same time as using English to explain ... grammatical structures. Vocabulary. Correct translation. Perhaps, because I'm thinking this way, I can't imagine myself conducting English classes in English. I can't stop thinking ... if I were a student, I wouldn't want to be taught in English. I wouldn't be able to understand what the teacher was saying. I wouldn't feel comfortable.

Struggling to find possible explanations for MEXT's expectations for change, Tomoko frequently referred to her previous in-class learning experiences. In her junior and senior high school days, the teacher-centered, textbook-based grammar translation method was primarily used to teach English subjects: "We were often asked to read aloud English texts in both [junior high and senior high] schools. But, there were very few communicative activities in senior high school." The grammar translation method was therefore the most familiar teaching approach for her. In other words, her "practical knowledge" (Golombek, 1998) of English teaching was formed when she was a junior and senior high school student, and it still affected the way that she, as a preservice teacher, thought about the possible approaches for teaching EFL classes in English. Similar phenomena were also observed in the other participants' data. Lortie (1975) argues that prior learning experiences in schooling play a crucial role in determining teaching beliefs and practices, and that teaching beliefs are formed on the basis of one's prior learning experience as a student rather than as a teacher (i.e. the apprenticeship of observation).

What appeared to be another crucial factor affecting the participants' perceptions was the lack of authentic experiences of being taught in English (see Table 6.1). It was hence speculated that gaining authentic experiences of being taught in English would positively affect teachers' attitudes and motivation toward using English as the medium of instruction in EFL classes. Makoto, however, pointed out the meaninglessness of such speculation. He had a study abroad experience with an English as a Second Language (ESL) program in Canada, stating that "Of course, classes were taught in English there." Makoto continued:

> Every lesson included many types of communicative activities. I really enjoyed interacting with my classmates and instructors through these

activities. I couldn't understand everything, though. If you ask me to teach the same way as those instructors did, I don't think I can do it ... First of all, I don't remember how they explained grammatical points ... The environment [indicating the distinction between ESL and EFL contexts] is different. We don't need to use English to live here [in Japan]. I think that ... the need to use English must be created.

Tomoko suggested that MEXT should make English an elective subject, and that "only students who are really motivated to learn English as a communication tool" should take EFL classes in senior high school. By doing this, MEXT may be able to support students who are interested in learning a different foreign language(s), while students who are highly motivated to learn English may be grouped and taught together in EFL classes. Sayaka implied that there were few opportunities for teachers to share information regarding class preparation procedures and instructional ideas to make English teaching effective. She also expressed the idea that there might be a "Japanese way" of teaching English that values the development of "linguistic sensibilities" and language awareness; hence it was not surprising when she said that she had decided to continue using Japanese as the medium of instruction in her EFL classes. Sayaka further mentioned that MEXT had sent a DVD to every senior high school so that inservice teachers could watch and learn from successful teaching practices with the use of English. However, detailed descriptions of class preparation procedures were not recorded on the DVD. Accordingly, context-sensitive, locally appropriate approaches may be called for; however, preservice as well as inservice teachers are not given ample opportunities to share information (particularly, information regarding instructional processes), transform practical knowledge, and develop as professionals in a cooperative or collaborative fashion.

6.4 Implications

Based on the research findings, the following implications can be proposed for policy makers, administrators, and teacher educators to develop and implement language education policy successfully in Asian EFL contexts in general and Japanese EFL contexts in particular:

(a) Policy makers, in collaboration with administrators, should reconsider students' right to choose a foreign language(s) to learn in school.
(b) Policy makers and administrators should conduct needs analyses of foreign language(s) in local school settings to clarify parents and students' needs.

(c) Policy makers should present opportunities for students, parents, teachers, administrators, and teacher educators to be involved in meaningful, constructive dialogue in the process of policy making.
(d) Teacher educators, possibly in collaboration with administrators, should provide ample opportunities for teachers (both preservice and inservice) to experience awareness-raising, reflection-type activities so that teachers can share process-oriented information and transform their practical knowledge and teaching beliefs.
(e) Teachers (both preservice and inservice) should explore and negotiate descriptive ways of teaching (as opposed to prescriptive ways of teaching) that are context sensitive and locally appropriate.

Collaboration and/or cooperation among policy makers, administrators, and teacher educators is vital to ensure the effectiveness of the implementation of any language education policy (Mahboob & Tilakaratna, 2012). All critical stakeholders need to become involved in discourse or discursive practices so that the process of policy making, as well as the implementation of policy, can be a collaborative/cooperative endeavor. Hence, policy making and implementation should be an inclusive, multi-stakeholder process. In addition, considering that *de facto* foreign language education is "English education" in Japan, it cannot be denied that students' right to select and study a foreign language(s) of their choice in school settings has been prejudiced. This problem should be solved (or at least, it should be politicized) as soon as possible in order for Japan to develop as a multilingual and multicultural society. It is hence suggested that policy makers, in collaboration with administrators (such as officers of prefectural boards of education), conduct needs analyses to investigate students' and parents' needs regarding foreign language learning at the local-school level. It is imperative and urgent for the government to create a system that reflects the outcomes of needs analyses in policy making and implementation.

In spite of the enactment of the new language education policy, senior high school teachers (both preservice and inservice teachers) may continue teaching EFL classes in exactly the same way as they were taught themselves, that is, using Japanese (i.e. through a teacher-centered, textbook-based grammar translation method) (cf. Pan & Block, 2011). By providing inservice and preservice training in which teachers can fully explore and effectively transform their practical knowledge and teaching beliefs, teacher educators and administrators can play an important role in the implementation of the new policy. The action of teacher educators and administrators may thus become a determining factor in the successful enactment of the policy.

In addition, as is evident in the present study, teachers will most likely end up as the main barrier to educational change unless they are given sufficient opportunities to explore and negotiate descriptive ways of teaching (i.e. context-sensitive, locally appropriate teaching approaches). Moreover, as this study implies, there is a tendency that teachers "often believe that they have little power to effect policy and do not view themselves as implementers of macro-level policies" (Mahboob & Tilakaratna, 2012, p. 8). Therefore, it seems urgent to equip teachers with the knowledge and skills to take part in political dialogue and discourse pertaining to education. More specifically, teachers need to acquire astute analytical skills to scrutinize the macro-structures of their educational, political context (Johnson, 2009). Teachers also need to acquire political tactics to engage in discursive practices so as to negotiate and change realities (see Shin, 2012).

6.5 Conclusion

The new language education policy, which has been enacted by MEXT in 2013, mandates that senior high school EFL teachers conduct all their classes in English. This new policy has generated repercussions among preservice teachers, inservice teachers, and teacher educators. There is no doubt that it adds to the pressure on both preservice and inservice teachers. The level of associated anxiety and pressure may vary among teachers due to differing school settings, employment status, teaching beliefs, and/or the way that they perceive realities. Likewise, how teachers react to the new policy implementation may also vary. Contextuality (Packer & Winne, 1995) of realities and issues is uniquely recognized and perceived by individual teachers.

Furthermore, the new policy certainly requires teachers to change their beliefs regarding English learning and teaching, as well as their pedagogical approaches and teaching practices. While the voices of policy makers and academics can be heard, the voices of teachers are rarely heard, and a dialogue in which teachers can engage with each other is especially lacking. This lack of dialogue is detrimental because it is local teachers, not policy makers, who have direct access to students and translate a top-down imposed policy into practice. This chapter hence presented an argument in support of the possibility of recognizing local teachers' roles and voices as an integral part of government policy making (cf. Farrell & Kun, 2007).

The limitation of the present study may be attributed to the low number of participants (i.e. four cases). All participants were Japanese teachers in an EFL setting. Furthermore, although the research methodology (particularly, the employment of GTA and member checking) might have minimized this possibility, it is likely that the researcher's role (interviewer) affected the objectivity of the data analysis and interpretations. Therefore, even though it was not a primary goal of this study, generalizability may be called into question. It should be stressed, however, that particularization, as opposed to generalization, was the research goal. A remark by Davis (1995, p. 441) is relevant here: "[o]ne of the common criticisms of qualitative studies is that they are not generalizable. On the one hand, a strength of qualitative studies is that they allow for an understanding of what is specific to a particular group, that is, what cannot possibly be generalized within and across populations." In this regard, the particularization of the studied cases should be taken as a strength.

Appendices

Table A6.1 Coding sample of Yuji

Segmented data	Property	Dimension	Label
I don't think MEXT fully understands what's really going on in schools.	Time Denial Object of denial Object of understanding Statement type Feeling/emotion	Present Complete MEXT's understanding Local school situations Criticism Negative	MEXT's understanding of local school settings
If MEXT had closely worked together with inservice teachers to develop the language education policy, the policy would have been totally different.	Mood Object of postulation Goal of work Result of postulation Degree of difference	Subjunctive MEXT's close, collaborative work with inservice teachers Development of the language education policy Differences in the policy Great ("totally")	Involvement of inservice teachers in policy making
MEXT staff don't have any understanding of the problems that inservice teachers face on a daily basis. It's sad ...	Time Denial Object of denial Object of understanding Description of problem Occurrence of problem Statement type Feeling/emotion	Present Complete MEXT staff's understanding Inservice teachers' problems Unspecified Daily Criticism Sadness ("Sad")	MEXT's understanding of inservice teachers' problems

Source: Primary data collected by the author.

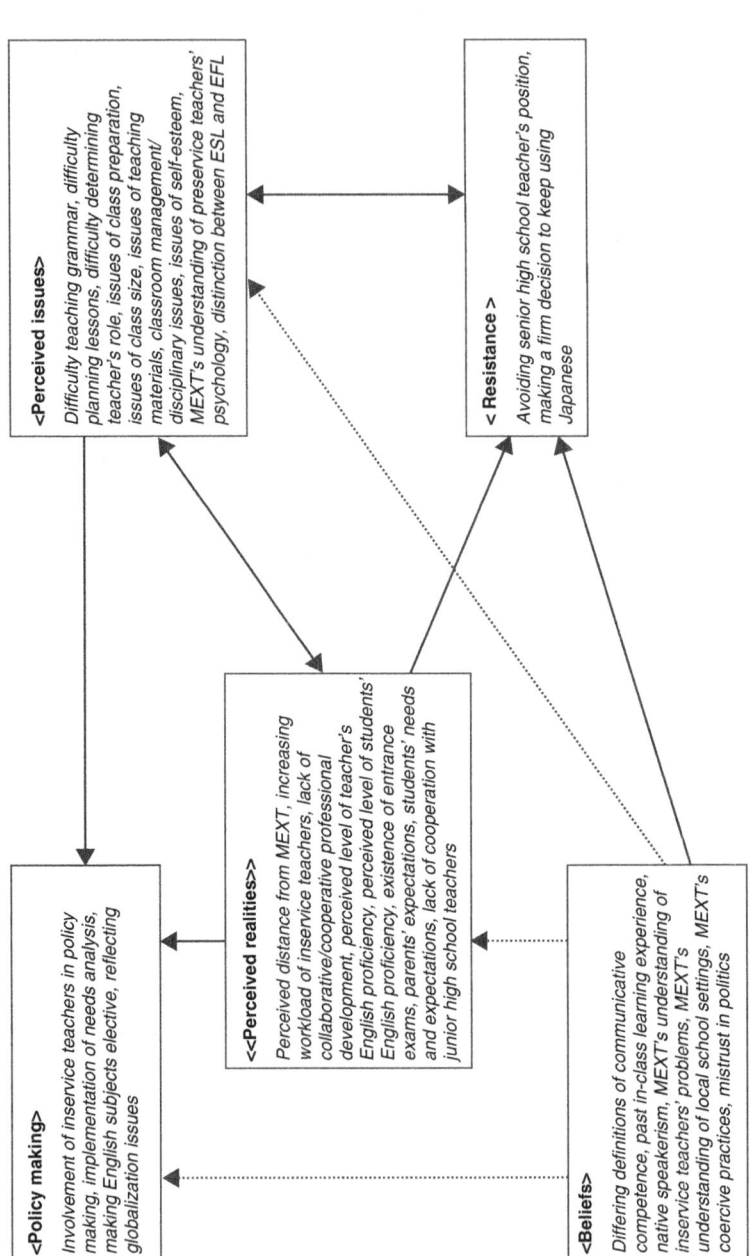

Figure A6.1 Sample concept map (subset)

Notes: << >> = Core category, < > = Sub-category, *Italics* = Label.
⋯▶ = Relation speculated based on data analysis.

Source: Primary data collected by the author.

Note

1. "[ ]" signifies information added by the researcher; "..." denotes places where part of the interview data is omitted.

References

Carson, T. (2005). Beyond instrumentalism: The significance of teacher identity in educational change. *Journal of the Canadian Association for Curriculum Studies, 3*(2), 1–8.
Connelly, F. M. & Clandinin, D. J. (1999). Knowledge, context and identity. In F. M. Connelly, & D. J. Clandinin (Eds), *Shaping a professional identity: Stories of educational practice* (pp. 1–5). London: Althouse Press.
Creswell, J. W. (1998). *Qualitative inquiry and research design: Choosing among five traditions*. Thousand Oaks, CA: Sage.
Cummins, J. (1979). Cognitive/academic language proficiency, linguistic interdependence, the Optimum age question and some other matters. *Working Papers on Bilingualism, 19*, 121–129.
Cummins, J. (1984). *Bilingualism and special education: Issues in assessment and pedagogy*. Clevedon, England: Multilingual Matters.
Davis, K. A. (1995). Qualitative theory and methods in applied linguistics research. *TESOL Quarterly, 29*(3), 427–453.
Eisenhardt, K. M. (2002). Building theories from case study research. In A. M. Huberman, & M. B. Miles (Eds), *The Qualitative Researcher's Companion* (pp. 5–35). Thousand Oaks, CA: Sage.
Erlandson, D. A., Harris, E. L., Skipper, B. L., & Allen, S. D. (1993). *Doing naturalistic inquiry: A guide to methods*. Newbury Park, CA: Sage.
Farrell, T. S. C. (2008). Critical incidents in ELT initial teacher training. *ELT Journal, 62*(1), 3–10.
Farrell, T. S. C., & Kun, S. T. K. (2007). Language policy, language teachers' beliefs, and classroom practices. *Applied Linguistics, 29*(3), 381–403.
Figal, G. A. (1999). *Civilization and monsters: Sprits of modernity in Meiji Japan*. Durham, NC: Duke University Press.
Freire, P. (1993). *Pedagogy of the oppressed*. New York: Continuum.
Gebhard, J. G. & Nagamine, T. (2005). A mutual learning experience: Collaborative journaling between a nonnative-speaker intern and native-speaker cooperating-teacher. *The Asian EFL Journal Quarterly, 7*(2), 48–66.
Gephart, R. P. (2004). Qualitative research and the academy of management journal. *Academy of Management Journal, 47*, 454–462.
Glasgow, G. P. (2012). Implementing language education policy to "conduct classes in English" in Japanese senior high schools. In A. Stewart, & N. Sonda (Eds), *JALT2011 Conference Proceedings* (pp. 399–407). Tokyo: JALT.
Golombek, P. R. (1998). A study of language teachers' personal practical knowledge. *TESOL Quarterly, 32*(3), 447–464.
Gorsuch, G. J. (2000). EFL educational policies and education cultures: Influences on teachers' approval of communicative activities. *TESOL Quarterly, 34*(4), 675–710.
Grossman, D. L. (2004). Higher education and teacher preparation in Japan and Hong Kong. *Nagoya Journal of Higher Education, 4*, 105–126.

Hargreaves, A. (1994). *Changing teachers, changing times: Teachers' work and culture in the postmodern age.* New York: Teachers College Press.
Johnson, K. E. (2009). *Second language teacher education: A sociocultural perspective.* New York: Routledge.
Lortie, D. C. (1975). *Schoolteacher: A sociological study.* Chicago: University of Chicago Press.
Lucien, E. (2001). *Japanese education in grades K-12* (ERIC Document Reproduction Service No. ED 458185). Washington, DC: Office of Educational Research & Improvement.
Mahboob, A. & Tilakaratna, N. (2012). A principles-based approach for English language teaching policies and practices (white paper). Alexandria, VA: TESOL.
Mann, S. & Tang, E. H. H. (2012). The role of mentoring in supporting novice English language teachers in Hong Kong. *TESOL Quarterly, 46*(3), 472–495.
Mâţă, L. (2012). Key factors of curriculum innovation in language teacher education. *World Academy of Science, Engineering and Technology, 66,* 512–520.
Maxwell, J. A. (1996). *Qualitative research design: An interactive approach.* Thousand Oaks, CA: Sage.
Maxwell, J. A. (2002). Understanding and validity in qualitative research. In A. M. Huberman, & M. B. Miles (Eds), *The Qualitative Researcher's Companion* (pp. 37–64). Thousand Oaks, CA: Sage.
McCarty, S. (1995). Practitioners of the liberal arts. *The Language Teacher, 19*(11), 43–44.
Merriam, S. B. (2001). *Qualitative research and case study applications in education.* San Francisco, CA: Jossey-Bass.
Ministry of Education, Cilture, Sports, Science and Technology of Japan [MEXT]. (2009). *Kotogakko gakusyushidoyoryo* [The course of study for senior high schools]. Retrived from http://www.mext.go.jp/a_menu/shotou/new-cs/youryou/kou/kou.pdf.
Ministry of Education, Cilture, Sports, Science and Technology of Japan [MEXT]. (2011). *Kotogakko gakusyushidoyoryo: Gaikokugo hen* [The course of study for senior high schools: Foreign language (English)]. Retrieved from http://www.mext.go.jp/a_menu/shotou/new-cs/youryou/eiyaku/__icsFiles/afieldfile/2011/04/11/1298353_9.pdf.
Moussu, L. & Llurda, E. (2008). Non-native English-speaking language teachers: History and research. *Language Teaching, 41*(3), 315–348.
Nagamine, T. (2008). *Exploring preservice teachers' beliefs: What does it mean to become an English teacher in Japan?* Saarbrücken, Germany: VDM Verlag.
Nagamine, T. (2012). A metaphor analysis of preservice EFL teachers' beliefs regarding professional identity. *The Asian EFL Journal Quarterly: Special Issue on Teacher Education, Identity and Development, 14*(2), 141–171.
Nishino, T. (2012). Multi-membership in communities of practice: An EFL teacher's professional development. *TESL-EJ, 16*(2), 1–21.
Packer, M. J. & Winne, P. H. (1995). The place of cognition in explanations of teaching: A dialog of interpretative and cognitive approaches. *Teaching and Teacher Education, 11*(1), 1–21.
Pan, L. & Block, D. (2011). English as a "global language" in China: An investigation into learners' and teachers' language beliefs. *System, 39,* 391–402.
Patton, M. Q. (2002). *Qualitative research and evaluation methods* (3rd edn). Thousand Oaks, CA: Sage.

Sakui, K. & Gaies, S. J. (2002). Beliefs and professional identity: A case study of a Japanese teacher of EFL writing. *The Language Teacher, 26*(6), 7–11.

Shin, S.-K. (2012). "It cannot be done alone": The socialization of novice English teachers in South Korea. *TESOL Quarterly, 46*(3), 542–567.

Stake, R. E. (2005) Qualitative case studies. In N. K. Denzin & Y. S. Lincoln (Eds), *The Sage handbook of qualitative research* (3rd edn, pp. 443–466). Thousand Oaks, CA: Sage.

Stewart, T. (2009). Will the new English curriculum for 2013 work? *The Language Teacher, 33*(11), 9–13.

Strauss, A. C. & Corbin, J. M. (1994). Grounded theory methodology. In Y. S. Lincoln & N. K. Denzin (Eds) *Handbook of qualitative research* (pp. 273–285). Thousand Oaks, CA: Sage.

Strauss, A. C. & Corbin, J. M. (1998). *Basics of qualitative research: Techniques and procedures for developing grounded theory*. Thousand Oaks, CA: Sage.

Suddaby, R. (2006). From the editors: What grounded theory is not. *Academy of Management Journal, 49*(4), 633–642.

Toulmin, S. E. (1990). *Cosmopolis: The hidden agenda of modernity*. Chicago: University of Chicago Press.

Vavrus, M. (2002). *Connecting teacher identity formation to culturally responsive teaching* (ERIC Document Reproduction Service No. ED 476689). Washington, DC: Office of Educational Research and Improvement.

Yamada, H. & Hristoskova, G. (2011). Teaching and learning English in English in Japanese senior high schools: Teachers' and students' perceptions. *Journal of Fukui-ken Eigo Kenkyu-kai, 69*, 3–33.

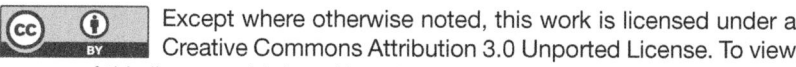 Except where otherwise noted, this work is licensed under a Creative Commons Attribution 3.0 Unported License. To view a copy of this license, visit http://creativecommons.org/licenses/by/3.0/

OPEN

7
An Alternative Approach to Foreign Language Education in Japan with a View toward Becoming a Multicultural Society

Mitsunori Takakuwa

7.1 Introduction

In compulsory education in public schools in Japan, foreign language education formerly began in lower secondary schools in principle. From 2011 it was introduced in elementary schools as well. Thus Japanese students in public schools are supposed to have the chance to learn foreign languages for at least several years during their compulsory education. Nonetheless, in reality, their choices are limited: they can learn only English, not other foreign languages, under the current national curriculum. English education is *the* foreign language education provided in compulsory education in Japanese public schools, and other foreign language education has been neglected. However, Japanese society is not as ethnically homogeneous as it has appeared to be (Burgess, 2007; Okubo, 2008; Tsuneyoshi, 2004). There are about two million foreigners registered in Japan, and more importantly, they are from various countries and regions, including where English is not primarily used (Ministry of Justice, 2012). Thus it can be said that Japan has now become a linguistically and culturally diverse society. Should we still continue to adhere to the "English education only" policy?

This study surveys foreign language education in Japanese compulsory education under the current national curriculum. It then examines the effectiveness of foreign language education in the context of Japan as a multicultural society, with special emphasis on schools with foreign children who have no knowledge of the Japanese language. Finally, the study sets forth an alternative approach to foreign language education, which is in line with Japanese society becoming increasingly multicultural and multilingual.

7.2 English education as the *de facto* foreign language education

In the academic year of 2011, starting in April and ending in March the following year, English education was officially introduced in elementary schools in Japan. Although the grade in which students start learning English varies from place to place, the national curriculum, or *the Course of Study*, for elementary schools specifies what is to be learned in grades five and six. This means that Japanese elementary school students will have started to learn English by the time they are in grade five at the latest. It should be noted that English education in elementary schools is formally called "Foreign Language Activities." Therefore, any other foreign language instead of, or in addition to, English could theoretically be taught. However, in reality, English is the choice of language as specified in the national curriculum formulated by the Ministry of Education, Culture, Sports, Science, and Technology (hereafter MEXT): "In principle English should be selected for foreign language activities" (MEXT, 2010). Thus in Japan "Foreign Language Activities" in elementary schools is practically synonymous with English education.

Japan adopts a nine-year-long compulsory education system from grade one to grade nine. Japanese students have an additional three years of "foreign" language education after graduating from elementary school. However, even at the lower secondary school level (grades seven through nine), foreign language education usually implies English education. The national curriculum for lower secondary schools lists "Foreign Languages" as the name of the subject to be taught along with other subjects, such as Japanese language, mathematics, and science. However, it is easy to recognize that only English is intended in the curriculum. There are three sections in the "Foreign Languages" curriculum for lower secondary students: overall objective, objectives and contents for each language, and lesson plan design and treatment of the contents (MEXT, 2011a). The first and third sections are brief, and much of the space is reserved for the second section. This extensive section is unevenly divided into two parts: "English" and "Other Foreign Languages." The way English education is implemented is explained in great detail. For example, one of the three subsections under the heading of "English" is "contents," which contains how four skills of English should be incorporated in language activities, how pragmatic functions of language should be treated in those activities, what phonological, lexical, or grammatical items of English should be taught, and how these items should be treated in class.

Compared to this detailed treatment of "English," the explanation of "Other Foreign Languages" in the same section, "Objectives and contents for each language," of the curriculum is markedly brief. Under the heading of "Other Foreign Languages" there is only one sentence, saying "Instruction for foreign languages other than English should follow the objectives and contents of English instruction" (MEXT, 2011a, p. 8). MEXT is the only agency in Japan to control education in general. As Seargeant (2009) pointed out, the Japanese educational system is highly centralized. Even when local governments set their own educational goals, they should follow the national curriculum. With the power and control that MEXT has, it specifies what to teach and how to teach it in great detail in the national curricula for academic subjects, as is the case with "English" described above. Thus, if MEXT had indeed intended to implement foreign language education other than English at the lower secondary level, it would have laid down the contents and the methodology of language teaching for other languages as well in the national curriculum. Instead, as we saw above, MEXT provided a very brief explanation in a single sentence. This lack of detailed explanation on foreign language education other than English suggests that MEXT does not take its implementation into serious consideration.

One could argue that MEXT's inclusion of this brief sentence implies that they are serious about implementing foreign language education other than English. However, this interpretation is highly unlikely, because it is practically impossible to follow the objectives and contents of English instruction when teaching other foreign languages. As mentioned above, the current national curriculum introduces English education in elementary school. The previous curriculum emphasized inculcating listening and speaking abilities in English. However, because English education would now be introduced at the elementary level, a revision was made to the curriculum such that lower secondary school students could develop their abilities in all four English language skills, because these skills would be built on the foundation of students' communication abilities, which were intended to be formed at the elementary school level (MEXT, 2011c; National Institute for Educational Policy Research, 2012). However, since foreign language activities at the elementary level are synonymous with English education, there is virtually no basis for foreign languages other than English. How can learners of a foreign language who have no knowledge of that language learn it effectively by following a curriculum that assumes they already have some prior knowledge of the language? This is akin to novice learners of a foreign language being forced to start their very first lesson at an intermediate level. If MEXT were serious about implementing foreign language education other than English, the organization would have developed another curriculum in which the objectives, instructions, and contents differed from those of English. Therefore, in reality, during the period of compulsory education in Japan both "Foreign Language Activities" in elementary schools and "Foreign Languages" in lower secondary schools are practiced solely through English education, and MEXT cannot be considered to be serious about implementing foreign language education other than English in compulsory education, despite the fact that Japan is a multicultural society.

7.3 English education for whom?

As we saw above, English education is the *de facto* foreign language education in the compulsory education system in Japan. It is true that English is among the most influential languages in the world today in the sense that it is primarily used in international communications in politics and businesses. However, it is also true that not everyone will be involved in such international communications. Among the biggest reasons to reallocate initial English education to elementary school level was that many Japanese people did not have good command of English even after about six to ten years of English education, including higher education, before it was introduced to elementary schools (Seargeant, 2009), and that starting to learn English at an earlier age was thought to be the solution to the Japanese people's lack of proficiency in English. That is, it was assumed that extending the period of English study would enable Japanese people to become proficient in it. This solution may work in some contexts, and may not in others. For the solution of making the period of English learning longer to work effectively, it should also be assumed that Japanese people's relatively poor English proficiency level, if indeed it exists, is due to the limited amount of time spent learning English. However, the factors that affect second language learning are more complicated (e.g. Andreou, G., Vlachos, & Andreou, E., 2005; Ellis, 2004). If one has no contact time with a target language, one is not likely to acquire it. If one lives in an environment in which the target language is primarily used and has much contact time with it by using it daily, one is likely to acquire it.

In this sense, increasing contact time with the target language may lead to enhancing learners' proficiency levels. But it is unknown how much contact time is enough for them to become proficient in the language on the continuum of contact time between zero and every day. Under the current national curriculum, Japanese fifth and sixth graders will experience English education for 35 periods (each a 50-minute class) per year—the same amount of time as is dedicated to "Moral Education." Would it be considered a significant amount of time to add 70 periods (roughly equaling 58 hours) of English lessons in the last two years of elementary schools?

Motivation is also an important factor in second language learning (e.g. Dörnyei, 2001; Gardner, 2010). In Japan many people do not need English to live their daily lives (Yano, 2008). Although some people may use English at work, they do not need it when buying groceries, commuting, going to hospitals, banks, or public offices, and so on. Two types of motivation can be introduced here: integrative and instrumental motivations concerning second language learning (Gardner & MacIntyre, 1991). Some learners are interested in the target language itself, the countries or regions in which it is primarily used, and the cultures associated with those who use it. Such learners can be said to have integrative motivation to learn the target language. Other learners tend to regard the language as some instrument or tool by which they can fulfill their desires to accomplish tasks in, say, business. These learners are thought to have instrumental motivation to learn the target language. In Japan, many people whose first language is Japanese do not have to use English. In such a situation, it appears difficult to encourage learners to maintain either type of motivation long enough for them to become proficient in the target language. Of course, there are some people who were able to learn it successfully with either or both types of motivation. It is likely that language teachers are among them. Other professionals or workers who use it for their business may also have been successful in maintaining motivation to learn it (Kubota, 2011; Seargeant, 2009). However, it is not as easy to maintain motivation to learn the target language as those who have been successful in being motivated may think it is.

Terasawa (2011) pointed out that the view that Japanese people have aspirations to learn English is misleading. A large-scale social survey of $n = 2,507$, which investigated the behaviors and thoughts of Japanese people based on the two-stage stratified random sampling (JGSS Research Center, n.d.), showed that about 40% of Japanese valued English skills either for their work or their personal life while the remaining of about

An Alternative Approach to Foreign Language Education in Japan   123

60% did not. More detailed analyses showed that, according to type of job, those who were professional workers valued English skills highly, whereas people in other occupations did not. In the "Professional" category, 69.9% of 113 male workers and 60.4% of 134 female workers put a relatively high valuation on English skills for their jobs. Also 63.7% of 113 male workers and 51.8% of 137 female workers valued English skills highly for their hobbies or personal relationships. The category of types of job that comes after "Professional" is "Managerial." In this category, 52.5% of 40 male workers and 25.0% out of four female workers valued English skills for their jobs, and 57.5% of 40 male workers and 75.0% of four female workers valued English skills highly for their hobbies or personal relationships. It should be noted here that the relatively high percentage of 75.0% may be due to the small sample sizw, that is $n = 4$ for this category. Thus caution is needed to evaluate this figure. For workers in other types of job ("Agricultural," "Skilled," "Semi-skilled," "Unskilled," "Clerical," and "Sales"), the highest percentage was 54.2% out of 168 male clerical workers who valued English skills highly. Thus it is safe to conclude that, except for those who are professional workers, the majority of Japanese people do not think English skills are important for their jobs and/or their personal lives.

From a slightly different perspective, it can be pointed out that among the parents of students who go to school and study English, the majority do not value English skills highly. The students also know that Japanese people do not need to use English in their daily lives. How can they be motivated to learn English then? It could be argued that English will be useful when visiting foreign countries or regions. However, the number of people who go overseas should be considered. Table 7.1 shows the total number of Japan's population, Japanese nationals overseas who stay overseas longer than three months, and Japanese overseas travelers (Japan National Tourism Organization, n.d.; Ministry of Foreign Affairs of Japan, 2011; Ministry of Internal Affairs and Communications, n.d.).

In Table 7.1 the number of Japanese nationals living in Japan is used to show a rough measure of how many Japanese people may need to use English after they study it under the national curriculum. Japan's total population is slightly larger than the number of Japanese nationals since the former includes other nationals living in Japan. As we can see, the number of Japanese nationals overseas is very small compared to Japanese nationals in Japan. Its ratio is less than 1%. The number of Japanese overseas travelers is much larger than that of Japanese nationals overseas. Still the number of Japanese overseas travelers accounts for

Table 7.1 Japanese population, Japanese nationals overseas, and Japanese overseas travelers

Year	Japanese population	Japanese nationals overseas	Japanese overseas travelers
2001	125,930,000	837,744	16,215,657
2002	126,053,000	871,751	16,522,804
2003	126,206,000	911,062	13,296,330
2004	126,266,000	961,307	16,831,112
2005	126,205,000	1,012,547	17,403,565
2006	126,286,000	1,063,695	17,534,565
2007	126,347,000	1,085,671	17,294,935
2008	126,340,000	1,116,993	15,987,250
2009	126,343,000	1,131,807	15,445,684
2010	126,382,000	1,143,357	16,637,224

Sources: Japan National Tourism Organization (n.d.); Ministry of Foreign Affairs of Japan (2011); Ministry of Internal Affairs and Communications (n.d.)

no more than 14% of that of Japanese nationals in Japan. Of course, it is unlikely that every one of the Japanese nationals overseas and Japanese overseas travelers has to be proficient in English, since some of them may go to countries or regions where English is not used primarily. However, for the sake of discussion, let us assume that everyone in these two categories would need to use English. Still the proportion of Japanese who need English is relatively small, and the conclusion that the majority of Japanese do not need English for their daily lives is tenable. Then why do Japanese students have to study English, among other foreign languages, for at least five years of compulsory education (grades five through nine), and probably for three additional years (grades ten through twelve) in upper secondary school? Do all of them have to learn it even when the majority of them are unlikely to need it? Maybe now is the time to consider whether English education should be the *de facto* foreign language education in Japan.

7.4 Diversity in Japanese society

As we have seen so far, the majority of Japanese people do not need English for their daily lives. Are there any other foreign languages they might encounter in Japan? Table 7.2 shows the number of registered foreigners and the breakdowns by nationalities (Ministry of Justice, 2012).

As Figure 7.1 shows, the number of registered foreigners gradually increased from 2001 and peaked in 2008, when over 2.2 million foreign residents were registered. After that the number declined, and, as of 2011, just over two million foreign residents were registered (Ministry of

Table 7.2 Number of registered foreigners and breakdowns by nationalities

	2001	2002	2003	2004	2005	2006	2007	2008	2009	2010	2011
Total	1,778,462	1,851,758	1,915,030	1,973,747	2,011,555	2,084,919	2,152,973	2,217,426	2,186,121	2,134,151	2,078,508
China	381,225	424,282	462,396	487,570	519,561	560,741	606,889	655,377	680,518	687,156	674,879
Korea	632,405	625,422	613,791	607,419	598,687	598,219	593,489	589,239	578,495	565,989	545,401
Brazil	265,962	268,332	274,700	286,557	302,080	312,979	316,967	312,582	267,456	230,552	210,032
Philippines	156,667	169,359	185,237	199,394	187,261	193,488	202,592	210,617	211,716	210,181	209,376
Peru	50,052	51,772	53,649	55,750	57,728	58,721	59,696	59,723	57,464	54,636	52,843
USA	46,244	47,970	47,836	48,844	49,390	51,321	51,851	52,683	52,149	50,667	49,815
Others	245,907	264,621	277,421	288,213	296,848	309,450	321,489	337,205	338,323	334,970	336,162

Source: Adapted from Ministry of Justice (2012).

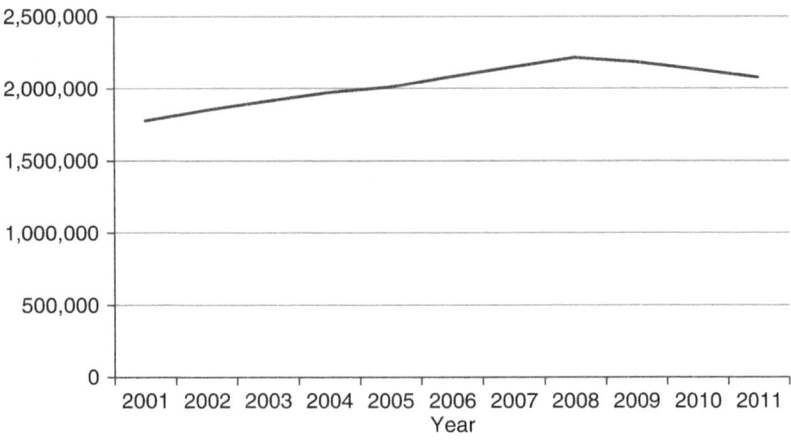

Figure 7.1 Total number of registered foreigners in Japan
Source: Ministry of Justice (2012).

Justice, 2012). Out of the total number of 2,078,508 registered foreigners, Chinese constitute about 33%, Koreans constitute about 26%, and both Brazilians and Filipinos constitute about 10% (see Figure 7.2).

Table 7.2 and Figures 7.1 and 7.2 show that the majority of registered foreigners originally came from Asian and South American countries. Because no data are available for the first language of these registered foreigners, we cannot be sure of which languages they use primarily. However, the fact that in these Asian and South American countries English is not primarily used as the first language of those who live there suggests that not everyone from these countries is proficient in English to the extent that they can live their daily lives using English without any difficulty. Then what would happen in terms of communication if the majority of Japanese who do not need and thus do not use English for their daily lives meet these foreigners from Asia and South American countries in Japan? Theoretically, it is possible to use English to communicate with each other. However, this type of communication requires that both parties be proficient in English. Whether the foreigners can use English or not, the majority of Japanese do not. Thus this type of communication seems rare in reality. Another scenario is for both parties to use Japanese. Anecdotally this type of communication seems much more common than the first one (Kubota & McKay, 2009). This is not surprising in that there are many foreigners who have lived in Japan and become proficient in Japanese. Even those foreigners who are not

An Alternative Approach to Foreign Language Education in Japan 127

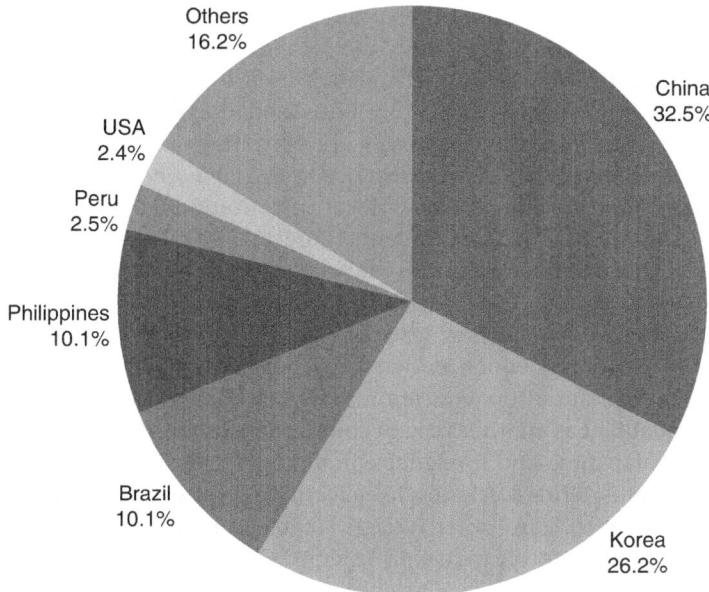

Figure 7.2 Percentage of registered foreigners by nationality in 2011
Source: Ministry of Justice (2012).

so proficient in Japanese are likely to be aware that it is primarily, and exclusively in most cases, used in Japan, and that they are expected to communicate in Japanese while they are in Japan. This type of communication is consistent with the language policy with which the Japanese government has put assimilation pressure on them (Tsuneyoshi, 2004; Vaipae, 2001). Japan has not actively accepted immigrants (Kanno, 2008; Sato, Okamoto, & Miyao, 2009). As it is rapidly becoming an aging society (Ministry of Health, Labour and Welfare, n.d.), it seems to have come to realize that, without people from outside the country, it is very difficult to sustain such a rapidly aging society. Currently there are about two million registered foreigners, which accounts for less than 2% of Japanese population. Thus these foreigners are considered minority groups compared to the mainstream Japanese nationals. For the minority groups, about 79% of whom are people from Asian and South American countries, the Japanese government has been trying to help them acquire Japanese. Also at present many local governments, along with the Japanese government, offer important notices and instructions concerning the civil service in Chinese, Korean, Spanish, and Portuguese, as well as Japanese and English. If some areas have a relatively large number of other minority groups whose first language is not among those listed above, the local governments may translate notices and instructions into languages used by these groups as well or instead. However, apart from translated documents, face-to-face services in the minority languages are very limited. Such services by which foreigners will receive assistance in the civil services in their first languages are often provided by local organizations, including NGOs and NPOs, not by local governments (Burgess, 2007; Tsuneyoshi, 2004). The fact that services in minority languages are limited in Japan is not surprising given that the majority of Japanese people are not proficient even in English, which they learn at school for several years, let alone in other languages, which are virtually neglected in foreign language education in compulsory education as we saw above. However, would it not be qualified as another type of communication in the present Japan that both Japanese and foreigners should try to learn each other's language? That is, while foreigners keep learning Japanese, Japanese people could also try to learn other foreign languages in addition to English. This would allow both parties to interact with each other in two-way communication.

7.5 Foreign language education in line with internal internationalization

Like the English, the majority of Japanese do not need other foreign languages either since they can live their daily lives in Japanese unless they swiftly become aware of the necessity to learn foreign languages mentioned above. Thus English and other foreign languages are similar in terms of usefulness for the majority of Japanese in their daily lives. However, a difference between them can be found in terms of the number of registered foreigners living in Japan, as we saw in Figure 7.2. Although no data are available for how many of these registered foreigners actually have a language closely associated with their countries of origin as their first language, it can be safely estimated that there is at least a slightly larger chance for Japanese to encounter foreigners whose first language is, or who have a good command of, Chinese, Korean, Portuguese, or Spanish than those with English. In this sense Japan can be regarded as a multicultural and multilingual society. Thus it is just as well worth learning other foreign languages as it is to learn English. The word *kokusaika*, which literally means internationalization, is often heard in many contexts in Japan (Ertl, 2008). However, internationalization is usually associated with English, not with other foreign languages. This seems to be due to the assumption that internationalization occurs when Japanese people go abroad, that is, when the direction of internationalization is outbound. Japanese people have an image of their going abroad, and thus they come to a conclusion that they need English outside Japan. However, as we saw above, internationalization does not occur unidirectionally. The opposite form of internationalization occurs when foreigners come from outside Japan. In this type of internationalization, which is called internal internationalization (Tsuneyoshi, 2004), the direction is inbound, and knowledge of the first languages of the foreigners will enhance communication between them and Japanese people. In other words, there is a sizable conflict regarding internationalization for Japanese people. In internationalization in its traditional sense, they believe they have to use English, although this is not always true, and thus they try to learn and use it for communication with foreigners, even when they go to countries or regions in which English is not primarily used. Thus Japanese people may believe that learning English is important, and English education as the *de facto* foreign language subject in compulsory education in Japan supports this view. In contrast, in internal internationalization, Japanese people believe they have only to use Japanese, and English if necessary, and thus they do not try to learn other foreign languages even if the foreigners who use them as their first language outnumber those who use English as such. This may be partly because Japan tries to assimilate foreigners into Japanese society by making them learn Japanese on one hand and neglecting foreign language education other than English in the compulsory education system on the other. Implementing foreign language education other than English in compulsory education may lead to resolving this conflict.

7.6 Foreign children in schools

There is another valid reason to teach foreign languages other than English in the compulsory education system in Japan. As we saw above, at present there are about two million registered foreigners in Japan. The number of these figures has been decreasing slightly, partly because of the recession after the subprime mortgage crisis in 2008 and because of the Great Earthquake in Japan in 2011. However, the number of children whose first language is not Japanese and who need special assistance in the Japanese language at school has not decreased. MEXT (2011b) reported the following numbers of those children (see Table 7.3).

The numbers in Table 7.3 show students in all the public elementary schools, lower and upper secondary schools, and other types of schools,

Table 7.3 Number of foreign children who require Japanese language instruction

Year	Foreign children who need Japanese language instruction
2001	19,250
2002	18,734
2003	19,042
2004	19,678
2005	20,692
2006	22,413
2007	25,411
2008	28,575
2009	(–)
2010	28,511

Source: MEXT (2011b).

which include schools for the educationally challenged. Data for 2009 are missing because MEXT decided to conduct this survey every other year after 2008. A glance at this table suggests that the number of foreign students who need Japanese language instruction peaked in 2008, and it may have started to decline, given that the total number of registered foreigners peaked in 2008 and has declined since then (see Table 7.2 and Figure 7.1). However, we cannot be sure about this, since, as stated above, the data are missing for 2009, and will be missing every other year after that, and thus we do not and will not have sufficient data to verify the interpretation of the data given above.

There is one thing we can reasonably conclude. Whether the number of foreign children who need Japanese language instruction stays the same or is decreasing, the total number of schools that host such students has increased since 2005, as in Table 7.4.

In other words, the possible decrease in numbers of such children, which might be related to the decrease in the total number of registered foreigners, does not affect the number of schools that host such students. Of course, it is possible that the number might have been higher in 2009 than in 2010, and we cannot be sure about this since no data is available for 2009. Still we can safely conclude that the number has increased since 2008, when the number of registered foreigners has, and the number of foreign students who need Japanese language instruction also seems to have, started decreasing. This brings up another issue for discussion. That is, how do schools accommodate foreign students who need Japanese language instruction? As Burgess (2007) pointed out, additional teachers are dispatched for those schools that host a certain

Table 7.4 Number of schools hosting foreign children requiring Japanese language instruction

Year	Schools hosting foreign children who need Japanese language instruction
2001	5,296
2002	5,130
2003	5,231
2004	5,346
2005	5,281
2006	5,475
2007	5,877
2008	6,212
2009	(–)
2010	6,423

Source: MEXT (2011b).

number of such students. This assistance does not seem sufficient, but it still is better than providing no support. About 80% of the schools that host such foreign students have four or fewer of them (MEXT, 2011b), and it is often the case that no additional teacher is dispatched for them (Burgess, 2007; Tsuneyoshi, 2004). Does having four foreign students require the school's teachers to make significantly less effort than having five of them? The line drawn between these cases is arbitrary. In fact, even having one such student requires teachers to make tremendous efforts. In the Japanese compulsory education system, at least one teacher is assigned to each class as a homeroom teacher, who takes care of the students in the class in terms not only of the students' academic progress but their school lives in general. Even when there is only one student in a class who needs Japanese language instruction, if the homeroom teacher does not speak their first language, the teacher has to make extra effort just to communicate with the student, let alone to take care of the student's school life in general. To make matters worse, it is often the case that the parent or parents of such a student may not have knowledge of the Japanese language. Thus, if the teacher wants to talk to the parent(s), an interpreter may be needed. Otherwise, negotiations between them would be likely to fail. Apparently, the teachers and the schools need much more support than they now receive from both national and local governments. Currently, local volunteers who have knowledge of the first language of the students who need Japanese instruction come to school and help them in class. However, not every school has those volunteers nearby. The most important thing is for the schools and teachers to be able to offer such support to those students.

So how can teachers and schools systematically accommodate these students and negotiate with their parent(s) when local volunteers are not available? This is when we should come back to the discussion of foreign language education in Japan.

7.7 Conclusion

As we saw before, English education is the *de facto* foreign language taught in elementary and lower secondary schools in Japan. That is, in Japan's compulsory education system, students in public schools study English as a foreign language, but not other languages. It is true that English is widely used around the world and, thus, to learn English is potentially useful. However, the majority of Japanese can live their daily lives without it. That is, English is a language that is useful, but not always necessary, for them. If so, they do not have to learn English to the extent that they are expected to become as proficient in it as those who use it as their first language. As we saw before, Japan is now a multicultural as well as multilingual society to a certain extent. For the majority of Japanese there are slightly higher chances to communicate in languages other than English inside Japan, although the likelihood is still low. Whether the target language is English or any other foreign language, it is not easy to become as proficient in it as those who use it as their first language with merely a few years of foreign language education in the country. This is mainly due to the fact that no foreign language is prevalent in Japan. However, if we can set the goal of foreign language education as to become proficient in it to the extent that Japanese people use it according to their goals and purposes, we can safely reduce the number of class periods for English in the compulsory education system, and make room for other foreign language education.

Thus, by introducing education in other foreign languages as well, we can not only teach other foreign languages to Japanese students, but also make them realize that English is not *the* foreign language but simply one of the foreign languages in the world. If Japanese students have knowledge of other foreign languages, students who come from overseas and use them as their first languages may feel more comfortable at school. It is also possible that some of the Japanese students may become teachers with such knowledge and help those students who come from outside Japan in their first languages. Because Japanese society is rapidly aging, it is anticipated that an even larger number of foreigners will be needed to sustain it. This will make Japan increasingly multicultural and multilingual. Knowledge of foreign languages will then become key in the near future.

References

Andreou, G., Vlachos, F., & Andreou, E. (2005). Affecting factors in second language learning. *Journal of Psycholinguistic Research, 34*, 429–438.
Burgess, C. (2007). "Newcomer" children in non-metropolitan public schools: The lack of state-sponsored support for children whose first language is not Japanese. *Japan Forum, 19*, 1–21.
Dörnyei, Z. (2001). *Motivational strategies in the language classroom*. Cambridge, UK: Cambridge University Press.
Ellis, R. (2004). Individual differences in second language learning. In A. Davies & C. Elder (Eds), *The handbook of applied linguistics* (pp. 525–551). Malden, MA: Wiley-Blackwell,
Ertl, J. (2008). International peripheries: Institutional and personal engagements with Japan's *Kokusaika* movement. In: N. H. H. Graburn, J. Ertl, & R. K. Tierney (Eds), *Multiculturalism in the new Japan: Crossing the boundaries within* (pp. 82–100). New York, NY: Berghahn Books.
Gardner, R. C. (2010). *Motivation and second language acquisition: The socio-educational model*. New York: Peter Lang.
Gardner, R. C. & MacIntyre, P. D. (1991). An instrumental motivation in language study: who says it isn't effective? *Studies in Second Language Acquisition, 13*, 57–72.
Japan National Tourism Organization (n.d.). *Visitor arrivals, Japanese overseas travelers*. Retrieved from http://www.jnto.go.jp/jpn/reference/tourism_data/pdf/marketingdata _outband6411.pdf
JGSS Research Center (n.d.). *JGSS-2010*. Retrieved from http://jgss.daishodai.ac.jp/ english/surveys/sur_jgss2010.html.
Kanno, Y. (2008). Language minority education in Japan. In A. Creese, P. Martin, & N. H. Hornberge (Eds), *Encyclopedia of language and education* (Vol. 9, pp. 237–248). New York: Springer.
Kubota, R. (2011). Questioning linguistic instrumentalism: English, neoliberalism, and language tests in Japan. *Linguistics and Education, 22*, 248–260.
Kubota, R. & McKay, S. (2009). Globalization and language learning in rural Japan: The role of English in the local linguistic ecology. *TESOL Quarterly, 43*, 593–619.
Ministry of Education, Science, and Technology (MEXT) (2010). *The course of study for elementary schools: Chapter 4 foreign language activities*. Retrieved from http://www.mext.go.jp/component/a_menu/education/micro_detail/__icsFiles/afieldfile/2010/10/20/1261037_12.pdf.
Ministry of Education, Science, and Technology (MEXT) (2011a). *The course of study for lower secondary schools: Chapter 9 foreign languages*. Retrieved from http://www.mext.go.jp/component/a_menu/education/micro_detail/__icsFiles/afieldfile/2011/04/11/1298356_10.pdf.
Ministry of Education, Science, and Technology (MEXT) (2011b). *Nihongo shido ga hitsuyo na gaikokujin jidoseito no ukeirejokyoto ni kansuru chosa (Heisei 22 Nendo) no kekka ni tsuite* [The results of the survey on the reception situation of foreign students who need Japanese instruction (Academic Year 2010)].

Retrieved from http://www.mext.go.jp/b_menu/houdou/23/08/__icsFiles/afieldfile/2011/12/12/1309275_1.pdf.
Ministry of Education, Science, and Technology (MEXT) (2011c). *The revisions of the courses of study for elementary and secondary schools.* Retrieved from http://www.mext.go.jp/english/elsec/__icsFiles/afieldfile/2011/03/28/1303755_001.pdf.
Ministry of Foreign Affairs of Japan (2011). *Kaigai zairyu hojinsu chosa tokei* [Annual report of statistics on Japanese nationals overseas]. Retrieved from http://www.mofa.go.jp/mofaj /toko/tokei/hojin/11/pdfs/1.pdf.
Ministry of Health, Labour and Welfare (n.d.). *Section 4 response to a society with a decreasing birth rate: Focusing on childrearing support measures.* Retrieved from http://www.mhlw.go.jp/english/wp/wp-hw4/honbun.html.
Ministry of Internal Affairs and Communications (n.d.). Table 1. Population by sex (as of October 1 of Each Year): total population, Japanese population (from 2000 to 2010) [Data file]. Retrieved from http://www.e-stat.go.jp/SG1/estat/Xlsdl.do?sinfid=00 0013168601.
Ministry of Justice (2012). *Kokuseki (shushinchi) betsu gaikokujin torokushasu no suii* [Changes in the number of registered foreign nationals by major nationality (place of origin)]. Retrieved from http://www.moj.go.jp/content/000098590.pdf.
National Institute for Educational Policy Research (2012). *Lower secondary education in Japan.* Retrieved from http://www.nier.go.jp/English/EducationInJapan/Education_in_Japan/Education_in_Japan_files/201203LSJ.pdf.
Okubo, Y. (2008). "Newcomers" in public education: Chinese and Vietnamese children in a buraku community. In N. H. H. Graburn, J. Ertl, & R. K. Tierney (Eds), *Multiculturalism in the new Japan: Crossing the boundaries within* (pp. 171–187). New York: Berghahn Books.
Sato, K., Okamoto, K., & Miyao, M. (2009). Japan: Moving towards becoming a multi-cultural society, and the way of disseminating multilingual disaster information to non-Japanese speakers. *Proceedings of the 2009 International Workshop on Intercultural Collaboration, USA* (pp. 51–60). doi:10.1145/1499 224.1499234.
Seargeant, P. (2009). *The idea of English in Japan: Ideology and the evolution of a global language.* Bristol, UK: Multilingual Matters.
Tsuneyoshi, R. (2004). The "new" foreigners and the social reconstruction of difference: The cultural diversification of Japanese education. *Comparative Education, 40,* 55–81.
Terasawa, T. (2011). Japanese people's valuation of English skills: Sociometric analysis of JGSS-2010. *JGSS Research Series, 8,* 47–57.
Vaipae, S. S. (2001). Language minority students in Japanese public schools. In M. G. Noguchi, & S. Fotos (Eds), *Studies in Japanese bilingualism* (pp. 184–233). Clevedon, UK: Multilingual Matters.
Yano, Y. (2008). Comment 5. *World Englishes, 27,* 139–140.

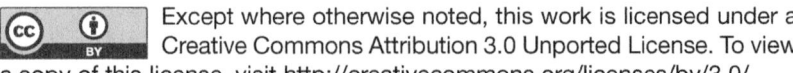

Except where otherwise noted, this work is licensed under a Creative Commons Attribution 3.0 Unported License. To view a copy of this license, visit http://creativecommons.org/licenses/by/3.0/

Part III
Migration and Citizenship

OPEN

8
Female Domestic Workers on the Move: Examining Global Householding and Global De-Householding in Today's World

Rieko Karatani

8.1 Introduction

Blown in by a windstorm from the East, Mary Poppins came to the Banks' home at Number 17 Cherry Tree Lane, London. The main character of P. L. Travers' children's novel, published in 1934, is allegedly the world's best-known "nanny."[1] The Banks' household is a traditional one. Mr Banks works in a bank in the City of London, leaving the task of hiring a suitable nanny for their children to Mrs Banks alone. Mrs Banks places a job advertisement in the newspaper, specifying a strong letter of recommendation as a requirement. Thus, a female employer decides the employment conditions of and negotiates with the female employee—a woman directing another woman.[2] In the Banks' home, the nanny is to work in a live-in environment, sleep in a nursery room, and have one day off every other Thursday. Even then, of course, it is not a full day, but only the afternoon between 1:00 p.m. and 6:00 p.m. In the eyes of the nanny's employer, there exists neither labor standard legislation nor any basic rights for laborers or employees.

The International Labour Organization (ILO) estimates that today there are up to 100 million Mary Poppinses around the world. It claims that these women are forced to bear even tougher conditions than the main character of Travers' children's novel.[3] It is an airplane, not an east wind, that brings them to developed countries, such as Britain, from developing countries such as the Philippines. They arrive in high numbers to look after families in host countries, leaving their own families behind. Female overseas workers are also increasingly participating in other sectors traditionally considered to be "women's work," such as health care and nursing for the sick and elderly (Ehrenreich & Hochschild, 2002; Kingma, 2006). Their basic rights, including days off each week, set hours, and minimum wage, have often been ignored, as if they have been forced into modern-day slavery.

This chapter analyzes the situation of today's Mary Poppinses in developed countries and beyond from an international relations scholarship perspective. In doing so, it focuses on the household as the basic unit of social reproduction, and aims to reveal the causes and effects of its reconfiguration beyond national borders. The conditions of female migrant workers are by no means simply a deal between a powerful and a not-so powerful woman. Rather, both women form part of a rapidly growing phenomenon described as "global householding."[4] Such a phenomenon is not confined to one region, but is prevalent all over the world. Asia is certainly not immune from it.

This chapter concentrates on three tasks. First, by examining the "security"[5] and "insecurity" of female overseas domestic workers (FODWs), it aims to incorporate the perspectives of both "gender"[6] and migration studies into the discipline of security studies. Within the study of International Relations (IR), security studies have traditionally focused on the military concerns of states. Recently, towards and since the end of the Cold War, security studies has undergone enormous changes, its scope of study being greatly expanded to cover non-military dimensions of security (Buzan, 1991). The field may nonetheless still lack analytical frameworks that integrate these wider issues into a holistic notion of security. "Global householding" is a vastly understudied, if not completely ignored, subject within security studies, despite involving an increasing number of countries and affecting so many people's lives both in positive and negative ways.

Second, this chapter attempts to explain how constraining regimes are in fact currently constructed in a multi-layered form, subsequently strengthening the "insecurity" of FODWs. It then demonstrates that these multi-layered regimes at national, regional, and global levels, whether upheld in practice or circumvented, have become a constitutive part of this "global householding" phenomenon. "Insecurity" for FODWs stemming from legal restrictions is found not only at a national level, but also within additional layers of regional and global jurisdiction. Scholars in gender and migration studies have examined the legal as well as psychological elements of the insecurities of women, especially female migrants, who accept live-in domestic jobs and are forced to work long hours under tough working conditions.[7] IR scholarship can further show

Female Domestic Workers on the Move 139

that the processes of "global householding" are increasingly occurring all over the world, and these women are subject to the multiplicity of the constraining national, regional, and global regimes.

Third, this chapter tries to challenge the state-centric academic analysis, and concentrates instead on the household as the space where individuals of different backgrounds meet and pool diverse resources for the purpose of ensuring the continuity of the collective unit. Within the household, we communicate and negotiate daily with one another, with efforts to establish what this volume calls the interactive "multiculturality," on which the basis of the convivial relationship is formed. By demonstrating that households are undergoing transformation due to population movements (one of the main forms being labor migrations), this chapter highlights how our differences are currently confronted and overcome through our daily contacts and interactions. Specifically, this analysis demonstrates that "global householding" has become a prevalent livelihood strategy in both developed and developing countries. Mary Poppinses are no longer localized characters in one region, but have been globalized and regulated. While such workers might help to secure access to the world for those who can afford to hire them, this process also makes the workers themselves and their families become even more insecure. By underestimating the impact of "global householding," either localized or temporary, we risk missing the "actually existing" struggles caused by global population movement and transactions.

The next section explains the causes of the widespread "feminization" of migration and introduces the concepts of "global householding" and "global de-householding." The chapter then examines how the disciplines of international relations and security studies deal with the "security" and "insecurity" of FODWs. To explore the "security" and "insecurity" of FODWs, this chapter draws on gender studies by adopting the analytical framework of the so-called "gendered geographies of power" (Pessar & Mahler, 2003, pp. 812–846), a research concept focusing on the ability of each female individual to act as an agent in today's world. It questions the extent to which each female individual is capable of acting as a potential agent, i.e. what determines their agency and what influences their ability to fulfill their power as an agent? This leads to the following section, which focuses on the way national, regional, and global regimes do indeed constrain such agency and thereby threaten the "security" of FODWs.

In conclusion, this chapter argues that whenever mothers or daughters go abroad as FODWs, their family members back home are exposed to "insecurity," most likely to a similar degree as the FODWs themselves. Possibly some FODWs in host countries become empowered, (re-)gaining an agency they never possessed in their home nation. Nonetheless, the "insecurity" of the family back home can only be overcome through substantial changes in the "geographies of power" in both the host and home countries. With both FODWs and their families in sight, this chapter suggests in its final analysis that we cannot conclude that the emerging activities of FODWs represent a great sign of "insecurity reduction" if one thereby ignores the inherently double-sided dimension of the problem. It also emphasizes that the nexus of global householding and global de-householding affects our lives in today's globalized world, and no one, whether in Europe, Africa, or Asia, can be free from the changes—and even crises—caused by the reconfiguration of the household beyond national borders. Thus, we are hard-pressed to find a new framework in which to analyze this global phenomenon.

8.2 The "feminization" of international migration

8.2.1 The "feminization" of international migration explained

For Castles and Miller (2009), "feminization" is one of six key words describing the international movement of people since the 1980s.[8] It is true that women have been moving abroad for as long as their male counterparts. However, these two scholars emphasize the increasing volume of female migration since the 1980s as remarkable. Structural changes in the industry sector and more active female participation in the labor market, as well as new demands from aging populations in developed countries, have made overseas female workers an increasingly indispensable workforce in the care and homemaking fields (Pessar & Mahler, 2003). These fields are traditionally defined as "women's work." They tend to pay very little and involve hiring temporary or even irregular workers. A large percentage of overseas female workers are employed in live-in situations. Altogether, their unique plights—being underpaid, insecure, dependent, and isolated—have received little academic attention so far.[9]

Numerous studies have already revealed the reasons for the increasing number of female overseas workers (Gregson & Lowe, 1994; Enloe, 2000, pp. 177–194). Building on such scholarship, this chapter emphasizes that the social and economic conditions of the sending countries contribute to the trend as much as those at the receiving end. Two contributing factors are the introduction of structural adjustment policies (SAPs) in the 1990s and the existing "domestic servant culture" among middle-class families in many less developed countries. Generally, welfare spending has been reduced to meet the targets set by SAPs. Thus, the poor become poorer and their standard of living plummets.[10] Foreign companies in export promotion zones tend to create high demand for young female workers, but lower demand for their male counterparts. Once young women then enter the waged labor market, they naturally aim for higher wages, whether the jobs they seek are offered domestically or abroad. As long as they are well paid, they might not hesitate to venture overseas and send more money back home. Without public welfare support, it is they who need to fend for their aging parents and young siblings.

In addition, it has long been quite common in the developing world to hire home servants. As such, a so-called "domestic servant culture" has prevailed for some time. It is often the case that FODWs had already worked as domestic servants in their own countries when they took the step of going abroad (Connell, 2008). While working as a servant in a middle-class family in their home countries, many FODWs at the same time allot a portion of their income to employing a servant to look after their own family. Hence, an economic "food chain of domestic work" emerges. At all levels of the chain, people become accustomed to relying on outside helpers in their own houses, whether they actually like it or not. With family care in the hands of waged servants, it is the drive for the highest wage, be it in the home country or in a foreign land, that entices them to work abroad. At the upper end of the chain, wealthy families in the developed world successfully obtain low-waged domestic workers by extending their hunt globally. In so doing, they may raise their standard of living, resulting in more time and money for themselves. To support the high standard of those now rich in time and cash, the FODWs, in contrast, suffer global separation from their own loved and treasured families.

8.2.2 "Global householding" and "Global de-householding"

In this chapter, the key concepts used to analyze female migration are "global householding" and "global de-householding." The concept of "global householding" was developed by Michael Douglass of Hawaii University and his present research group (Douglass, 2006). With increasing global movements of people, he renews his focus on the concept of "household." The importance of "household" in the world-system was emphasized by Immanuel Wallerstein more than two decades ago (Smith, Wallerstein, & Evers, 1984). According to Douglass, today's "household" is undergoing enormous changes due to low fertility rates and the longevity prevalent throughout the developed world.

In addition, governments worldwide have increasingly privatized social services, and thus providing care for the elderly and infants has become too great a burden for each household to bear on its own. With the population rapidly aging and shrinking, the households of developed countries are seeking help from abroad, mostly from developing countries. As a result, quite a few "households" in this globalized world are supported by financial and physical inputs beyond national borders, and are thereby successively transformed into "global households," or rather forms of "global householding" (Douglass, 2006, pp. 421–425). Douglass summarizes the major features of "global householding" as the increasing attempts to form and sustain households through global movements and transactions among household members through various means such as marriage, child-bearing and adoption, and hiring foreign domestic helpers and caregivers (Douglass, 2006, pp. 424–425).

To supplement this idea, this chapter introduces an additional dimension to "global householding," namely "global de-householding." By hiring FODWs, an employer's family indeed experiences "global householding." It clearly improves their quality of life by having FODWs do the cooking and cleaning, for example. At the same time, however, the FODWs' own families back home face "global de-householding," losing an important family member who could have looked after them and improved their quality of life as well. In a sense, one of the most important features of today's "insecurity" of FODWs is that it is by nature globalized beyond national jurisdiction. The conditions for both concepts, "global householding" and "global de-householding," occur simultaneously and are inseparably interlinked. Furthermore, whether it is regarded as "global householding" or "global de-householding" depends on whose viewpoint we assume and the extent to which we see ourselves as autonomous agents in the process.

"Global householding" and "global de-householding" are relational concepts in that they involve the countries and family units at both the sending and receiving ends. The extent of their effects depends on the relationship between those who move across and those who stay within national borders. As pointed out, it has long been common for upper class families in developed Western European countries to hire live-in maids. The same can be said for the wealthy in developing countries. In developing countries, such live-in maids were also often alienated and exposed to long working hours under tough conditions. Today's Mary Poppinses, nonetheless, are mainly from developing countries, leaving their families behind to work long and hard in the rich world. Thanks to FODWs, those who live in developed countries may be freed to concentrate their energies on waged jobs and enjoy more leisure time. Thanks to "global householding," they can choose what to do and what not to do. Furthermore, some may actively further advance "global householding" by sending their own children to study or work abroad in the quest for higher wages. Ultimately, they choose whether or not to expose themselves to the "global householding" phenomenon. In contrast, most FODWs venture abroad toward something they cannot gain in their home countries, such as economic advancement, or social or political freedom.

From the viewpoint of FODWs coming from the Philippines, for example, the "global householding" of their employer in Britain is based on their own "global de-householding." Under these circumstances, such Filipinas are deprived of the choice of caring for their aging parents and growing children. Some academics are concerned that the children of FODWs may suffer psychological loss, thus falling into "insecurity" in return for the economic gains accrued (Parreñas, 2005). Essentially, the "global householding" of families in developed countries always exists against the background and mostly at the expense of the "global de-householding" of those in less affluent countries. Moreover, as pointed out earlier, FODWs are denied the opportunity to act as independent actors with the ability to claim their own rights and their own "security" in host countries. Consequently, the actual costs of upholding a high level of "security" for those families who opt for "global householding" are simply transferred, in the form of "global de-householding," to the FODWs and the families they leave behind. These two concepts should therefore be examined together to demonstrate that these developments are two sides of the same coin. When viewed as a pair, they present a complete picture of the rewards and penalties arising from these global phenomena.

8.3 The "security" and "insecurity" of FODWs

8.3.1 What do we mean by the "security" and "insecurity" of FODWs?

Since the UNDP *Human Development Report* was published in 1994, its key concept, "human security," has inspired a heated debate among scholars and practitioners. Numerous studies have attempted to clarify the relationship between "human security" and the conventional understanding of "national security" in IR. Some scholars argue that the newly suggested concept of "human security" could be further differentiated to distinguish between "human security," which is provided by societal institutions and services, and "personal security," which comprises the maintenance of life and existence (Hatsuse, 2003). With regard to FODWs, the immigration legislation and policies of the receiving country often assume their dependency on the male member of the family, simply ignoring the fact that the FODWs travel independently to work and support themselves. This often results in the denial of their capacity and their legal right, as individuals, to claim "human security." Such deprivation of institutional protection and societal services consequentially leads to the erosion of their "personal security," ultimately their very life and existence. In this chapter, "security," unless specified, refers to "human security," deprivation of which ultimately threatens the "personal security" of FODWs and their families.

It is important to note that immigration, nationality, and labor-related legislation and policies in most countries today are unlikely to be explicitly discriminatory against women. In their written form, they appear to be value-neutral. However, as mentioned, when actually implemented they became gendered in the sense that women are regarded as individuals who do not work or reside on their own account. Their entry statuses are often based on that of male members of the family, preventing women from accepting a waged job or remaining in the country if they get divorced or lose their male partner. In reality, as previous research has demonstrated, FODWs are placed under the triple burdens of gender, ethnicity/race, and occupation (Anderson, 2000, pp. 1–8). Thus, neutral-sounding legislation and policies play a key role in rendering FODWs' "insecurity" invisible, leaving the triple burdens of FODWs intact.

Worse, as the following section demonstrates, FODWs today face not only national legislation and policies that implicitly exploit and discriminate against them in comparison to male migrants, but also regional and global regimes. In combination, they remove the plights and exploitation of FODWs from public view. This triple layer of national, regional, and global regimes, which enhances the "insecurity" of FODWs, is the main characteristic of today's migration control mechanism. It is therefore vital to shed light on this complex multi-layered mechanism by unwrapping it, layer by layer, and examining how each layer works in combination with the others to prevent FODWs from pursuing their "security."

8.3.2 What does security studies learn about the "insecurity" of FODWs from migration and gender studies?

Towards and since the end of the Cold War, according to Krause and Williams (1996, p. 229), three main factors have determined the course of development in the field of security studies: first, dissatisfaction among some scholars of security studies regarding the emphasis on states and the traditional military-centric approach of neo-realists; second, an urgent need to respond to the challenges arising from a post-Cold War security order; and third, a strong desire for the security studies discipline to become more relevant to contemporary concerns. Broadly, Krause and Williams point out three directions in which the so-called "new thinking on security" debate is heading (Krause & Williams, 1996, pp. 229–230). The first approach aims to broaden the scope of security studies with the purpose of including non-military issues under the concept of "security." The second trend is to deepen the agenda of security studies by flexibly adjusting the level of analysis from that of individual or human security to that of international or global security. The third group maintains the state-centric approach, but focuses its analysis on diversified forms of inter-state security cooperation, such as common, cooperative, collective, and comprehensive cooperation (Krause & Williams, 1996, p. 230). The traditional approach in the field sees states, groups, or individuals as givens, and treats threats external to these givens in the search for solutions to remove such threats. In contrast, the first and second approaches mentioned above focus on the process through which threats against an individual or group are constituted as "social facts" (Krause & Williams, 1996, pp. 242–243). Their interest therefore lies in who—a government, business enterprise, or charismatic person—defines "security" for particular issues—economic well-being, military build-up, or environmental degradation—and in the process, under what conditions do they effectively provide it (Krause & Williams, 1996, pp. 242–243).

Among the scholars within this "new thinking on security," Buzan and those who contributed to his work (1998) engage in "the most thorough and continuous exploration of the significance and implications of a widening security agenda for security studies" (Huysmans, 1998, p. 480). Nonetheless, even their efforts are criticized for failing to pay attention to the concept of "security" on the basis of gender.[11] This lack of attention, Hansen (2000) insists, results from one of the two main shortcomings of security studies, namely "security as silence."[12] According to Hansen, "security as silence" occurs in situations where the potential subject of security is forced to either remain silent or likely face even greater "insecurity" if the particular situation should receive attention. FODWs fit well into this category. As "women," they face enormous pressures to tolerate lesser "security," whether in their home country or receiving countries. In addition, as "overseas workers," their entry status often depends entirely on their employers, thus depriving them of any chance of challenging their bosses. In particular, for "irregular" or "illegal" female workers, the only remaining option is to remain silent in spite of their constant "insecurity." Regardless of whether remaining silent is instigated by force or by one's own will, unless the resulting "insecurity" surfaces, the phenomenon will never become a subject of security studies. Consequently, the "insecurity" of FODWs has remained under-studied until very recently. Those researchers who try to introduce gender perspectives into security studies argue that the concept of "security" needs to be redefined in a way that reflects the economic, political, or social conditions surrounding a particular individual or group.[13] Whether one feels "secure" or "insecure" depends on one's position. Thus, what should really be examined are the economic, political, and social structures within which "security" and "insecurity" are constructed (Tickner, 1997, p. 624).

In the 1990s, migration studies researchers began to learn from gender studies, thus becoming exposed to a new understanding of "security." Since the late 1980s, they had already begun rectifying the stereotype of a migrant being male and single. Yet, their efforts fall short of transforming their analytical approach wholeheartedly; female migrants are still often simply added alongside their male counterparts as further issues of concern. Some critics thus described this new approach in migration studies as "adding women and stirring" (Curran et al., 2006, p. 209). In the early 1990s, academic interest within the field further shifted to network formation in a transnational setting, especially on the basis of, and with an emphasis on, race, ethnicity, and nationality. Meanwhile, those academics sympathetic and devoted to gender perspectives became concerned that what they had learned in the late 1980s might once again be forgotten in the new agenda. This time, in paying attention to gender issues in the context of transnational settings, they attempt to present analytical frameworks under which one does not merely "add women and stir," but that rather bring "gender" as a relational concept into a holistic perspective. This new analytical framework focuses on the way in which gender relationships are constructed beyond national borders. Henceforth, the treatment and identity of FODWs also becomes subject to transnationally constructed gender relationships (Donato et al., 2006, pp. 3–26).

Among various scholarly works that aim to bring gender into migration studies, that of Pessar and Mahler presents an analytical framework based on "gender geographies of power (GGP)" (Pessar & Mahler, 2003, pp. 812–846). This deserves special attention. The GGP framework has four key concepts as its main constitutive pillars. These are "geographical scales," "social location," "power geometry," and "imagination." First, according to Pessar and Mahler, gender—a relational concept—operates within "geographical scales" that comprise multiple spatial and social scales across transnational spaces. At the same time, gender ideologies and relations are continuously reaffirmed and reconfigured within each constituent "geographical scale." "Social location," as the second component of this analytical framework, refers to people's positions within interconnected power hierarchies, which are created through various socially stratifying factors such as history, politics, economics, geography, and kinship. Since the hierarchies of each factor operate at various levels and affect the "social location" of individuals or groups, Pessar and Mahler emphasize that social location is always fluid and not fixed. Certain advantages and disadvantages are conferred according to one's "social location." Furthermore, "social location" determines the types and degrees of agency one can exercise. Pessar and Mahler call this "power geometry," which is the third component of their framework. The fourth component is "imagination." In examining agency, they emphasize that it not only implies people's ability to influence others and their surroundings, but also their cognitive power to initiate change. Suppose that two people are in the same "social location." One might simply be buried, whereas the other might intend to fight back thanks to "imagination."

Focusing on "power geometry" makes us aware that it is not only crucial how transnational "geographical scales" are formed; it is also who and what controls their formation that plays the key role in understanding the "security" and "insecurity" of today's FODWs. This general understanding draws our attention to multiple-layered migration regimes, which are touched on in the next section. Such layers of legality reflect the intentions of the powerful within today's "geographical scales." Given that various regimes intend to keep FODWs in their current "social position"—invisible—it may still be possible for FODWs themselves to transform their "power geometry" through "imagination." Taking "imagination" into consideration, the GGP framework suggests that not all FODWs should remain powerless, exploited, and controlled by employers and governments in their host and home countries. It recognizes that their "social location" can shift. "Power geometry" is malleable, and some FODWs could someday fulfill the roles of initiators, refiners, and transformers. To frustrate such challenges from FODWs, however, powerful players—national governments being the main players in this case—continue to strengthen confining mechanisms, among which migration regimes comprise the most explicit and concrete form. They play an important role in depriving FODWs of "imagination" and maintaining the current "power geometry." In building multiple-layered migration regimes at the global, regional, and local levels, national governments of both developed and developing countries aim to control the transnational "geographical scales" in which they are predominant.

8.4 National, regional, and global regimes surrounding FODWs

8.4.1 National regimes

Currently, governments in Western developed countries adopt citizenship- and immigration-related legislation and policies that reflect an "anti-immigrant, pro-immigration" nature.[14] The purposes of these types of policies in relation to FODWs are two-fold. First, to keep them marginalized in the society, they force FODWs to accept only certain types of occupation and working conditions. Second, they enable the host government to increase the volume of incoming FODWs for the purpose of upholding the "security" of its nationals in exchange for the FODWs' "insecurity." For example, the work permit system not only distinguishes between immigrants with legal or illegal entry status, but also ties the former to certain jobs and certain working conditions. In the view of governments in developed countries, what they need is not "immigrants in general" but "those who fulfill a certain job." Thus the main aim of currently implemented immigration regimes is to link immigrants to precisely those jobs that nationals neither wish to have nor dare to fill. In this way, host governments can enjoy the benefits of introducing foreign workers who will work for the nation's citizens and raise their level of "security" at very little cost.

Taking the British case as an example, British legislation and policies in the migration-related field no longer include explicitly discriminatory terms and provisions against female migrants. On further scrutiny, however, some legislation and policies are applied in a way that might be disadvantageous to women. Three areas where discriminatory practices against immigrant women may abound are the right of entry, residence, and employment; of family reunion; and of family formation in the form of marriage. First, given that a woman enters the country as the "spouse" or "child" of a legal male entrant, her right to enter and reside subsequently depends on the right of her husband or father. Under the status of "spouse" or "child," such women are consequently prevented from accepting paid work. Suppose a woman enters a country as a legally independent immigrant. In this case, a typical job for her, such as domestic worker or carer, tends to be less likely than other jobs to confer her with permanent residency. As a result, migrant women are subject to a higher risk than their male counterparts with regard to losing their legal entry status and being deported, for example in the case of divorce for married women or unemployment for independent migrant women. In 1979, the British government abolished the visa category for overseas domestic workers (ODWs). Instead, they created a special category to allow the wealthy to bring their domestic workers with them (Bhabha, 1994, pp. 173–184; Anderson, 2000, pp. 86–107). This category, however, was specifically linked to wealthy entrants, and their accompanying domestic workers were not allowed to change employer lest their entry status be stripped. Until 1998, when immigration regulations regarding ODWs were amended, such workers had to endure severe working conditions and even violence from their employer for fear of being deprived of their legal status and thus being deported.

The second set of barriers experienced by immigrant women arises in connection to family reunion. The fundamental right to family reunion is enshrined in the European Convention of Human Rights, for example. However, it is usually provisional and governed by a set of regulations. The required access to adequate accommodation and the necessary proof of sole responsibility for childrearing are two examples that often work against women in Britain. With their low wages, FODWs find it difficult to secure their own accommodation to fulfill the requirements of immigration rules. Worse, most FODWs often live with their employers; thus, they have no option of bringing their children even if they wished to. A thornier regulation that implicitly discriminates more against women than the housing one does is that of "sole responsibility," a regulation introduced in 1968. Under the 1968 Commonwealth Immigrants Act, immigration rules allowed immigrants to bring their children only if they as parents residing in Britain had "sole responsibility" for the child's upbringing (Home Office, 2005, Chapter 14.5). These provisions, although unintended by the then government, worked against many immigrant women from Caribbean countries. Some researchers suggest that immigration officers either consciously or subconsciously believe in the male breadwinning model, and thus think that the male member of the family (father or grandfather in this case) determines where the family should be located (Bhabha, 1994, pp. 31–39). It is therefore difficult for mothers to bring their children to Britain if their fathers or grandfathers, unemployed as they may be, reside in their home countries.

The last case of implicit disadvantage for migrant women relates to international marriage. The British government introduced the "primary purpose rule" in the 1980s. Until this rule was abolished in 1997, those who wished to bring spouses or fiancé(e)s had to prove the genuineness of the marriage and that it was the primary reason for coming to Britain. Although this rule itself did not include sexually discriminatory phrases or conditions, its application tended to be harsher towards women. A general stereotype was that male immigrants were more of a threat to the labor market than their female counterparts. In consequence, when immigrant women applied to the Home Office to invite their husbands or fiancés, they were investigated more thoroughly than immigrant men were. It was also the case that British immigration rules in relation to marriage were based on the prevalent understanding of marriage under British law. Consequently, women in polygamous marriages were not considered as wives, and second wives were prevented from entering Britain as spouses. Also, so-called child wives under 16 years of age were not admitted as either a spouse or fiancée.

Regardless of the long history of female migration, female migrants even today remain invisible with regard to policy making and research. As pointed out in the previous section, governments select certain types of migrants, and in receiving them, they attempt to maintain the current "power geometry." Inflows of live-in overseas domestic workers may reduce the burdens of domestic chores and appear beneficial to female nationals with waged jobs. In reality, reliance on FODWs keeps intact and reinforces traditional stereotypes of "women at home doing housework" and "women taking care of the elderly and childrearing at home." All in all, this may actually prolong the unfair treatment of women. In sum, "anti-immigrant, pro-immigration policies" not only determine the "social location" of female migrants but also that of female nationals at the same time. Women, whether nationals or immigrants, are kept in a weaker "social location" and their agency still depends on male members of the family. In general, only a few lucky women take up paying jobs, forcing other unlucky women to take over domestic chores, doing so under the conditions set by the current "power geometry" of male dominance and female subjugation.

8.4.2 Regional and global regimes

Traditionally, national governments have claimed the exclusive authority to control who enters, stays in, and leaves their territory. Yet, national governments are now aware that they need to act together to tighten control over the international movement of people. Thus, they have established a form of inter-state cooperation to deal with the growing volume. In the field of migration control, therefore, both regional and global levels of control mechanisms are added, complementing national policy instruments designed to uncover undocumented or overstayed foreign migrants and deter asylum-seekers. It is true that national governments are also delegating policy implementation to municipal and local sectors, conferring upon them, for example, the competence and authority to check suspicious cases.[15] Nevertheless, such sectors are subject to their national governments and do not generally take their own policy initiatives. This chapter thus concentrates on the development of regional and global migration control policies, focusing on those of the European Union (EU), and on global cooperation in the form of international conventions.

It may be true that regional and global institutions such as the EU and the United Nations (UN) exert only an indirect and non-compulsory influence on national policies. Nevertheless, they may play an important role in advancing some kind of agenda and changing our mental frame of perception. The idea of universal human rights is the prime example, and has been greatly promoted since the end of the Second World War by international and regional organizations and through various international conventions (Donnelly, 1986, pp. 599–642). Human rights activists and groups, in the face of domestic deadlocks, bypass national governments. They seek support from international organizations to have them exert pressure from abroad to change national policies. Through the "boomerang effect" (Keck & Sikkink, 1998), they wish to ensure that national governments admit cases of human rights violation and rectify them. This certainly also applies to the subject of this chapter. When the maltreatment and invisibility of FODWs come to light, regional and global institutions may be able to affect national policies. Possibly, the current "power geometry" may shift through these regional and global regimes, and FODWs might finally be able to speak up and improve their "security."

Recently, the UN and regional organizations such as the EU have become extremely active in promoting multinational cooperation to combat the trafficking of migrants (United Nations General Assembly [UNGA], 2000a, b). Although promoters of multinational cooperation claim that remedies for victims of trafficking are the prime purpose, the actual practice of existing cooperation appears to concentrate on controlling and regulating the international movement of people. Actual help for the victims is supposed to be left to national governments, but concrete actions seem to be slow to evolve. Contrary to the high hopes of human rights academics and activists, neither regional nor global regimes in the field of migration are aiming to shift the "power geometry" in favor of migrants. They are more likely to deny the potential agency of migrants who have already been rendered powerless, and to uphold the very "power geometry" that works against them. Some academics even suggest that national governments deliberately advance regional and global regimes with the intention of avoiding the national judiciary and furthering control over migrants (Guiraudon & Lahav, 2000, pp. 163–195). In a sense, the establishment of regional and global regimes diversifies the means of national government, and expands the merits of the existing "power geometry." Furthermore, the levels of control mechanisms interactively strengthen each other.

If we look at the actual provisions of international conventions, we find that the term "gender" appears frequently within them. Relevant international organizations, such as the UN, have for some time actively promoted awareness of "gender-related" issues. After nearly 20 years' preparation, the UN finally adopted the International Convention on the Protection of the Rights of All Migrant Workers and Members of their Families (ICMW) in 1990. As the "first comprehensive universal codification of migrants' rights" (Cholewinski, 1997, p. 199), a migrant worker is defined in Article 2(1) as "a person who is to be engaged, is engaged, or has been engaged in a remunerated activity in a State of which he or she is not a national." This definition of migrant workers is considered the most comprehensive in any international instrument concerning migrants, and is thus praised in itself as a "major accomplishment" (Hune, 1987, pp. 123–124). Obviously, migrant women form part of the category of "migrant workers" and should be protected as such. They are also supposed to receive protection as members of migrants' families (Article 1). Specifically, Article 1 declares that the ICMW applies to all migrant workers and their families "without distinction of any kind," such as on the basis of sex. Article 7 also prohibits discrimination on the grounds of sex with respect to the rights provided for in the ICMW. To clarify the intent of sexual equality, the drafters of the convention decided to use the terms "he or she" and "his or her" instead of "he" and "his" towards the end of the preparatory process (Hune, 1991). They could not have made it clearer that all the convention's provisions are applicable to both migrant men and women.

Migrant workers are, according to the convention, to be treated equally to nationals with regard to economic, social, and cultural rights. For example, employment conditions (Article 25), social security (Article 27), emergency medical care (Article 28), and access to education

(Article 30) are specifically mentioned as areas where equality should be guaranteed. Furthermore, Articles 26 and 40 provide migrant workers with the right not only to partake in trade union activities, but also to "form associations and trade unions in the State of employment." The right to education is also widely conferred upon migrant workers, as seen in Article 43, for example. It grants migrant workers and nationals equal access to vocational guidance, training, and retraining facilities. Migrant women who had been treated as invisible even in their home countries might be able to make use of the opportunities provided by the convention to improve their "social location."

Even as a member of a migrant's family, female migrants can receive access to vocational guidance and training under Article 45, although the extent of access is limited in comparison to that stipulated in Article 43. In addition, the convention provides the possibility for migrant women who have entered a country as a dependent or spouse to remain and reside there even after the death of a migrant worker or the dissolution of their marriage (Article 50). To save family members in the case of a migrant's death or divorce, the provision imposed the obligation on states to take into account the length of their stay and authorize them to remain and even work. Even though it does not grant them an absolute right to remain in the country of employment, this special consideration to family members was a welcome addition for migrant women whose residential status was conditionally based on the status of their husbands or fathers.

Despite these provisions, the ICMW has received considerable criticism for not paying sufficient attention to migrant women since its enactment (Hune, 1991, pp. 800–815). The biggest criticism arises from the fact that the convention fails to go beyond the "add women and stir" approach. As Hune (1991, pp. 812–813) suggests, the ICMW drafters did not consider that the concept of "labor" may not mean the same to women as to men. As mentioned earlier, a number of migrant women are employed in the care and housekeeping fields. These fields have for a long time been considered as "women's fields," in which they are supposed to excel by nature. As a result, jobs related to domestic chores, childrearing, and elderly care, for example, are often paid very little or next to nothing. To some people, these jobs do not qualify as "waged labor," as they do not require any special skills or talent, since women are supposed to be born with such skills. The ICMW simply aims for sexual equality, but does not intend to tackle these implicit assumptions or the notion that "female-type work" is inferior to "male-type work." In addition, the convention does not consider that female migrants have to play the role of primary caregiver for children and family members, spending more time than their male partners at home to perform household chores. Given that equal access to "labor" between nationals and migrants is guaranteed, female migrants, in contrast to males, need further public support from their host countries before they can accept employment. Without waged employment, migrant women may continue to rely on their spouses and remain invisible in the host society. As previously pointed out, seemingly neutral terms such as "labor" and "laborer" are often defined in a way that might disadvantage women, and thus require redefinition to change the existing "power geometry." Ultimately, the ICMW does not aim for the fundamental transformation of the "power geometry," but rather for the alleviation of the plights of migrants within given circumstances.

At the level of regional regimes such as the EU, issues relating to migrant women are also handled with the "add women and stir" approach. The frequent appearance of the term "gender" in EU publications might not yet have resulted in the improvement of the "social location" of women in general. EU social policies have gone to great lengths to establish equality between women and men, especially in terms of access to labor markets (Ackers, 1998, p. 2). Not only policy makers but also academics are seeking the best way to achieve equal treatment between the sexes at the EU level. A voluminous amount of research has been conducted on gender equality in labor markets for quite some time.[16] As mentioned with regard to the global regime, while current EU policies may improve the "social location" of EU working women in employment, they are not intended to challenge the current "power geometry" of FODWs. They simply allow EU women with a job to be treated in the same way as EU men, as long as the traditional "white male breadwinning model of family relations" remains intact. In other words, according to Ackers, all residents of the EU are classified into several categories on the basis of citizenship, gender, and access to employment, and are prioritized according to a combination of these three factors (Ackers, 1998, p. 40). Within the hierarchy of people legally resident in the national territory, those males who contribute to the labor market and hold citizenship are ranked first. Next are female spouses with citizenship, as they are acting as women are "supposed to"—that is, being supportive of male citizens. Illegal migrants aside, the remainder of the pecking order is as follows: working female citizenship holders, citizenship holders not active in the labor market—single mothers and the elderly, for example—employed legal male migrants, and a small number of

Female Domestic Workers on the Move 155

female migrants holding skilled jobs. Unfortunately, FODWs are still at the very bottom (Ackers, 1998, p. 40).

Finally, seemingly neutral concepts and categories such as "labor," "laborers," and "waged labor" have all been defined in a male-dominant world. Thus, they intentionally or unintentionally tend to lower women's "social location." Peterson declares that regimes based on male experience and male understanding cannot really account for women (1996, pp. 11–28). Accordingly, three options are suggested: "either females cannot be added (they are marginalized), or they must become 'like men' (they are masculinized), or *they are included, and the meaning of the category is transformed to include femaleness.*" (Peterson, 1996, p. 17, emphasis in original). So far, the current regional and global regimes include women by forcing them to "masculinize" themselves for fear of being "marginalized." It is obvious that traditional concepts, categories, and stereotypes need to be transformed to include femaleness if we are to aim to fundamentally challenge the "power geometry" on women's behalf and to improve their "social location." Currently, regional and global regimes might work favorably for some women who become "masculinized." To other women, the vast majority perhaps, they merely complement national regimes that make women accept more "insecurity" than men. For FODWs, today's multiple-layered regimes—national, regional, and global—form an even more starkly oppressive environment than before.

8.5 Conclusion

This chapter has attempted to make three points. First, today's FODWs are not singularly glued to a certain "social location" by national regimes. Rather, they are triply fixed in their social and legal cage by the two additional layers of regional and global regimes. At a superficial glance, the emergent regional and global regimes in the field of migration offer a glimmer of hope in that they seem concerned with the plights of FODWs and appear to offer a remedy for them. In reality, they are favorable only to a small group of women who are willing to accept the current "power geometry." FODWs remain, as always, powerless and invisible. Worse, their "insecurity" is triply fixed. Second, emergent regional and global regimes do not aim to challenge the current "power geometry" and FODWs' resulting "social location" at the very bottom in any host country. Regional and global regimes may only indirectly influence national governments and policy makers, provided their "boomerang effect" is felt. Yet, today's regional and global regimes relevant to migration are established to protect "laborers" and "migrants" as they are currently understood. By accepting these concepts, these regimes, albeit inadvertently, may be supporting, reinforcing, and cementing the current "power geometry."

Third, as migrant women move across national borders, so too does their "insecurity." Unfortunately, space limitations restrict this chapter from providing further examination of the above cases in Britain or additional examples outside of Europe. We nonetheless find in today's world the prevalence of "insecurity" that crosses borders to the families of FODWs back home in return for the "security" of nationals in their country of employment. As mentioned earlier, the benefits of "global householding" are reaped by people in developed countries at the expense of the damage of "global de-householding," which is shouldered by those in developing countries. Of course, the perception of the phenomenon as "global householding" or "global de-householding" differs depending on timing and the focus of analysis. Yet, by presenting the two concepts together, we can highlight a lopsided relationship between FODWs and their families back home *vis-à-vis* their employers in the host countries. Once aware of the zero-sum elements of "global householding" and "global de-householding," we can take a further step to reveal how these are currently consolidated and even strengthened. Emerging regional and global regimes neither guarantee "security" for FODWs nor prevent "insecurity" from being transferred to their own families, let alone saving them. Worse, most FODWs are from developing countries where social welfare systems are barely existent. While the family members left behind—especially the elderly and infants—may benefit economically by receiving money, they certainly lose out psychologically.

The previous section cited Peterson, who stressed the need to transform traditional concepts and categories, as they were formed through male experience and thus oblivious to the experience of women. Otherwise, the current "power geometry" surrounding FODWs will remain unchanged. Recently, some academics have paid attention to networking and the mutual assistance in which FODWs are actively engaged, claiming that they constitute burgeoning "political activities" and portraying them as signs of change (Kofman et al., 2000, pp. 163–191). In line with this argument, Kofman and others, for example, dispute conventional understanding with regard to the political rights of migrants. They insist that while FODWs might be devoid of voting rights, they are devoid of other types of political activities within the host society as well. Through community groups and networks, FODWs are in constant contact with each other and even with the host population. Taking a wider definition of "politics," Kofman and others try to perceive FODWs not as "objects of political discourse," but as "participating subjects" (p. 163). Since most FODWs in their home countries were afforded limited access to any kind of political activity, they may be more liberated in their countries of employment, thus finding themselves in a much stronger "social location." To some academics, therefore, FODWs might be accredited with the "power to effect change" (Hardy-Fanta, 1993, p. 30). Undoubtedly, FODWs are not always submissive, invisible, and passive objects of exploitation and oppression. Legal exclusion from the formal political process without the right to vote in a way encourages FODWs to become more active in forming associations and networks in their daily lives.

Pessar and Mahler's analytical framework—"gender geographies of power"—introduced and applied in this chapter, presents "imagination" as one of the four main components. Considering people in similar "social positions," some remain subdued while others take the initiative to challenge the system. The root of these different reactions lies in "imagination." Therefore, FODWs' networks and community campaigns might some day provide a strong initiator for change and result in a more tangible challenge to the current "power geometry." Even so, one of the three main arguments of this chapter was the emergence of multiple-layered regimes that threaten the "security" of FODWs. Whatever activities FODWs may be involved in within their country of employment and residence, such activities need to go beyond national borders before they can ever lead to a shift in "power geometry" in a transnational arena. There is no doubt that we should encourage the burgeoning political activities of FODWs, but at the same time, we should not expect too much from them. Ultimately, challenges to and alteration of the "power geometry" should come from those with power. Only they can build counter-regimes of transnational "geographical scales" and transform the "power geometry" in favor of the powerless. Only with their concession and willingness can we establish a truly multicultural space in which differences in power, gender, wealth, and so on are intensively negotiated, and even reconciled.

Notes

Professor, Faculty of Policy Studies, Kansai University. This chapter is based on a presentation given at an international conference—"Global Migration and the Household in East Asia"—in Seoul, on 2–3 February, 2007. The author is grateful for all the comments from the floor.

1. Persons who look after children on a contract basis are referred to in various ways, for example as a "nanny," "au pair," "maid," and "child-minder." The definitions of these terms may differ according to the country and era. In Britain, for example, "au pair" is a legal immigration status, denoting a person who matches the required conditions of age, country of origin, and employment details. "Child-minders" are required to register themselves in Britain, while "nannies" and "maids" lack any form of legal definition. "Nannies" usually concentrate on childrearing at the employer's house, whereas "maids" are responsible for all kinds of housework chores as well.
2. Anderson (2000, p. 7) emphasizes the role of a "female" employer who often hires female overseas domestic workers (FODWs) under oppressive working conditions.
3. The ILO convention concerning decent work for domestic workers (no. 189) came into entry in 2013 in order to combat deplorable working conditions, labor exploitation, and abuses of human rights. Although the number of domestic workers is steadily increasing all over the world, only 12 countries so far have ratified this convention.
4. Douglass (2006). Professor Michael Douglass' research program at Hawaii University introduces the term "global householding." The term "household" includes members based on fictive family relationships, such as nannies, who take the childrearing role over from birth parents, and live-in overseas carers, who look after elderly members of a family. In contrast, the term "family" is usually restricted to biological members. Nowadays, many "families" in both developed and developing countries may have members working or residing abroad. As the volume of movement of people beyond borders increases, so does the number of families who, for their livelihoods, depend on money sent from abroad by family members or who hire workers from abroad to perform their household chores. In sum, it is more appropriate to use the term "household" or even "householding" than "family" to describe how people in the globalized world live and conduct their daily lives.
5. "Security" can mean both "human security," which is protected by social institutions, and "personal security," which implies the maintenance of one's life. In the case of FODWs, the threat to their "human security" by global, regional, and national regimes tends also to threaten their "personal security," leading them into conditions of "insecurity."
6. There does not yet exist an authoritative definition for "gender." The author follows Pessar and Mahler and defines "gender" as a "process, as one of several ways humans create and perpetuate social differences." Pessar and Mahler (2003, p. 813) also consider "gender" as a structure "embedded in institutions." The author agrees with this view, seeing "gender" as part of a complex web of institutionalized social relationships that determines one's power within a society.
7. For the case of Britain, see Bhabha and Shutter (1994) for example.
8. Castles and Miller (2009, pp. 8–9). Five other characteristics are "globalization," "differentiation," "acceleration," "politicization," and "proliferation of migration transition."
9. Kofman et al. (2000). Their work is one of the recent pieces of academic research to have systematically surveyed the plights and treatment of FODWs.

10. Chang (2000) emphasizes the impact of SAPs on pushing female laborers in developing countries to developed countries to seek higher paid jobs.
11. Hansen (2000), Steans (2006, pp. 63–77), Tickner (1997, pp. 611–32, 2001, pp. 36–64). These scholars emphasize the importance of combining gender and security studies in general.
12. Hansen (2000, pp. 287, 294–9). The other shortcoming, according to Hansen, is what she terms "subsuming security." She argues that gender-based insecurity tends to be treated as an aspect of national or religious security, and that female victims are not regarded as a "referent object." Unless recognized as a "referent object," they cannot become the subject of security studies.
13. Tickner (2001, pp. 36–64) provides a thorough survey on the way security studies is developing by learning from feminist perspectives.
14. Chang (2000, pp. 30–31) points out the differences between pro-immigration policies and pro-immigrant policies. According to Chang, the former simply encourages the inflow of immigration, which does not necessarily mean that it is friendly toward immigrants. It is therefore possible to have a pro-immigration and anti-immigrant policy at the same time.
15. Guiraudon (2000, pp. 249–69). Since the 1980s, quite a few developed countries in Western Europe have begun to involve local and municipal governments in migration control mechanisms. Concentrating on the case of the EU, Guiraudon, for example, has worked on the vertical diversification of migration control mechanisms, both upward to an international level and downward to a local level.
16. See, for example, Gregory, Sales, and Hegewisch (1999) and Council of Europe (1996). These works are typical examples of research conducted in the 1990s.

References

Ackers, L. (1998). *Shifting spaces: women, citizenship and migration within the European Union*. Cambridge: Polity Press.
Anderson, B. (2000). *Doing the dirty work? The global politics of domestic labor*. London: Zed Books.
Bhabha, J. & Shutter, S. (1994). *Women's movement: Women under immigration and nationality and refugee law*. London: Trentham Books.
Buzan, B. (1991). *People, states and fear*. Hemel Hempstead: Harvester Wheatsheaf.
Buzan, B., Wæver, O., & de Wilde, J. (1998). *Security: A new framework for analysis*. Boulder: Lynne Rienner.
Castles, S., & Miller, M. J. (2009). *The age of migration: International population movements in the modern world* (4th edn). London: Macmillan.
Chang, G. (2000). *Disposable domestics: Immigrant women workers in the global economy*. Cambridge: South End Press.
Cholewinski, R. (1997). *Migrant workers in international human rights law: Their protection in countries of employment*. Oxford: Clarendon Press.
Connell, J. (Ed.) (2008). *The international migration of health workers*. London: Routledge.
Council of Europe (1996). *Joint specialist group on migration, cultural diversity and equality between women and men, final report of activities* (EG-MG, 2 rev.).

Retrieved form http://www.coe.int/t/dghl/standardsetting/equality/03themes/gender-equality/EG-MG(1996)2_en.pdf.
Curran, S., Shafer, S., Donato, K., & Garip, F. (2006). Mapping gender and migration in sociological scholarship: Is it segregation or integration? *International Migration Review*, 40, 199–223.
Donato, K., Gabaccia, D., Holdaway, J., Manalansan, M., & Pessar, P. (2006). A glass half full? gender in migration studies. *International Migration Review*, 40, 3–26.
Donnelly, J. (1986). International human rights: a regime analysis. *International Organisation*, 40(3), 599–642.
Douglass, M. (2006). Global householding in Pacific Asia. *International Development Planning Review*, 28(4), 421–45.
Ehrenreich, B., & Hochschild, A. R. (2002). *Global women: nannies, maids, and sex workers in the new economy*. New York: Henry Holt and Company.
Enloe, C. (2000). *Banana, beaches and bases: Making feminist sense of international politics* (2nd edn). Berkley: University of California Press.
Gregory, J., Sales, R., & Hegewisch, A. (1999). *Women, work and equality: The challenge of equal pay in a deregulated market*. London: Macmillan.
Gregson, N. & Lowe, M. (1994). *Servicing the middle classes: Class, gender and waged domestic labour in contemporary Britain*. London: Routledge.
Guiraudon, V. (2000). European integration and migration policy: Vertical policy-making as venue shopping. *Journal of Common Market Studies*, 38(2), 249–269.
Guiraudon, V. & Lahav, G. (2000). A reappraisal of the state sovereignty debate: The case of migration control, *Comparative Political Studies*, 33(2), 163–195.
Hansen, L. (2000). The little mermaid's silent security dilemma and the absence of gender in the Copenhagen School. *Millennium*, 29(2), 285–306.
Hardy-Fanta, C. (1993). *Latina politics-Latino politics*. Philadelphia: Temple University Press.
Hatsuse, R. (2003). "Nihgen no anzenhosho" ron no houkousei [Directions for the studies of "human security"], *Gendaishakai kenkyu* [Contemporary Research], 4/5, 81–95.
Home Office. (2005). *UK visas diplomatic service procedures entry clearance vol. 1 general instructions* (Chapter 14.5).
Hune, S. (1987). Drafting an international convention on the protection of the rights of all migrant workers and their families. *International Migration Review*, 21, 123–127.
Hune, S. (1991). Migrant women in the context of the international convention on the protection of the rights of all migrant workers and members of their families. *International Migration Review*, 25, 800–815.
Huysmans, J. (1998). Revisiting Copenhagen: Or, on the creative development of a security studies agenda in Europe. *European Journal of International Relations*, 4, 479–505.
Keck, M. E. & Sikkink, K. (1998). *Activists beyond borders*. Ithaca: Cornell University Press.
Kingma, M. (2006). *Nurses on the move: Migration and the global health care economy*. London: ILR Press.
Kofman, E., Phizacklea, A., Raghuram, P., & Sales, R. (2000). *Gender and international migration in Europe*. London: Routledge.

Krause, K. & Williams, M. C. (1996). Broadening the agenda of security studies: politics and methods, *Mershon International Studies Review, 40,* 229–254.

Parreñas, R. S. (2005). *Children of global migration: Transnational families and gendered woes.* Stanford: Stanford University Press.

Pessar, P. R. & Mahler, S. J. (2003). Transnational migration: Bringing gender. *International Migration Review, 37,* 812–846.

Peterson, V. S. (1996). Shifting ground(s): Epistemological and territorial remapping in the context of globalization(s), In E. Kofman, & G. Young (Eds), *Globalization: theory and practice* (pp. 11–28). New York: Pinter.

Smith, J., Wallerstein, I., & Evers, H. D. (1984). *Households and the world-economy.* London: Sage Publications.

Steans, J. (2006). *Gender and international relations: Issues, debates and future directions* (2nd edn). Cambridge: Polity.

Tickner, J. A. (1997). You just don't understand: troubled engagements between feminists and IR theorists. *International Studies Quarterly, 41*(4), 611–632.

Tickner, J. A. (2001). *Gendering world politics.* New York: Columbia Univ. Press.

United Nations Development Program (1994). *Human development report 1994: New dimensions of human security.* New York: Oxford University Press.

United Nations General Assembly (2000a). Protocol against the smuggling of migrants by land, sea and air, supplementing the United Nations Convention against transnational crime. *Treaty Series.* (Vol. 2241, p. 507, Doc. A/55/383). New York: United Nations.

United National General Assembly (2000b). Protocol to prevent, suppress and punish trafficking in persons, especially women and children, supplementing the United Nations Convention against transnational organized crime. *Treaty Series.* (Vol. 2237, p. 319, Doc. A/55/383). New York: United Nations.

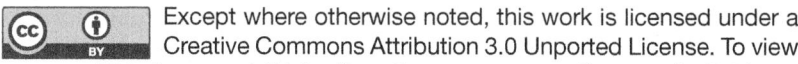 Except where otherwise noted, this work is licensed under a Creative Commons Attribution 3.0 Unported License. To view a copy of this license, visit http://creativecommons.org/licenses/by/3.0/

OPEN

9
Multiculturalism Policies and the Stepwise International Migration of Filipino Nurses: Implications for Japan

Maria Reinaruth D. Carlos

9.1 Introduction

As a result of globalization, labor migration and migrant integration are inevitable yet uncomfortable bedfellows. From the point of view of the host society, the entry of workers from another nationality or culture might solve a domestic labor shortage, but at the same time it will raise serious questions regarding how migrants can be integrated in the society. In what aspects of the community and to what extent will they be allowed to participate in the host society? Multiculturalism policies have been established as frameworks for integration; some have earned praise for their success in some migrant-receiving countries and endured criticisms in many other countries. This chapter presents the case of stepwise migrant nurses from the Philippines to provide one perspective on how multiculturalism policies becomes important predictor of the pattern of international labor migration.

The objectives of this chapter are three-fold: (1) to examine the stepwise migration behavior of Filipino nurses, especially how and why it happens; (2) to determine how multiculturalism policies impact the choice of transit and final destinations in the process of stepwise migration; and (3) to look at the links between stepwise migration and multiculturalism policies, specifically in Japan, which has begun accepting Filipino nurses under a government-to-government arrangement called the Japan-Philippines Economic Partnership Agreement (JPEPA). Given the tendency toward stepwise migration among Filipino nurses, the weakness of the JPEPA scheme as a source of a stable long-term nursing workforce, and the limited capability of the Japanese government to effectively and immediately implement "top-down" multiculturalism policies, this chapter suggests a strategy of encouraging circular migration of foreign nurses in order to alleviate shortage of nurses in the future and at the same time to promote multiculturalism in this country.

An emphasis of this chapter is on the "stepwise" migration of nurses, where they sequentially work in several countries as transit points or stepping stones until they reach their most preferred and final destination. The "stepping stone" strategy has been mentioned in several previous works on nurse migration (see Buchan, Jobanputra & Gough, 2005; Buchan et al., 2005; Dumont & Zurn, 2007; Kingma, M., 2008; Matsuno, 2009), but few have elaborated on how and why this phenomenon occurs. Nurses from the Philippines do follow (and are likely to follow) the stepwise migration pathway. By going through several transit points rather than straight to the most preferred destination, they are able to use their time efficiently while waiting for opportunities in the most desired destination and to accumulate resources—human, financial, social, and political—for use in the transit points or to be transferred to the next destination.

There is also the question of how stepwise migrants distinguish between a transit destination and a final one. This is particularly relevant considering the emerging issue of nurse retention. Two factors prompt stakeholders' deep concern on the retention issue. First, in light of the aging population, it is important to have a stable source of experienced nurses in the workforce. Therefore, ongoing training of foreign-educated nurses can be one strategy for overcoming future projected shortages. Second, training nurses takes time and incurs costs, and the longer the nurse stays, the higher the possibility of recovering this investment. Even in Japan, the attention of policymakers and those on the ground has been gradually shifting from recruiting and employing foreign nurses to retaining them in the workplace.

The multiculturalism policies (or lack of them) that nurses consider important in their choice of final or transit destinations are explored in this chapter. Specifically, three basic components or aspects of multiculturalism policies and practices will be investigated, namely, (1) access to labor markets and equal treatment of locals and foreigners in the workplace, (2) access to citizenship, and (3) family reunification. These multiculturalism policies on the national level as well as multicultural practices in the workplace influence migrant decisions through their impact on the economic (salary, labor conditions, and security of tenure) and social (availability of family support, recognition, sense of self-worth, and belongingness in the workplace) determinants of stepwise migration.

Japan began receiving foreign nurses in 2008 under a government-to-government economic partnership agreement. Under this scheme, nurses from the Philippines and Indonesia are initially accepted as "candidates," and their stay beyond three years is only permitted if they pass the National Licensure Examination conducted in the Japanese language. Five years have passed, but the results are very limited in terms of the number of nurses who were recruited, the number who qualified to stay beyond three years, and the number of those who chose to stay after getting the Japanese license. While multiculturalism policies are deemed important in attracting and retaining foreign nurses in this country, their formulation and more so their implementation has been slow, primarily because of the political, economic, and social implications, of which the Japanese stakeholders are wary. Given these domestic circumstances, coupled with the tendency for Filipino nurses to engage in stepwise migration, this chapter suggests the alternative, albeit mid-term, measure of encouraging "circular migration." This will not only create a stable pool of foreign nurses, but also introduce and contribute to multiculturalism on the ground (multiculturalism from below). This undertaking, in turn, can be an instrument for this country's national and local governments to initiate complementary "top-down" multiculturalism policies.

The empirical evidence on the dynamics of the stepwise migration pattern and its relationship with multiculturalism will be drawn from data gathered from fieldwork conducted in Singapore, Australia, the UAE, Japan, and the US. The fieldwork component comprises two parts: (1) implementation of a common survey questionnaire (through snowballing), with a few items redesigned to be compatible with the current labor migration policies of a specific destination; and (2) semi-structured interviews with some of the respondents and stakeholders. The questionnaires were implemented as follows: Singapore (March 2010, March 2011); Dubai, the UAE (October 2010); and Sydney and Darwin, Australia (October 2012). The numbers of nurse respondents[1] are as follows: 72 in Australia, 53 in Singapore, and 48 in the UAE. In the US, interviews with stakeholders were conducted in June–July 2012 in Washington DC, Los Angeles, CA, and Union, NJ. Information on multiculturalism policies, immigration rules and procedures was taken mostly from announcements in official government websites and newspapers.

This chapter is organized as follows: in the next section, the analytical frameworks on stepwise migration, multiculturalism, and multiculturalism policies to be used in this chapter will be presented. In Section 9.3, results of a study on the working of stepwise migration are analyzed, followed in Section 9.4 by a discussion of how multiculturalism policies affected nurses' choices of transit and final destinations. In Section 9.5, Japan's current scheme for accepting Filipino nurses is examined from the perspectives of its labor shortage of nurses and multiculturalism. The final section summarizes and concludes this chapter.

9.2 Analytical framework—stepwise migration and multiculturalism

Simply defined, stepwise international migration is a pattern, pathway, or strategy in which migrants move from one transit country (the stepping stone) to the next until they reach the most preferred destination. It is a series of rational decision-making processes that involve constantly assessing the labor and migration conditions and policies in several destination countries as well as the migrants' own capabilities and resources with the objective of moving to a better or more preferred destination, until the most preferred final destination is reached (Carlos & Sato, 2010, 2011).

A stepwise migration pattern differs from the conventional patterns of migration in three ways. First, this migration pattern consists of multiple stages, with the migrant's movement from one stage (destination) to another following some form of hierarchy. This differs from a one-time movement from the origin to the destination by permanent migrants or from circular migration wherein the migrant moves back and forth between one origin and one destination. Second, stepwise migrants are not simply "transients" who spend just a week or a month in one destination. Third, this pattern has a dynamic nature in which the migrants themselves actually make a series of decisions—either at the beginning of their journey (departure from the source country) or along the way to the most preferred and final destination. Their journey may be planned, to some extent, from the beginning, but it may also be unplanned (Paul, 2011).

Recent empirical studies, such as Carlos and Sato (2010, 2011) and Paul (2011), show that nurses' decisions on how they treat a destination depends on the country's economic performance, its historical and political affiliation with the sending country, and its ambiguous and unpredictable policies on the recruitment and employment of foreign workers. This chapter looks at multiculturalism policies in the destination as another important factor that strongly influence the migrant's decision on whether to stay in one destination or to leave for the next one.

The concept of multiculturalism was introduced in the 1960s, and in the years that followed debates on what multiculturalism is and why and how it should be implemented have gradually become the center of discussions about migrant integration. In recent times, the 9/11 incidents in the US and social unrest involving migrants in France and Germany necessitated the re-examination of multiculturalism as a form of integration. Some alternative, but equally controversial, ideas such as "interculturalism," "civic integration," and "social cohesion" have been introduced. They are not completely distant in meaning from multiculturalism, but they build on, and are therefore, compatible with multiculturalism. Moreover, multiculturalism programs and practices have only changed their titles, and are still based on the same ideas and principles (Banting & Kymlicka, 2012, p. 15; Cantle, 2012).

The working definition of multiculturalism that is adopted in this study is derived from Tariq Modood:

> Multiculturalism refers to the struggle, the political mobilization but also the policy and institutional outcomes to the forms of *accommodation* in which *"differences"* are not eliminated, are not washed away but to some extent recognized. Through both these ways, group assertiveness and mobilization, and through institutional and policy reforms to address the claims of the *newly settled, marginalized groups*, the character of "difference" is addressed; ideally, a negative difference is turned into a positive difference, though in most contemporary situation(s), something of each is likely to be simultaneously present [emphasis added]. (Modood, 2013, p. 36)

For Modood, multiculturalism is one mode of integration,[2] in which cultural, political, and other forms of (negative) differences, as identified both by the integrating group (often the newly settled minority) and the other groups (majority and the "traditional" minority groups), are recognized and put to use for the good of the larger group (positive difference). Moreover, these differences are addressed by using two main tools, as follows: through assertion by and mobilization of *all* groups (not only the integrating group), and through the implementation of a set of policies by the government on the national and local levels. Effective multiculturalism policies should not be meant to eliminate differences among the groups; instead, they should cultivate a vision for the common good of the multicultural society despite these differences. Neither is multiculturalism a "cure-all" prescription to prevent and resolve conflicts among groups in a society. Furthermore, to be able to channel negative differences into positive differences, groups should not just be recognized but also appreciated so they can feel a greater sense of belonging and thus dedication to the common good.

In reality, however, it is difficult to differentiate multiculturalism policies from other types of policies related to immigration. In the opinion of Banting and Kimlycka (2012), "there is no universally-accepted definition of 'multiculturalism policy' and there is no hard and fast line that would sharply distinguish multiculturalism policies from closely related policy fields, such as anti-discrimination policies, citizenship policies and integration policies" (p. 6). Therefore, we define multiculturalism policies on a broad spectrum; that is, as a wide range of policies that can be employed to accommodate new group identities and new norms in the public sphere. Furthermore, we limit our analysis to the following three areas of multiculturalism policies: (1) access to labor market and equal rights and benefits in the workplace, (2) access to citizenship, and (3) family reunification. These three areas are the most essential components of multiculturalism policies that motivate foreign workers in general and stepwise migrant nurses in particular to stay in a destination.[3]

9.3 Stepwise migration among Filipino nurses

This section will discuss how and why stepwise migration has become a common practice among Filipino nurses, as indicated by the results of the fieldwork in three destinations.

9.3.1 Do Filipino nurses engage in a stepwise migration strategy?

In order to determine whether Filipino nurses engage in stepwise migration, we first inquired about their work experience before coming to the current destination. The survey results show that some respondents have worked in countries outside the Philippines at least once. The percentage of those who have work experience abroad is highest for Australia at 35.4%, followed by the UAE (31.9%), and then Singapore (15.4%). In addition, whereas all respondents in Singapore had some work experience in the home country, some nurses in Australia and the UAE did not have any. This is because in Australia and the UAE, alternative migration pathways other than obtaining a working visa, for which a Philippine license is often required, are available to Filipino nurses, as mentioned above.

Another interesting trend is that the majority of those who had experience working outside the Philippines had previously been based in the UK, Ireland, the Kingdom of Saudi Arabia (KSA), and other counties in the Middle East. Of these countries, the KSA emerged as the most popular, with the exception of the UK for nurses based in Australia. Apparently, this is because the KSA has been actively recruiting nurses from the Philippines since the 1970s. From 2004 to 2010, about 70% of all newly hired nurses processed by the Philippine Overseas Employment Administration (POEA) were deployed to this country (Philippine Overseas Employment Administration, n.d., Table 14). Having easy access to nursing jobs in the KSA through POEA-accredited recruitment agencies, fast processing and immediate deployment at an affordable cost largely contribute to its popularity as an initial destination.[4]

For those currently working in Australia, the UK (18.5%) and Ireland (9.2%) also emerged as formerly popular places for Filipino nurses to work. These countries faced nurse shortages from the late 1990s until the mid-2000s, and they allowed entry of Filipino nurses on work visas that could later be converted to permanent residency visas and then citizenship. Their numbers peaked in 2001 and declined thereafter, when despite, the bilateral agreement on the recruitment of Filipino nurses forged by the two governments in 2002, recruitment was unilaterally stopped by the UK government, to the surprise of the Philippine government. There were two reasons: self-sufficiency in their nursing workforces has been achieved and there was competition from nurses coming from within the EU (Carlos, Sato & Caragay, 2009, pp. 77–81).

9.3.2 How do Filipino nurses engage in stepwise migration?

To further understand how stepwise migration took place among the nurses in this study, their pathways and period of stay in each destination was mapped (see Appendix Table A9.1). The results revealed two trends. First, migrant nurses stay in one destination for a considerable period, usually years. This length of stay is necessary because the resources required to move to the next destination often take time to accumulate, particularly human and political resources (i.e. experience, skills, and citizenship). For nurses currently in Australia, the longest times spent in previous destinations were 13 years in the KSA, 11 in Libya, and 11 in the UK. Stepwise migrant nurses in the UAE also spent as long as 15 years in the KSA. On the other hand, very few respondents in Singapore had more than 5 years' experience in other countries.

Second, compared to those who are based in Singapore and the UAE, many who now work in Australia had passed through several transit destinations, the most popular being the UK and Ireland. One interviewee who left the Philippines in 2000 said that compared to those originating directly from the Philippines, "it was much easier and less expensive to come to Australia with the UK passport, UK experience, and a UK nursing license." Given these advantages, we can infer that Filipino nurses who possess a passport from the UK or Ireland are more likely to engage in stepwise migration to Australia.

9.3.3 Why do Filipino nurses engage in a stepwise migration strategy?

Evidently, the tendency for nurses to take a roundabout pathway and pass through several transit destinations instead of heading directly to the most preferred final destination is a rational strategy. It allows for the accumulation of resources in the transit destinations that are not readily available in the Philippines but are required in the more preferred destinations. Moreover, it is seen as a rational strategy in light of the unpredictable and ambiguous nurse-migration policies of these destinations.

The findings imply that *transferrable* and *useful* resources in the forms of human resources (skills and license, as mentioned above), economic resources, social networks, and political resources (citizenship) can be accumulated in an previous (initial and transit) destinations, motivating nurses to work there first and engage in this stepwise strategy. In a focused group discussion (FGD) conducted among respondents who engaged in stepwise migration (Darwin, October 25, 2012), the nurses admitted that having several years of experience in one transit destination was much more preferred over the experience obtainable in the Philippines. Moreover, having a license appears to be a valuable asset in some cases because it enables the nurse to work right after arrival in a more/most preferred destination. Employers prefer nurses who have work experience overseas because it is considered proof of better nursing skills and knowledge, familiarity with modern medical instruments, and ability to work in a multicultural setting. Indeed, Filipino nurses target human resources in the destination to make them more *marketable* in the next destination.

The nurses also accumulate the economic resources to cover the expense of moving to the next destination, such as recruitment fees, examination and review fees, settlement costs, and transportation costs. Because of the low salary of nurses in the Philippines, these nurses prefer to work outside the country for much higher pay so they can save for such expenses. Social networks (social resources) in the destination—such as Filipino friends and families, the Filipino community in general, international recruitment agencies, and co-workers from different countries—can also be easily accessed from a destination. These networks can provide more accurate information about other destinations, although recently the Internet has also become a source of information for recruitment, and about life and work in potential destinations. Some international recruitment agencies choose to establish temporary and permanent offices in the destinations rather than in the Philippines to avoid being subjected to the strict recruitment regulations of the Philippines and because employers prefer nurses with experience working overseas.

Most of all, many of the respondents value the citizenship (i.e. political resource) obtained in the destination through naturalization because this becomes a way for easy access to and more favorable employment conditions in the next destination. Traditionally, obtaining citizenship in a destination is highly valued by migrants because it will give them equal rights and privileges under the law of the destination country and will allow them to settle permanently without migration restrictions. Many destination countries also use citizenship to attract and retain foreign nurses. In the case of the Filipino nurse respondents, however, citizenship in a destination is even more significant because it enables them to enjoy the rights and privileges accorded by some other destinations to citizens of the country where they are naturalized.

As one example, several Filipino nurse respondents in Australia have acquired prior citizenship in the UK, which was advantageous in finding work in Australia and settling there. A respondent in Dubai planned to work in the UK, apply for citizenship, and then return to the UAE because by doing so she would receive a higher salary and could petition for her family's entry more easily than could her fellow Filipino nurses in the UAE. Another respondent from Australia pointed out that she wants to work in the KSA temporarily because her Australian citizenship and nursing license enable her to receive a salary and benefits that are tax free and much higher than that usually earned by Filipinos in the KSA. In contrast to the common notion that a migrant will stay if she becomes a naturalized citizen of the host country, the nurses in the study instead consider such access to citizenship as a way to move on to another destination.

Moreover, the time spent in one destination, which is considerable, is explained by the unpredictable labor migration policies in many preferred destinations. Whether, when, and how to recruit and accept foreign nurses is singlehandedly decided by stakeholders in these destinations. Respondents pointed out that staying in one destination is an efficient and effective way to spend time while waiting for the opportunity to work in the most preferred destination, which depends largely on immigration policy reforms that may take years to be approved. For example, the current visa retrogression policy (US Citizenship and Immigration Services, 2013) of the US prevents entry of Filipino nurses, despite them meeting requirements such as passing the Visa Screen Program administered by the Commission on Graduates of Foreign Nursing Schools (CGFNS) International and National Council Licensure Examination for Registered Nurses (NCLEX-RN). Instead of staying in the Philippines, many of them grab the opportunity to work first in a less preferred destination with migration that is more restrictive and labor conditions that and worse and have lower pay, but which has a shorter processing time and requirements that are easier to meet. Indeed, when the respondents were asked about their top three reasons for working in the current destination, 71.7% of those in Singapore and 59.6% of those in the UAE chose "having the opportunity because this country actively recruits nurses from the Philippines." In contrast, only 11.3% of the respondents from Australia chose this response. This finding confirms that countries that actively recruit nurses from the Philippines easily become immediate or initial transit destinations for its nurses, but not necessarily their final destination.

Finally, the fact that nursing is a relatively global profession also contributes to the feasibility of stepwise migration. Nursing skills and knowledge have basic commonalities in many countries, allowing their accumulation and transferability among destinations. There are countries where the license is honored under a mutual recognition scheme so that nurses can begin working with minimal orientation from the new employers. Such is the case in Australia for licenses obtained in the UK (as explained above), Ireland, and New Zealand. The licensure or board examinations act as an objective way of assessing the nursing skills and knowledge accumulated elsewhere and evaluating their transferability across countries.

From these findings, it can be inferred that there is indeed some sort of hierarchy in the preferred destinations of stepwise migrants. However, such rankings do not seem to be determined prior to their first departure from the Philippines, and they will go wherever there is an opportunity to work. As they move along their stepwise pathway and accumulate resources overseas, the succeeding decision-making process to determine whether to stay or move and when to move to the next destination becomes more systematic and predictable.

9.3.4 To stay in the current destination or move to the next one?

To further verify whether the current country is a final or a transit destination, the respondents were asked about their future plans. The responses show that while only 8% of the respondents in Australia had plans of leaving that country to work in another destination, more than half of the respondents in Singapore (54.7%) and the UAE (79.6%) had plans to do so. Moreover, a considerable percentage of the respondents in these two transit countries were still undecided on whether to stay or move to the next destination.

Such trends were further confirmed by asking the respondents how long they planned to stay in the current destination to work. About 80% of those in Australia wanted to remain in the country for more than an additional 10 years, and about 70–80% of those in Singapore and the UAE had shorter-term plans to stay in these countries no more than five additional years. The shorter (mid-term) plans to stay in Singapore and the UAE imply that the respondents consider these countries as transit points, and that they are potential stepwise migrants who will live in multiple destinations over their lifetimes. In contrast, respondents in Australia had a relatively long-term plan for working there; many even indicated "until retirement," which suggests that this country is considered a final destination.

The decision to stay in the current destination or seek greener pastures somewhere else arises from essential differences among the destinations and preferences of the migrants themselves. For one, the destinations differ in their geographical distance from the Philippines, with Singapore being the nearest and the UAE the farthest. Some respondents value the idea that they can go home anytime if they work in Singapore. To be able to land a job as a nurse in Singapore, Australia, or the UAE several years of work experience, either in the home country or in another destination, is required. However, licensing procedures differ. Currently, in Australia, nurses who hold a license and have experience working in previous destinations, such as Canada, New Zealand, the Republic of Ireland, South Africa, the UK, or the USA, are exempted from appearing for the Australia Nursing Board Exam (Australian Health Practitioner Regulation Agency, 2013). On the other hand, Singapore requires that all nurses from the Philippines possess a Philippine nursing license and a recommendation from the employer to be eligible for the Singaporean Nursing Board Exam (Singapore Nursing Board, 2013). Respondents in the study indicated that in Singapore, obtaining a working visa before entering the country is the main pathway available for

Filipino nurses, whereas in Dubai (UAE), Filipinos can first enter the country to join relatives or as tourists, then take the Nursing Board Examinations after arrival and find employment. If aspirants pass and find an employer within a year, they can be granted a nursing license and a work visa (Dubai Health Authority 2013, p. 53). Australia also provides several pathways for Filipino nurses. They can come as students to enroll in graduate programs in accredited Australian universities, as dependents of a family member who is a migrant, as students taking the bridging program for nurses, and as nurses with a license from an approved country such as the UK, Ireland, or South Africa (Australian Government Department of Immigration and Border Protection, 2013).

In addition to these factors related to geographical distance and the foreign-worker recruitment system, subsequent decisions also depend on how they are accommodated in the destination through multiculturalism policies, the details of which will be discussed in the next section.

9.4 Multiculturalism policies as a determinant in the choice of transit and final destinations

Of the different factors that distinguish a transit destination from a final one, multiculturalism policies can be considered crucial, especially from the perspective of the retention of nurses. While Australia has been openly promoting multiculturalism, the UAE and Singapore seem to be strikingly conservative in their policies and practices, as elaborated below. These differences affect migrants' long-term plans rather than the initial decision to migrate.

In the following discussion, countries are classified on a spectrum reflecting the extent to which multiculturalism is implemented and the nature of multicultural policies, with Australia, as an active promoter of multiculturalism and multiculturalism policies toward one end, and Singapore and the UAE toward the other end.

9.4.1 "Easy entry–easy exit" transit destinations: The case of Singapore

The recruitment of Filipino nurses to Singapore has been ongoing since the early 1990s, which is later than recruitment to Middle East countries, where Filipino nurses have been employed since the Marcos administration in the 1970s.[5] Singapore represents a group of destinations that allow easy entry because of its organized recruitment system, in which the private sector, including hospitals and care home administrations as well as private recruitment agencies, are actively involved and are cooperative in bringing in foreign nurses (Personal communication with a recruiter in Singapore: March 19, 2008). At the same time, however, nurses consider these destinations only as stepping stones, and their stay in these countries can very well facilitate their easy exit to a more preferred destination.

That it was relatively easy and faster to find work in Singapore compared to the US, Australia, and other receiving countries was evident in the interviews. Because of the acute nursing shortage and need to fill positions as soon as possible, and the efficient and transparent system of processing immigration papers in terms of what documents are needed and the adoption of online application software, the entire recruitment process from application to employment usually takes one to two months, compared to years in the case of the US. Applications can be lodged through relatives in Singapore, partner recruitment agencies in the Philippines, or via the Internet. Compared to their counterparts in other countries, Singaporean employers and the Singapore Nursing Board play a greater role in recruitment. They even come to the Philippines to administer the licensure examination and conduct interviews. The recruitment fee is also less expensive and paid using an easier repayment scheme compared to those in other countries. In 2009, the recruitment fee ranged from $1,500 to $3,000, which is paid by the Filipino nurses in installments after their arrival in Singapore. It is also relatively easy for Singaporean employers to decide on hiring foreign nurses because they do not pay any fees to the recruiter, and they are also assured that nurses who do not perform well during the six-month probation period can be "returned and replaced with another nurse from the Philippines" (Personal communication with a recruiter in Singapore: March 19, 2008).

While Singapore sets two conditions for institutions to be eligible to hire foreign nurses, these do not seem to hinder their recruitment and employment. Based on Singaporean immigration rules, the recruitment and employment of a foreign nurse depends on two conditions: the total number of foreigners employed does not exceed the quota (called the dependency ratio ceiling), which is generally about 10–15% of the total workforce in 2008, and also that the employer is willing to pay a monthly foreign worker's levy of about $250–390.[6] An administrator of a nursing home, when interviewed in March 2010, emphasized that it is more costly to employ foreign nurses because of the levy and housing and food subsidies. Nevertheless, they are willing to employ foreign nurses because there is a general shortage of nurses owing to the unpopularity of the profession among Singaporeans and that many nurses leave nursing either to raise a family or go overseas (Interview with administrator of a nursing home, March, 20, 2008).

While Singapore and some Middle Eastern countries openly and actively recruit foreign workers, their conditions after arrival in the destination are often highly dependent on their salary, job category, nationality,[7] and type of visa. By setting rules based on these criteria, the government is able to selectively accept "desirable" foreign workers. The foreign workers in Singapore are categorized according to their skills, with domestic helpers and construction workers at the bottom (categorized as unskilled) and skilled professionals on top. Filipino registered nurses are considered "mid-level skilled" workers. They receive an "S pass" visa,[8] with which they enjoy a greater number of and better privileges than do foreign workers in the construction and other services sectors, but these privileges are fewer and less superior than those afforded to professionals engaged in IT, education and research, pharmaceuticals, and other high value-added sectors. For those who have a "work permit" (domestic helpers, healthcare assistants, and waiters/waitresses) or "S" pass status, the employer has to pay the foreign worker's levy (tax). In contrast, the foreign worker's levy is not required when "professionals" holding an Employment Pass ("E" pass) or Personalized Employment Pass (PEP) are employed.

One of the nurses' privileges concerns family reunification. Nurses can only bring in their immediate family members (spouse and unmarried biological and/or legally adopted children below age 21) as dependents if their monthly fixed salary is at least $2,800.[9] While many of the respondents could meet this salary requirement, they chose not to petition for dependent visas because of the high cost of living in Singapore, including costs of housing and children's education, which are not subsidized by the government or by the employer. They are also not allowed to apply for dependent visas for their parents and parents-in-law. Many nurses opt to bring their families in simply for a vacation, since the Philippines is only a three-hour flight from Singapore.

In Singapore, citizenship through naturalization is generally not granted to foreign workers unless they marry a local or there are extraordinary circumstances.[10] Dual citizenship is strictly disallowed. Application for permanent residency requires that the applicant holds at least an S pass and proof of employment, but satisfying these requirements is not an assurance that the application will be approved. Permanent residency status is important if Filipino nurses plan to stay in Singapore to work because they can find jobs more easily with this status. In addition, employers prefer permanent residents because they are no longer included in the foreign workers' quota and the employer does not need to pay the levy for them. However, ironically, permanent residency is tied to employer sponsorship; the permanent residency and re-entry permit to enter and exit Singapore are both issued with specific validity dates (usually three to five years), and they can only be renewed by showing proof of employment (Immigration and Checkpoints Authority, n.d.).

While there are no official policies discriminating against Filipino nurses in the workplace, respondents claimed that they are *at the mercy* of the local hospital administrators from the time they arrive in Singapore. Filipino nurses come to Singapore on a temporary/probationary nursing license issued by the Singapore Nursing Board, which is valid for six months and renewable for another six months. Nurses who do not receive a good evaluation after this period will be repatriated. Those who are initially employed as healthcare attendants or nursing aides need to be promoted first to enrolled nurses and then to registered nurses, both of which depend on the initiative of the employer. If the employer deems their performance unsatisfactory, their initial two-year contract will not be renewed, and they will have to return to the Philippines. They are not allowed to find another employer, unless they leave the country first.

9.4.2 The preferred "in-between" transit destinations: The UK and Ireland

Based on the stepwise pathways revealed by the respondents, the UK[11] and Ireland are considered the more preferred transit destinations for Filipino nurses for many reasons. First, compared to Singapore and the UAE, it is not as easy to enter the UK and Ireland because they have more prohibitive requirements regarding work experience and licensing. Second, access to recruiters for these destinations is quite limited in the Philippines because many are often based in other transit destinations, like Singapore and the UAE, where interviews are also conducted. Third, these destinations offer higher salaries and better benefits than the initial transit destinations.

A last and perhaps most important difference from the initial transit destinations is that these countries provide opportunities for migrant workers to become citizens provided they have lived in the country for a specified period. Obtaining citizenship in these second-transit destinations increases the probability of being hired in a more desired destination because of favorable policies and mutual agreement schemes (such as those among the Commonwealth countries) concerning employment and the status of citizens' stays in these destinations.

One interviewee from Australia said, "When I was in the UK, everyone was eyeing UK citizenship because we wanted to go to Australia. It was easy for me to come to this country because of my UK passport. In fact, I began working in the wards only a week after arrival." One interviewee in the UK also said, "now that I have a UK passport, I am planning to return to the UAE because I will earn more compared to Filipino nationals there." Further studies are necessary to determine what other "in-between" transit countries are considered by these nurses and how access to citizenship not only affects their decision-making process in choosing destinations, but also influences their identity formation, sense of belongingness, and ideas on nationalism and multiculturalism.

9.4.3 Final destinations: Australia and USA

Not surprisingly, the US is the top destination because of its historical and cultural affinity with the Philippines.[12] Buchan et al. (2005) and Buchan, Jobanputra, & Gough (2005) observe that a majority of nurses from other source countries are also inclined to target the US as a destination. It is the traditional destination for Filipinos who wish to pursue the American dream, as it has what Paul (2011) calls "place reputation." In addition, the Philippine nursing curriculum is patterned after that of the US, so less adjustment is required in the workplace. A very large Filipino community is also available to support newly arrived nurses. Moreover, that foreign nurses can have varied career options and a clear career pathway in the US contributes to its popularity as a final destination. In a telephone conversation with a Filipino nurse based in Maryland in June 2012, he noted, "while in other countries, there are very few options for nurses, especially Filipino nurses, in the United States there is career development or job promotion. ... Here in the US, if you really work hard, you get recognized, you get promoted, you get compensated, *kahit sino ka pa* [whoever you are]." Filipino nurses in the US not only find opportunities to work in hospitals, but also in other fields such as home nursing care, medical insurance, and nursing-related businesses. They have assumed important positions where they work, such as vice-president of a health care company or head nurse in a hospital.

This study also showed that, in addition to the US, Australia was the other country most preferred by respondents. There are several reasons why Filipino nurses want to remain there for long periods. Australia offers one of the highest salaries and best benefit schemes, such as six weeks' annual leave, among the destinations. Opportunities for career growth, citizenship, and family reunification are good, and Australia appeals to personal preferences such as the less severe weather and shorter distance to the Philippines compared to the UK and Ireland. Respondents also mentioned Australia's positive environment for raising children and the advantage of having "lots of space" when building a family.

Compared to transit destinations, there are many types of visas and migration pathways available to aspiring nurses, both temporary and permanent, in Australia.[13] However, for most of these pathways, considerable professional nursing experience and a high level of English language proficiency are necessary to obtain a professional nursing license and tenured employment. However, these language and skills requirements have become more difficult in the past decade. For example, to avail oneself of any of the permanent residency visas, the foreign nurse should achieve a minimum International English Language Testing System (IELTS) score of six points in all skills (reading, writing, speaking, and listening) in one sitting. To apply for most of the visas, the Filipino nurses should be nominated or sponsored by an employer, many of whom prefer nurses who are trained in specialized fields like psychiatric nursing, renal care, or theatre or surgical nursing. An option for those who lack the skills and language is to get a nursing-student visa. However, while there are no initial requirements for skills and language proficiencies, students are required to provide proof of ability to fund their education. Therefore, the easier way to get to Australia is to go initially to a transit destination such as the UK, Ireland, the US, Singapore, or Canada to gain experience and licensure and to save money.

Once employed as registered nurses in an Australian public hospital, the salary, benefits, and labor conditions are the same as those of local nurses. Nurses can negotiate with hospital administrators and the government through the nurses' association, which all nurses are allowed to join. Each state or territory has its own Public Sector Nurses' and Midwives' Enterprise Agreement[14] that contains provisions regarding the salary, allowed leave, security of tenure, and other labor conditions and is negotiated every three years. Moreover, the nurses' association stands behind its members. One Filipino nurse noted that, "if it were not for the nurses' association, I would have been laid off for alleged incompetency. *Ipinaglaban talaga ako ng union* [The nurses' association really fought for me]." This kind of support by a professional group and the sense of "belongingness" to a group, which are not readily found in transit countries, are highly appreciated by the Filipino nurses.

Since family reunification has been a vital part of Australian immigration policy, nurses can include their immediate family members in their application for a skilled worker visa, a relative-sponsored visa, or even a student visa. Converting a working visa to permanent residency also takes less time compared to many other destinations. One respondent was able to get permanent residence visas for herself and her husband through employer nomination barely a year after migrating to Australia on a working visa. This visa assures her and her family that they can stay and work in Australia on a permanent basis, receive subsidized healthcare, access certain security payments, and be eligible to apply for Australian citizenship. It also gives her family the opportunity to sponsor relatives from the Philippines. Another feature of Australia, being an immigrant country, is that it allows for dual citizenship. For naturalized Philippine-born nurses, this is an advantage if they want to enjoy the rights and privileges of a Filipino citizen, such as owning land and other real estate in the Philippines and long-term stays without the necessity of applying for a visa, while keeping a residence in Australia.

Finally, it is also noteworthy that the respondents cited the multicultural character of Australian communities, in terms of not only hosting migrants from many countries and having ethnic restaurants and groceries, but more importantly, in terms of the national and local government and the workplace providing opportunities to people of different origins and backgrounds to actively interact. For example, multicultural festivals (country days) and seminars are held to promote understanding of varied cultures, and free interpretation services in many languages are provided.

From the discussions above, it is clear that differences in multiculturalism policies in the destinations, particularly with regard to access to the labor market, citizenship, and family reunification, contribute to the stepwise migrant's decision whether to stay in one destination or move to the next one. If a country wants to keep a pool of foreign skilled nurses, especially in light of a serious shortage of nurses owing to demographic issues, the implementation of favorable multiculturalism policies is indispensable. In the following section, we look specifically at Japan, which has yet to find a long-term solution rather than a mere stopgap measure to address the future shortage of skilled nurses in the country.

9.5 Stepwise migration and multiculturalism: The case of Japan

9.5.1 The migration of Filipino nurses to Japan under the JPEPA scheme[15]

Japan began accepting nurses from Indonesia in 2008 and the Philippines in 2009. Under the provisions of JPEPA, which is a comprehensive treaty covering trade, investments, cooperation, and movement of natural persons, Filipino and Indonesian nurses are allowed to come to Japan as "candidate nurses." It took about eight years from the time the negotiations started until it was implemented, partly because the Japanese stakeholders were greatly divided in their opinions about whether and how to accept foreign nurses. Even without gaining national consensus, the agreement was ratified, and the first group of Filipino care-workers and nurses arrived in May 2009.

Under the original agreement, the Philippine government, through POEA, is in charge of recruiting and deploying "candidate" nurses, and the Japanese government, through the Japan International Corporation of Welfare Services (JICWELS) (2013) takes care of these nurses after they arrive in Japan. The Japanese government and Japanese employers share the cost of recruitment, deployment, education, and training, amounting to an estimated US$40,000 (excluding an average monthly salary of US$2,000 and an annual bonus of 2.6 times the monthly salary) per candidate nurse for three years, the initial period of the contract. If they pass the Japanese National Nursing Licensure Examination (NLE) within three years, then they can stay to work as professional nurses. If they fail, then they are obliged to return to the home country.

Statistics show disappointing results for the scheme in the first four years of its implementation. While the quota for Filipino nurses was set at 200 persons annually, the number deployed did not reach even half of this quota. According to statistical data from the Ministry of Health, Labor and Welfare of Japan (MHLW) (2013) and JICWELS, in the first four years of implementation of the scheme, only 237 were deployed to Japan and only 25 of them (10.5%) were able to pass the NLE. Moreover, there is high rate of pre-termination of contracts. For example, of the 93 persons who came in 2009, 31 ($\frac{1}{3}$) had left Japan (Carlos, 2013) before the completion of the initial three-year contract.

There are many reasons cited in the literature to explain this dismal performance, ranging from the language barrier, difficulty passing the licensure examination, difficulties in intercultural communication in the workplace, and other issues that are typical in a multicultural environment or workplace. The hospital employers also complained about the heavy burden imposed on them by the Japanese government to handle the financial expenses (which amount to more than half of the total expenses), education in language and skills, and training and management of the candidate nurses.

The Japanese government has acknowledged these problems and is now working toward several revisions of the scheme. It must be noted, however, that many of the problems identified and the solutions offered so far have been made on the assumption and expectation that the nurses will stay and become a stable source of labor in the long run. Below, we argue that Japan is more of a transit destination than a final one. It might not even be chosen as a transit destination given the limited transferrable resources that can be accumulated in this country.

9.5.2 Is Japan a transit point or a final destination?

Undoubtedly, Filipino nurses will choose Japan as a destination, but most probably only as a transit point. It is unlikely that Filipino nurses will settle in Japan for good under the current JPEPA scheme because of the country's substantial differences from the other potential final destinations mentioned above.

In addition to the lower salary and benefits in Japan compared to the US, Canada, and Australia, the lack of multiculturalism policies is expected to influence nurses' decisions about whether to remain in Japan. Access to labor in Japan is highly restricted to this government-to-government arrangement and is initially limited to three years and 200 nurses each year. Unlike Australia, there are no other pathways available for nurses educated overseas. Filipino nurses can be treated and compensated as professional nurses only if they pass the difficult licensure examination. In the meantime, they perform in the workplace as assistant nurses or nursing aides. Unlike in Australia, the provisions of the labor contract are mostly left to the decision of the employer. Consequently, especially in the first two years of the implementation of the JPEPA scheme, there was a notably wide gap in the salary and benefits and other labor conditions among the candidate nurses in the same batch.

With regard to family reunification, employers do not allow foreign candidate nurses to bring in even immediate family members. Employers also generally discourage taking long holidays; candidate nurses are allowed only one to two weeks of return leave to visit relatives in the Philippines. Compared to those who are working in Australia and the US, the Filipino nurses in Japan need to pass the licensure examination within a specific period of three years. One revision to this scheme in 2012 allowed for those who did not pass within three years and returned home to come back to Japan on a short-term visa to retake the examination. Obtaining permanent residency is neither easy nor fast. Passing the NLE is a prerequisite, and foreigners with a working visa who do not have a special relationship with the Japanese (such as those who are born in Japan, are former Japanese nationals, or are the spouse or child of a Japanese national) are generally required to have worked in Japan for at least five years, before they are allowed to apply for permanent residency (Ministry of Justice of Japan, 2013a). To obtain Japanese citizenship, foreigners have to satisfy numerous requirements and undergo a lengthy procedure, as stipulated in the Nationality Law (Ministry of Justice of Japan, 2013b). Given these conditions, Filipino nurses are not likely to consider Japan as a final destination.

However, Japan does have some qualities similar to those of other transit destinations. The JPEPA scheme provides Filipino nurses with the opportunity to leave the Philippines. They need pay only for their passport, health examination, and other documents required by the Philippine government for all overseas workers (subscription to health insurance and the migrant welfare fund) because the rest—the bulk—of the costs for recruitment, deployment, and language and skills education/training are jointly shouldered by the Japanese government and the host institution (hospital). The requirements (a bachelor of science in nursing diploma, a Philippine nursing license, and three years' work experience), which are similar to those of Singapore and other transit destinations, are relatively easy to comply with. Like the other transit countries, Japan shows a trend towards discouraging permanent settlement and favoring a guest-worker migration policy.

One serious concern, however, is that Japan may not even be chosen as a transit destination, especially for those whose main objective in staying in one destination, like Singapore, the UK, Ireland, and the UAE, is to accumulate "transferrable" resources. The skills gained in Japan and the nursing license may not be accepted elsewhere, especially in the potential final destinations. Japanese citizenship, while it takes a considerable time to obtain, may not offer as many privileges as UK or US citizenship, especially in terms of preferential status in some more preferred destinations (like the Middle Eastern countries) in such matters as salary, benefits, and visa status/status of stay. Not even proficiency in the Japanese language, achieved while in Japan, will be useful in the next preferred destination.

Unfortunately, in order to retain foreign nurses, Japan still has much to improve in terms of formulating and implementing the basic multiculturalism policies discussed in this chapter. Moreover, Japan is not largely a country of immigration. Thus, the Japanese, especially the aging generations, generally have limited interaction with and are therefore less accustomed to foreigners in the workplace and serving as care providers. The government has long postponed relaxing immigration rules for foreign workers. While realizing the need for foreign workers to sustain economic development since the 1960s, stakeholders have been divided in their opinions on whether and on what terms foreign workers should be admitted. As a result, Japan has welcomed foreigners, not formally as "workers" from the "front doors" but from the "side doors" (spouses of Japanese nationals, industrial trainees, students, and Japanese descendants) and for a time, even from the "back doors" (undocumented foreign workers).

Specifically in the nursing care sector, given the impending serious shortage of nurses due to the aging population and the projected increase in competition to attract and retain foreign nurses, Japan's options may be declining. Unless steps are initiated to solve this problem now, it will be difficult to rely on foreign nurses in 10–15 years when the workforce shortage is expected to reach its peak. While there may be a large international pool of nurses willing to work in Japan, they may not be immediately available to work in Japanese hospitals and nursing homes. This is because, especially in the case of Japan, cultural competency and language proficiency are as important as skills and experience for workers in the nursing sector.

9.5.3 Circular migration as a mid-term solution?

In light of these circumstances, what can Japan do to sustain a steady supply of foreign nurses who are not only skilled in their jobs but also culturally and linguistically competent? One way is for this country to adopt a "revolving door" or circular migration policy in which the Filipino nurses are able to go back and forth between the Philippines and Japan to practice their profession. The requirements for passing the NLE could be relaxed to encourage Filipino nurses to take it; for example, administering it partly in English or in simplified Japanese, giving the foreign nurses more chances to pass the examination, or giving more time and resources to prepare. Access to the labor market can be improved by exploring other feasible ways to bring in Filipino nurses, such as granting student loans and/or scholarships to potential nurses or establishing agreements between medical institutions in the Philippines and Japan to develop and share human resources. Like many transit countries, employers can develop a system to assure Filipino nurses that they can return to their home country for a leave longer than one to two weeks as part of their work contract. Given the geographical proximity between Japan and the Philippines, allowing this is an alternative to bringing the families of Filipino nurses to Japan. Filipino nurses should be encouraged to return, and they should be given priority in recruitment. Human relations in the workplace can be improved by giving both Japanese and Filipino nurses opportunities for collaboration and interaction. These could assist the Filipino nurses in gaining appreciation for working and living in Japan despite the lack of a Filipino support group or family in the country. These initiatives could very well be undertaken by the private sector rather than the government, which has been limited because of its inability to gain consensus among the domestic stakeholders with regard to employing foreign nurses.

Although these measures might not be an incentive for Filipino nurses to make Japan their final destination, they can help alleviate the shortage of nurses by assuring Japan of a pool of qualified and competent foreign nurses to boost its workforce in the long run. Furthermore, these private initiatives can encourage, and would require, the Japanese government to formulate and implement multiculturalism policies in the following three areas: access to the labor market, access to citizenship, and family reunification. Finally, interaction between Filipino and other foreign workers with colleagues and patients in this service sector will be a good start in promoting multiculturalism in Japan in which "top-down" public policies and "bottom-up" private initiatives work hand in hand to promote migrant integration in this country.

Appendix

Table A9.1 Stepwise migration pathways of Filipino nurses in Australia, Singapore, and the UAE

Australia (n = 23)		Singapore (n = 8)		UAE (Dubai) (n = 15)	
Respondent number	Pathway	Respondent number	Pathway	Respondent number	Pathway
3	Phil (5) KSA (5) Ireland (2) Australia (9)	1	Phil (3) KSA (1) Singapore (2)	1	Phil (6) KSA (3) UAE (6)
4	Phil (3) Ireland (8) Australia (4)	2	Phil (6) KSA (2) Singapore (12)	8	Phil (9) KSA (1) UAE (19)
5	UK (8) Australia (3)	15	Phil (2) KSA (1) Phil (2) Singapore (2)	9	Phil (?) KSA (8) UAE (17)
8	KSA (2) UK (11) Australia (1)	26	Phil (3) KSA (3) Singapore (1)	11	Phil (5) KSA (2) UAE (2)
10	KSA (10) UK (3) Australia (1)	27	Phil (5) Kuwait (4) Singapore (1)	12	Phil (3) KSA (15) UAE (3)

Table A9.1 Continued

Australia (*n* = 23)		Singapore (*n* = 8)		UAE (Dubai) (*n* = 15)	
Respondent number	Pathway	Respondent number	Pathway	Respondent number	Pathway
11	Saipan (2) KSA (8 mos.) KSA (12) Ireland (2) Australia (9)	37	KSA (5) Singapore (2)	13	Phil (7) KSA (3) UAE (4)
12	KSA (13) UK (2) Australia (9)	38	Phil (1) Denmark (4) KSA (0.5) Singapore (17)	20	KSA (15) UAE (4)
14	Phil (2) Singapore (EN 3) New Zealand (4) Australia (1)	39	Phil (3) UAE (4) Singapore (1)	21	Singapore (2) UAE (3)
21	Afghanistan (1) UK (8) Australia (3)	40	Phil (4) KSA (2) Singapore (15)	22	KSA (2) Taiwan (3) KSA (2) UAE (3)
22	UK (11) Australia (1)			24	KSA (4) UAE (3)
25	Phil (8) Ireland (2) Australia (9)			33	KSA (4) UAE (3)
26	Libya (12) UK (3) Australia (14)			36	Phil (3) Jordan (2) Qatar (5) Phil (business) UAE (11)
34	KSA (3) Australia (23)			39	KSA (6) UAE (3)
37	Philippines (5) KSA (2) Australia (6)			43	KSA (5) UAE (10)
53	USA (8) Australia (1)			48	Phil (8) KSA (10) UAE (12)
59	Phil (5) UK (3) Australia (11)				
62	Phil (6) KSA (9) Australia (16)				

(*continued*)

Table A9.1 Continued

Australia (n = 23)		Singapore (n = 8)		UAE (Dubai) (n = 15)	
Respondent number	Pathway	Respondent number	Pathway	Respondent number	Pathway
67	Phil (8) UK (2) Australia (5)				
68	Phil (3) KSA (7) UK (11) Australia (3 months)				
69	Phil (4) KSA (10) Ireland (4) Australia (1)				

Notes: Only those respondents who have experience working in at least one overseas destination are included in this table. Numbers in parentheses indicate number of years spent working in the destination (except for Australia Respondent 68).
Source: Author's compilation.

Notes

All errors remain the responsibility of the author. For correspondence, write to rdcarlos@world.ryukoku.ac.jp.

1. The respondents in this study are holders of Philippine nursing licenses who work as staff nurses and nurse assistants/aides in the destinations.
2. The other forms of integration as articulated by Modood are assimilation, individualist-integration, and cosmopolitanism (Modood, 2013, pp. 146–155).
3. It must be added, however, that for some stepwise migrants, access to citizenship may not necessarily keep them in a destination. It is paradoxical that in some cases, access to citizenship through naturalization drives them to move to a more preferred country that cannot be reached directly from the country of origin due to restrictive, ambiguous, or unpredictable migration policies in the destinations, as argued by Carlos and Sato (2010).
4. The statistics exclude those who did not go through the POEA, such as those who left as tourists, dependents of Filipino migrants overseas, and students.
5. It is not exactly clear when Singapore began actively recruiting nurses from the Philippines. However, the results of the survey show that Filipino nurses were already working in Singapore in 2003–2004.
6. In June 2013, the worker's levy was raised over a staggered period of three years, evidently to moderate the growth of the foreign workforce inflow. For computations of the dependency ratio ceiling and levy per sector, see the Ministry of Manpower, Singapore. http://www.mom.gov.sg/Documents/services-forms/passes/Schedule_of_Levy_Changes_2013-015.pdf, accessed September 10, 2013.

7. For example, the approved source countries for the manufacturing sector are China, Malaysia, Korea, Taiwan, and Hong Kong only.
8. For details about the S-pass, see the Ministry of Manpower Singapore website: http://www.mom.gov.sg/foreign-manpower/passes-visas/s-pass/before-you-apply/Pages/default.aspx, accessed September 20, 2013.
9. However, this minimum required amount was raised to $4,000 in September 2012, making it more difficult for nurses to petition for their immediate family members. Refer to Ministry of Manpower, Singapore (2012).
10. Young foreign men may become Singaporean citizens if they complete the National Service military obligation.
11. For more details about the results of the survey and discussions on the situation and policies in the UK circa 2000, please refer to Carlos and Sato (2010).
12. For details about the history of Filipino nurse migration to the US, see Choi, 2003.
13. The visas available are as follows: (a) Nurses sponsored by an employer (Temporary Work (Skilled) Visa (Subclass 457), Employer Nomination Scheme and Regional Sponsored Migration Scheme); (b) Skilled Migration (Independent migrant, sponsorship by an eligible Australian relative or nominated by a state or territory government); (c) Working holiday; (d) Temporary visa option to do a bridging program to improve skills; (e) Training and Research (Occupational Trainee Stream) Visa; (f) Visitor (Business Stream) Visa (Subclass 600); (g) Student visa (Ministry of Immigration and Citizenship of Australia, 2013).
14. For the current provisions of the Public Sector Nurses and Midwives' Enterprise Agreement in Darwin, Northern Territories, see Office of the Commissioner for Public Employment of Northern Territories, Australia (2013).
15. For details, see Carlos (2013).

References

Australian Government Department of Immigration and Border Protection (2013). *Visa options for nurses*. Retrieved from http://www.immi.gov.au/skilled/medical-practitioners/visa-options-nurses.html.

Australian Health Practitioner Regulation Agency (2013). *Overseas practitioners*. Retrieved from http://www.ahpra.gov.au/Registration/Registration-Process/Overseas-Practitioners.aspx.

Banting, K. & Kymlicka, W. (2012). Is there really a retreat from multiculturalism policies? New evidence from the multiculturalism policy index. *The Stockholm University Linnaeus Center for Integration Studies* (SULCIS). (No. 2012, p. 4). Retrieved from http://www.su.se/polopoly_fs/1.103206.1349356509!/menu/standard/file/SUL CIS_WP2012_4.pdf.

Buchan, J., Jobanputra, R., & Gough, P. (2005). Should I stay or should I go? *Nursing Standard*, 19(36), 14–16.

Buchan, J., Jobanputra, R., Gough, P., & Hutt, R. (2005). Internationally recruited nurses in London: Profile and implications for policy. *The King's Fund Working Paper*. Retrieved from http://www.kingsfund.org.uk/publications/internationally-recruited -nurses-london.

Cantle, T. (2012). *Interculturalism: The new era of cohesion and diversity*. Hampshire, UK: Palgrave Macmillan.
Carlos, M. R. D., Sato, C., & Caragay, R. (Eds) (2009). The migration of health care workers from the Philippines: Japan as a potential host country for nurses and caregivers. *Philippines-Japan Conference on Migration Proceedings. Ryukoku University Afrasian Center for Peace and Development Studies Research Series, 8*. Retrieved from http://www.afrasia.ryukoku.ac.jp/jp/research/researchseries8.pdf.
Carlos, M. R. D. (2013). The stepwise international migration of Filipino nurses and its policy implications for their retention in Japan. *Afrasian Working Paper Series, 23*. Shiga: Ryukoku University Afrasian Research Centre.
Carlos, M. R. D. & Sato, C. (2010). The multistep migration of nurses: The case of Filipinos in the United Kingdom. *Journal of the Socio-cultural Research Institute of Ryukoku University, 12*, 5–34.
Carlos, M. R. D., & Sato, C. (2011). The multistep international migration of Filipino nurses: The propensity to migrate among Filipino nurses in Dubai. *Journal of the Socio-cultural Research Institute of Ryukoku University, 13*, 37–64.
Choi, C. C. (2003). *Empire of care: Nursing and migration in Filipino American history*. Durham, NC: Duke University Press.
Dubai Health Authority. (2013). *Dubai healthcare professionals licensing guide*. (pp. 51–53, p. 112). Retrieved from http://www.dha.gov.ae/EN/SectorsDirectorates/ Director ates/HealthRegulation/MedicalComplaint/Documents/Dubai%20 Healthcare%20professional%20Licensing%20Guide%20-%20Final.pdf.
Dumont, J. -C. & Zurn, P. (2007). Immigrant health workers in OECD countries in the broader context of highly skilled migration. *International Migration Outlook Part III* (pp. 161–228). SOPEMI, Paris. Retrieved from http://www.oecd. org/els/ mig/41515701.pdf.
Immigration and Checkpoints Authority Singapore (n.d). Permanent residency services guidelines. Retrieved from http://www.ica.gov.sg/services_centre. aspx?pageid=231.
Japan International Corporation for Welfare Services [JICWELS]. (2013). *Gaikokujin kangoshi kaigofukushishi kouhosha ukeireno wakugumi, tetsuduki ni tsuite* [Framework and guidelines in the recruitment of foreign candidate nurses and careworkers]. Retrieved from http://www.jicwels.or.jp/files/ H26E59BBDE5868 5E8AAACE6988EE4BC9AE7ACAC1E983A8JICW.pdf.
Kingma, M. (2008). Nurses on the move: Historical perspective and current issues. *The Online Journal of Issues in Nursing, 13*(2) (Manuscript 1). Retrieved from http://www.nursingworld.org/MainMenuCategories/ANAMarketplace/ ANAPeriodicals/OJIN/TableofContents/vol132008/No2May08/Nurses onthemove.html.
Matsuno, A. (2009). Nurse migration: The Asian perspective. *International Labor Organization*. (pp. 1–23). Retrieved from http://www.ilo.org/wcmsp5/groups/ public/---asia/---ro-bangkok/documents/publication/wcms_160629.pdf.
Ministry of Health, Labor and Welfare of Japan [MHLW] (2013). *Dai hyakunikai kangoshi kokkashiken goukaku joukyō* [Announcement on the successful examinees of the 102nd nurses national licensure examination]. Retrieved from http:// www.mhlw.go.jp/stf/houdou/2r9852000002xz4d-att/2r98 52000002xz8r.pdf.
Ministry of Immigration and Citizenship of Australia (2013). *Visa, immigration and refugees: Via options for nurses*. Retrieved from http://www.immi.gov.au/ skilled/medical-practitioners/visa-options-nurses.htm.

Ministry of Justice of Japan [MOJ] (2013a). *Eiju kyoka ni kan suru gaidorain* [Guidelines concerning permanent residency permit]. Retrieved from http://www.moj.go.jp/nyuukokukanri/ kouhou/nyukan_nyukan50.html.

Ministry of Justice of Japan [MOJ] (2013b). *The nationality law.* Retrieved from http://www.moj.go.jp/ENGLISH/information/tnl-01.html.

Ministry of Manpower Singapore (2012). *Review of dependent privileges for work pass holders for implementation.* Retrieved from http://www.mom.gov.sg/MOMDoc/ Dependant_Privil eges_FAQ.pdf.

Modood, T. (2013). *Multiculturalism.* Cambridge, UK: Polity Press.

Office of the Commissioner for Public Employment of Northern Territory, Australia (2013). *Northern territory public sector nurses and midwives 2011–2014 enterprise agreement.* Retrieved from http://www.ocpe.nt.gov.au/__data/assets/pdf_file/ 0007/53359/FWA_approved_Nurses_Agreement_2011-2014.pdf.

Paul, A. M. (2011). Stepwise international migration: A multistage migration pattern for the aspiring migrant. *American Journal of Sociology, 116*(6), 1842–86.

Philippine Overseas Employment Administration [POEA] (n.d.). *Overseas employment statistics 2010.* Retrieved from http://www.poea.gov.ph/stats/2010_Stats.pdf.

Singapore Nursing Board (2013). *Registration/enrollment for foreign trained nurses.* Retrieved from http://www.healthprofessionals.gov.sg/content/hprof/snb/en/leftnav/ registration_practising_certificate/registration_enrolment/internationally_qualified_nurses_midwives.html.

US Citizenship and Immigration Services (2013). *Visa retrogression.* Retrieved from http://www.uscis.gov/portal/site/uscis/menuitem.5af9bb95919f35e66f614176543f6d1a/?vgnextoid=a294b16dedc0f210VgnVCM100000082ca60aRCRD andvgnextchannel=aa290a5659083210VgnVCM100000082ca60aRCRD.

Except where otherwise noted, this work is licensed under a Creative Commons Attribution 3.0 Unported License. To view a copy of this license, visit http://creativecommons.org/licenses/by/3.0/

OPEN

10
Who Benefits from Dual Citizenship? The New Nationality Law and Multicultural Future of South Korea

Shincha Park

10.1 Introduction

An individual with dual citizenship has long been regarded as "deviant" in the modern nation-state system.[1] The Hague Convention on Nationality of 1930 established the principle of a single allegiance by an individual to a polity—"one nationality for one person"—in order to clarify to which state an individual owed a military obligation (Faist & Kivisto, 2007, p. 32).[2] Under such a principle, a state authority reserved political, economic, social, and civil rights for its citizens, and only those who had these rights were treated as moral equals and enjoyed full securement of their interests, properties, and identities. As the world has become more and more divided and institutionalized through international law and treaties, each individual has been strongly connected to a specific nation-state. Dual citizenship has thus been perceived as an abnormal situation for the modern nation-state. However, policy makers today are starting to see dual citizenship as an opportunity to promote economic development and to solve such social problems as a declining birth rate and aging population, rather than as a threat to sovereignty and social integration.

Since an increasing number of individuals hold dual or plural citizenship today, the principle of a single allegiance is being challenged and the state authorities are attempting to reinterpret and reconstitute the boundary between the nation and the citizen. This is an issue not only for migrants moving to a new place, but also for people in diaspora.[3] Many migrant-sending countries have been trying to build networks with their diaspora populations during the last few decades, including India, China, Italy, Russia, the Philippines, Morocco, Greece, Turkey,

Hungary, Mexico, and South Korea. The development of transportation and communication technologies has not only accelerated migration but also helped those who emigrated, and their descendants, to stay connected to their "home country" from wherever they live. As a result, migrant-sending countries have introduced new policies to encourage emigrants and diaspora to "return" to their "home country," although such policy changes are introduced not for the welfare of the diaspora population but are usually in the economic and political interests of the state authorities. The question of dual citizenship has become an unavoidable one for both sending and receiving countries. It is often seen as a sign of growing transnationalism and the declining power of the nation-state over individuals' lives, since individuals with dual or plural citizenship are assumed to be relatively free from the constraints of the disciplinary and controlling power of the state while enjoying a transnational life beyond territorial boundaries. However, such an understanding appears to be misleading when we look closely at the growing acceptance of dual citizenship, which shows an interesting duality: it is usually seen as a sign of the transnationalization of an individual's activities and belongings, but it is also, in a sense, a new political institution to expand the power of the state beyond its territorial boundaries. Then, what does this change suggest? What impact and significance does dual citizenship have for each of the actors—government, immigrants, and diasporas—involved? Who benefits from dual citizenship?

In order to take a step toward answering these questions, this chapter will look at the case of the New Nationality Law of South Korea that started to recognize dual citizenship, although in a limited way, and will consider the aims, implications, and limitations of this new policy. Responding to the rapid increase in non-professional migrant workers and international marriages, as well as an aging population and declining birth rate (Lim, 2009), South Korea has introduced several policy changes since the 1990s. This study focuses especially on the dual citizenship policy introduced with the revision of the Nationality Law in May 2010 (effective since January 1, 2011). With this policy, the South Korean government seems to be trying to attract more skilled and talented immigrants, to develop connections with such skilled immigrants and with overseas Koreans, and to support the social integration of marriage immigrants and their children. While such a policy change shows South Korea's move toward a multicultural society, it is simultaneously bringing about new problems to resolve. As it is still a new policy, looking at what are and will be the consequences of this change may help us to gain a thorough understanding of the impact of dual citizenship on the modern nation-state and on the lives of modern individuals.

10.2 Citizenship and dual citizenship in the modern nation-state system

The notion of a specific territorial boundary encompassing a group of people, as well as the specific forms of government that developed, followed the advent of the modern nation-state in 16th and 17th century Europe. Various political institutions, such as territorial management, centralized authority, control of the nobility, taxation systems, and welfare institutions, were established in the process of state formation. With the development of modern nationality laws in the 19th and 20th centuries, it has become a common practice of the state to delineate inhabitants of its territory as citizens, by the institutions of citizenship and nationality—either by ancestral lineage or by birth. The nation-state came to hold the authority to decide who the "citizen" is and what rights and duties they possess (Hollifield, 2008; Koslowski, 2001).

As the volume and frequency of human migration has increased in a globalized world, more and more people today are living outside the country of their citizenship, and consequently the number of individuals who possess or seek dual citizenship is on the rise. Some commentators say that the question of dual citizenship is the point at which transnationalization of citizenship appears most prominently (Bloemraad et al., 2008, p. 167; Faist, 2007, p. 1), and it puts states under pressure to reformulate traditional citizenship and encourage transnational activities of migrants. Is it really a sign of the declining power of state authority, though? If that is the case, then how do we explain the fact that more and more countries are starting to recognize dual citizenship today?

There is a growing body of literature on the issue of dual or plural citizenship, as more countries have started to recognize it over the past two decades. However, as a relatively new subject, there are not yet enough studies to lead us to concrete theorization. Researchers have addressed variously the reasons for its increase around the world. Some argue that those countries with a large emigrant population will allow dual citizenship; others argue that the increasing movement of people is a consequence of an ever more globalized world in the post-Cold War era, or the shifting character of conflicts to internal ones, or the development of universal human rights norms. In addition, such domestic factors as the development of gender equality, pressure from emigrants, and growing social problems like labor shortages and an aging society are also responsible for the change (Faist & Gerdes, 2008; Koslowski, 2006). While some countries recognize dual citizenship, however, they do not extend it to immigrants living within their territorial boundaries, as in the case of the Philippines, Taiwan, and Poland. Others, such as the US, are not officially in favor of dual citizenship, but the Supreme Court and State Department recognized people to hold citizenship of multiple countries (Bloemraad et al., 2008, p. 168). The question is why attitudes toward migration policy and dual citizenship vary between countries even when they share similar social, economic, and political conditions.

It is undeniable that economic and political interests are strong driving forces behind the recognition of dual citizenship. However, other factors, such as historical experiences and ideologies, have also had an undeniable influence on the patterns of citizenship and nationality policies around the world today, as well as other social conditions, such as nationalist sentiment or images of immigrants as a threat to the native community in a given society. Recognition of dual citizenship may help immigrants to be acknowledged as equal members in a society and may protect them from discrimination by alleviating the boundary between citizens and "foreigners." However, the classification and criminalization of migrants have been major practices of social control by the authorities, and the "otherness" of migrants can easily be translated into "fear" and "threat." Also, if core political rights are reserved as a privilege of citizens, recognition of dual citizenship may convey a sense of devaluation of national citizenship and may appear as a betrayal by the state; from the perspective of native citizens with single nationality, those with dual citizenship may seem to enjoy more advantages by belonging to multiple polities.

Dual citizenship is often seen as a manifestation of transnationalism, or transnationalization of citizenship. In fact, the number of states permitting dual citizenship has been increasing in recent years, and so has the number of individuals who hold dual citizenship by birth or by choice. However, this does not instantly mean the declining power of state authority over citizens. Dual citizenship policy is rather an attempt by state authority to adjust to, and to re-establish its role and status in, the rapidly changing global environment. The question of dual citizenship is thus a field of negotiation between conflicting forces, including: protecting the privileges of citizens at the cost of the rights of non-citizens; trying to extract more economic benefit from foreign labor by granting permanent residency or dual citizenship; finding a solution to social problems like an aging society and declining birth rate; increasing the options and opportunities of the diaspora community by dual citizenship; or enabling immigrants to stay mobile so that they can easily move to better opportunities. Although there are substantial differences in attitudes toward dual citizenship between countries, the question of dual citizenship is becoming an important item on the agenda of policy makers around the world, regardless of whether they recognize it or not. In the following section, the focus will turn to the dual citizenship policy of South Korea, and its implications for how it is changing (or will change) society.

10.3 South Korea's new nationality law and dual citizenship policy

Owing to rapid economic development since the late 1980s, labor shortages have been one of the urgent issues faced by the South Korean economy. The influx of foreign workers consequently transformed South Korea from a labor-sending to a labor-importing country. In response to increasing migrants and the growing social problems like declining birth rate, South Korea has been introducing remarkable changes into their immigration and citizenship policies since the mid-1990s (Lee et al., 2006; S. Lee, 2005). These changes have also aimed to attract more migrant workers to stay permanently and to prevent Korean nationals from renouncing their Korean citizenship. The primary goal of these policy changes is to promote economic development while alleviating social problems.

The revision of the Nationality Law in May 2010 (effective since January 1, 2011) opened the door to dual citizenship. It was the latest development in this series of changes made to immigration policies and related legal structures,[4] including providing immigrant workers and foreign investors with easier access to the Korean economy, and allowing more overseas Koreans to work and stay in South Korea. With regard to overseas Koreans, the Kim Young-Sum administration initiated the New Policy for Overseas Koreans in 1993, which led to the establishment of the Globalization Project Committee in 1995 and the Overseas Koreans Foundation in 1997 in an attempt to strengthen ties between overseas Koreans and promote their rights and interests, as well as participation in the country's development.[5] The succeeding Kim Dae-Jung administration introduced the Overseas Koreans Act in 1999, which granted partial citizenship to overseas Koreans.[6] Policies that also cover non-Korean immigrants include: the Foreign Industrial Trainee Program, which started in 1991; successive Employment Permit Systems (EPS)[7] from 2004 onward; the Act on the Treatment of Foreigners in Korea of 2007; abolition of the Family Registry Law with the patrilineal family system, which was replaced by the Law on the Registration of Family Relationship in 2008;[8] and the Multicultural Family Support Act of 2008.[9] Among these policies, the EPS and the Overseas Korean Act were important steps in extending, albeit partially, the scope of citizenship before the introduction of the New Nationality Law of 2010. What these policy changes show is an orientational shift in South Korea's policy since the 1990s to actively utilize migrant labor rather than control them to ensure social cohesiveness.

The New Nationality Law of 2010 is characterized by: (1) the relaxation of requirements for the naturalization of competent immigrants; (2) the relaxation of the obligation to give up a foreign nationality upon naturalization (limited acceptance of dual citizenship); (3) the acceptance of dual citizenship based on a pledge not to exercise their foreign nationality inside the country; and (4) the prohibition of expatriation without completing military service. The New Nationality Law allows holding dual citizenship for immigrants upon naturalization to South Korea. The recognition of dual citizenship seems to be the government's attempt to attract more talented immigrants to the country and to integrate immigrant brides and their children into society. It also aims to keep ties with overseas Korean communities, as well as those who emigrate for career and education, so that they can contribute to the development of the national economy and that the assets and pensions of aged overseas Koreans can be brought into the country.

The question of dual citizenship has been debated in South Korea since the early 1990s, but it was seen negatively at first because of concerns that it could be used to avoid military service or that it might cause a problem with the family registration system. However, as a consequence of the continuing outflow of the population (especially young and talented individuals), as well as the need for further foreign investment to recover from the economic crisis of 1997, granting partial citizenship for overseas citizens and the recognition of dual citizenship have become important on the agenda for the development of the state. In addition, the pressure from Korean communities in the US, as well as the organization of Korean adoptees abroad,[10] has increased since the turn of the century.

Consequently, South Korea's dual citizenship policy sets several limitations on who is eligible to take such citizenship. The policy excludes:

those who hold two nationalities as a result of "overseas birth";[11] male citizens who have not completed their military service; foreign spouses of Korean nationals who could not maintain their marriage due to unforeseeable reasons (such as death or disappearance of the Korean spouse); foreigners living in the country for more than 20 years (namely, the Chinese minority); overseas Koreans under the age of 65 (regardless of their citizenship); and low-skilled migrant workers.[12] For overseas Koreans, the age restriction and the military obligation are the main obstacles. In fact, the overseas Korean community in the US has been calling for the Korean government to lower the age restriction. The current president, Park Geun-Hye, has been speaking about lowering the age requirement for overseas Koreans from 65 to 55 since her presidential election campaign—due probably to securing the voting by overseas Korean citizens beginning with the presidential last election (December 2012). With regard to immigrants with no Korean origin, there are already several requirements to fulfill before obtaining a permanent or long-term residency visa or before applying for naturalization. This makes it difficult for semi- or low-skilled migrant workers to have dual citizenship in South Korea.[13] Thus, South Korea's New Nationality Law can also be seen as an attempt to attract skilled migrant workers as well as Koreans educated abroad to return, while marginalizing low-skilled and poorly educated migrant workers, maintaining the national security system, and encouraging the economic activities and investments of overseas Korean citizens under the auspices of the state.

These concerns are not unique to South Korea, as the question of dual citizenship has been under debate in many other countries. However, the reaction to these questions and the changes made to policies differ, even among countries of similar social and economic conditions. Among Asian countries, for instance, Singapore and Japan have a similar, or even higher, economic status compared with South Korea. These three countries also share common social problems today, including an aging population, labor shortages, and a declining birth rate. However, neither Singapore nor Japan officially acknowledges dual citizenship. With its strictly polarized immigration policy, Singapore provides liberal and preferential conditions for highly skilled and talented professionals to work, while putting such constraints on low-skilled workers as not allowing family reunions and marriage with Singaporean citizens (Cho, 2011; Low, 2011). These "global talents" tend to be highly mobile, though, while permanent residents are often reluctant to become naturalized citizens because of the military service obligation, and many young Singaporeans are willing to leave the country for their career or education, if given the chance (Yeoh & Lin, 2012). This has made Singapore increasingly dependent on non-resident migrant workers. As a consequence, today the Singaporean government is under strong pressure from both non-resident citizens and non-citizen residents to start recognizing dual citizenship. The Japanese government too has been reluctant to open its door to low- or semi-skilled migrants. Official acceptance of immigrant labor is limited to "through the side door," such as granting Long-term Resident visa to Japanese descendants, allowing trainees on the Technical Intern Training Program not to be treated as immigrant labor, and accepting candidate nurses and candidate care workers from Southeast Asia under the Economic Partnership Agreement (Carlos, 2012). A social environment unfavorable to outsiders may also prevent immigrants from becoming a member of Japanese society, which is reflected in the fact that the rates of permanent residency and naturalization show no significant difference from those in Singapore and South Korea, despite the fact that Japan has no mandatory military service for male citizens.

There are, of course, problems regarding the treatment of, or range of discrimination against, low-skilled migrant workers in South Korea. Nevertheless, South Korea did introduce a dual citizenship policy, albeit limited. While there may be several complex factors that led the government to implement the policy, a major one may be the rapid and massive transformation in the composition of the population due to growing immigration since the 1990s. The development of such social problems as an aging population and declining birth rate also had an undeniable influence on migration and citizenship policies. Another factor may be the historical experience of having large emigrant populations as a consequence of colonization, decolonization, war, and economic difficulties, which have developed into an abundant "resource" for networking, especially after the economic crisis in the late 1990s. Migration to Western countries, especially to the US, has long been a strong preference for many South Koreans in search of better work and educational opportunities, and it has now developed into lively networks and communities of overseas Koreans generating the "culture of migration" in South Korean society. South Korea's policy of limited acceptance of dual citizenship may be driven by economic interest rather than universal human rights norms or diaspora welfare. Yet its limited nature and exclusion of low-skilled migrant workers show the government's concern with the issue of competing loyalties and obligations, as well as immigrant integration and political cohesion. While South Korea seems to be shifting toward a multicultural society with the

New Nationality Law, it has brought about a new set of problems for society to overcome. That said, the rest of this chapter will discuss what implications the dual citizenship policy has for the changes happening, or that will happen, in South Korean society.

10.4 Dual citizenship, transnationalism, and transnational nationalism

While scholars of globalization have argued that there are increasingly more transnational or postnational spaces for individuals, civil organizations, and NGOs to develop a transnational civil society, outside the modern state structure and the system of international society (e.g. Appadurai, 1996; Ong, 1999; Sassen, 1996; Soysal, 1994), such a contrast between national and transnational is misleading. Both practices are often mutually dependent, and transnational activities can be embedded within the very structure of the state and interstate system, helping to reconstitute the state itself (Bauböck, 2003, p. 701; Varadarajan, 2010, p. 25). In a similar vein, dual citizenship has been a disturbing factor for the modern nation-state with regard to the principle of single allegiance, and it is often seen as a sign of growing transnationalism that enables individuals to transcend exclusionary nationalism. Dual citizenship, however, does not necessarily have to conflict with nationalism, but nationalism can play an important role in both the implementation and practice of policies targeting overseas Koreans. In fact, migrants today maintain connections with their families, friends, co-villagers, religious colleagues, and business partners with the help of communication, transportation, and financial mechanisms. Such cross-border social networks enable them to engage in the economic, social, and political life of their country of origin, while simultaneously encouraging the sending countries to develop such connections for their own advantage.

The growing volume and frequency of transnational activities of migrants—migrant transnationalism—can, in a cumulative way, have enough impact to change the state sovereignty and social life of people in both the sending and receiving countries (Portes, 2003; Vertovec, 2004). On the one hand, therefore, "dual citizenship is an enabling device for transnational practices" (Bauböck, 2003, p. 715), as it gives individuals such rights as unconditional right of entry, right to bring in family members, right to own property, right to access welfare, and right to security and protection. On the other hand, though, it is part of a national project to re-establish and reinstitute the role and sovereignty

Who Benefits from Dual Citizenship? 199

of states in a changing global environment and to engage with diaspora for national development. As Varadarajan writes:

> the diasporic reimagining of the nation that characterizes the production of the domestic abroad is not a process that is driven by diasporas themselves. It is [...] a peculiar form of transnational nationalism that has been embraced by states at the same time as they embark on programs of neoliberal restructuring. (2010, p. 49)[14]

In terms of South Korea, overseas Koreans have long entered into transnational activities across state boundaries in business, education, artistic activities, social movements, and political participation (Lee & Park, 2008). They not only establish and maintain ties with Korean society through such cross-border activities, but also extract various benefits.[15] The media—newspapers, satellite television, and the Internet—may play an important role in this process, since they enable people to communicate and share information within and beyond diaspora communities that network across borders, as well as to interlink the social lives of diaspora communities and South Korea through common cultural resources such as TV programs and music. The development of such connections has made the South Korean government aware of the usefulness of diaspora networks to attract investment and human resources from overseas Koreans, and possibly strengthen economic, political, and cultural ties between their host countries and South Korea. However, it is also true that there is a significant difference between Korean diaspora communities in the degree of their transnational activities and engagement with South Korea.

South Korea has introduced a series of policies for its diaspora population since the 1990s that has extended the boundary of political belonging, albeit partially, beyond its territorial boundary. This was due to the changes in the political and economic environment following the end of the Cold War as well as political democratization at home, the economic crisis of 1997, and the growing numbers of overseas Koreans. The New Nationality Law of 2010 extended the boundary further by partially recognizing dual citizenship. The dual citizenship policy can be understood as an attempt to reimagine the nation through the expansion of the scope of citizenship. In other words, it is a project of state-initiated transnational nationalism, with the aim of improving the political and economic standing of South Korea in international society by attracting talented migrants and developing diasporic engagement.

It is, however, difficult to evaluate how successful the dual citizenship policy is in attracting and providing an opportunity for immigrants and overseas Koreans to enjoy full citizenship in South Korea. Although it has only been two years since the enactment of the New Nationality Law in January 2011, statistics shows that the number of those who acquired South Korean nationality has not increased drastically compared with previous years, but it rather decreased: about 13,000 people got South Korean nationality in 2012, while it was about 19,000 in 2011 and 18,000 in 2010 (Table 10.1). The number of citizenship renunciations has also decreased, though still exceeding the number of naturalizations. While there is no concrete data on the rate of dual citizenship holders/applicants among the number of naturalizations and renunciations, it may be assumed that, overall, the interest in dual citizenship among immigrants and overseas Koreans without Korean citizenship is not so high. On the other hand, however, the rate of citizenship renunciations among those who hold dual citizenship is decreasing since the enactment of the New Nationality Law. Therefore, the expectation of the government from the dual citizenship policy is "to stop the net outflow of population and to contribute to the increased economic competitiveness of the country."[16]

There are still several obstacles to be removed before the dual citizenship policy brings about further social changes. For instance, mandatory military service still pushes Korean males with dual citizenship to choose foreign citizenship over Korean citizenship, and it also makes immigrants unwilling to naturalize, in order to avoid the duty for their

Table 10.1 Acquisition and loss of nationality in South Korea from 2007 to 2012

	2007	2008	2009	2010	2011	2012
Naturalization	8,480	11,512	25,035	16,303	16,085	10,540
Recovery	1,781	3,740	1,708	1,010	2,264	1,987
Acquisition	119	125	205	267	316	240
Reacquisition	158	122	129	543	899	616
Loss	22,802	20,163	21,136	22,131	21,472	17,641
Renunciation	726	276	886	733	1,324	823
Other	696	154	708	1,448	1,722	1,365
TOTAL	34,762	36,092	49,807	42,435	44,082	33,212

Note: 'Other' includes numbers for decision of nationality, choice of nationality, and keeping of nationality.
Source: Ministry of Justice, South Korea, *Churipgug-oegugin-jeongchaek-tonggye-yeonbo 2012* [Korea Immigration Service Statistics 2012], *pp.614–615*.

children. In addition, for non-Korean immigrants, except those who are married to a Korean citizen,[17] requirements for naturalization, such as length of residency and residential status, occupational and economic status, and knowledge of the Korean language, history, and culture, often become hindrances, as these may cost more than the benefit of holding dual citizenship. Moreover, the existence of a narrow ethno-racial concept of national identity becomes not only a barrier to social participation for immigrants, including overseas Koreans, but also leads to severe discrimination and exclusion that impede the development of multiculturalism in South Korea (Lim, 2009). Dual citizenship, then, may be no more than an instrumental choice for professional migrant workers and spouses of Korean citizens, which is where the debate about political belonging and national belonging rises to the surface.

Dual citizenship is a practice of transnational nationalism with which states attempt to expand the boundary of the nation and the citizen. At the same time, transnationalism of diasporas—for instance, associations of Korean American and Korean adoptees lobbying for dual citizenship—is also inextricably linked with nationalism (Ang, 2001). Such forms of nationalism directed to/from outside territorial borders, however, have the potential to change the narrow view of nationalists who put sole importance on the home country, and to enable immigrants and diasporas to express their multiple and multilayered identities. If this is the case, South Korean society can overcome its narrow concept of national identity and belonging based on the dichotomy of inside/outside (against immigrants) and purity/impurity (against overseas Koreans), and start to embrace not only co-ethnic "brethren" but also every stakeholder in society as part of the nation.

10.5 Is dual citizenship a step toward a multicultural society?

When thinking about the cultural diversity of South Korean society, there are broadly two issues of concern. One is the relationship of South Korean society with immigrants, including immigrant workers and immigrant brides who are not of Korean origin; and the other is its relationship with overseas Koreans, regardless of their citizenship status.

With regard to the latter group, the overseas Korean population mainly comprises people of Korean origin in China, North America, Japan, former USSR countries, and Koreans adopted overseas, some of whom carry Korean citizenship and some not. There are also Korean communities in South America, Europe, Australia, and New Zealand, which are a source of return migration. Just considering the variety of locations, it is possible to say that there is already a multicultural diversity within a population group categorized as "Korean." These Koreans, with varying social, cultural, and linguistic backgrounds, are connected to South Korea with the help of the development of communication and transportation. Some of them "return" to their "home country" in order to find jobs or educational opportunities, or to satisfy their desire to identify with their ancestral land. However, it is not easy for second or third (or later) generations of overseas Koreans to be a part of South Korean society. A closer look reveals that their cultural differences are not regarded equally in the society, and they quite often face discrimination and marginalization because of differences in language, cultural behavior, and social experience, such as education and military service (Kibria, 2002). Since the enactment of the New Nationality Law in 2011, many Koreans who were adopted overseas are returning to South Korea in order to recover their Korean citizenship and to work and study.[18] However, they too come to feel that they are "foreigners" in society for having a different language and social experiences.

Such experiences are the consequence of the narrow ethno-racial concept of national identity, in which not only non-Korean immigrants, but also "mixed-blood" and overseas Koreans, are marginalized and discriminated against as not being "true" Korean. Especially among overseas Koreans, the Korean Chinese have been facing serious discrimination in South Korea for decades (Chung, 2008; S. Lee, 2005). Most Korean Chinese come as low-skilled labor migrants or as brides, and they have often been treated unjustly at work and at home: their common ethnic origin and language places them only slightly above other low-skilled migrant workers. Such treatment of Korean Chinese was evident in the Overseas Koreans Act of 1999, which at first excluded Korean Chinese, ethnic Koreans in the former USSR countries, and some Koreans in Japan. Although the Act was amended later due to opposition from civil society and the Chinese government, each Korean group from different locations was still treated unequally and hierarchically within the amended Act: the highest privilege was given to Korean Americans, while scant attention was given to Korean Chinese (Chung, 2008; Park, 1996). It is also reported that Korean businessmen's imposition of their business models and cultural practices on their ethnic Korean business partners in the former USSR countries is creating an extremely negative reaction among these ethnic Koreans (Hübinette, 2009, p. 58). This demonstrates that there is a hierarchical view against diasporas on the side of native Koreans; placing diaspora communities in a lower status than Koreans in South Korea. Taken as a treatise or an ideology, the idea of diaspora essentially contains the essence of differentiation. It bestows the "home country" with the authenticity and centrality for the national collective, without questioning the sociohistorical origin of the nation itself. It then establishes an unequal power relationship between those who are members of the "home country" and the diasporas outside.

In terms of immigrants of non-Korean origin, the government has introduced some policy measures during the last decade. Responding to the rapid increase in international marriages since the turn of the century[19] and providing support for these multicultural families, especially for foreign brides and their children, have become important items on the agenda. The South Korean government enacted the Act of Treatment of Foreigners in 2007, in which the protection of the human rights of foreigners and support for their social integration were addressed as being the duty of the state and local governments. One measure implemented by the Act was the social integration program for spouses of Korean citizens. The program provided its participants with certain incentives to obtain permanent resident status or naturalization. While it usually requires five years of residency with long-term residential status, written exams, and interviews in order to naturalize to South Korea, those who take the program receive an exemption from the written exams, and the time needed for the process is reduced.

Following the relaxation of requirements for resident status acquisition and the simplified naturalization process for spouses of Korean citizens, the government introduced the Multicultural Family Support Act in 2008 and established more than 200 Multicultural Family Support Centers around the country.[20] Local governments mainly operate these centers, providing such services as counseling for women and children, language education programs, working support programs, and organizing volunteer teams for these families. Together with the social integration of marriage immigrants, there was a question of the increasing number of children with dual citizenship as a consequence of the new Family Relationship Registration Act of 2008, which removed patrilineal civil registration. More recently, the Korean Immigration Service prepared the Basic Plan for Immigration Policy, in which immigrant integration and achieving multiculturalism are the recurring themes.[21] Although it is still a policy without a concrete and specific perspective, it shows the remarkable shift in South Korea's policy orientation, which could not have been imagined a few decades ago. One goal of the dual citizenship policy introduced in this context was to normalize the status of marriage immigrants and their children. It was, therefore, the growing social diversity in South Korean society that brought about the introduction of the New Nationality Law.

Further study and careful analysis are necessary before understanding whether South Korean society is moving toward accepting cultural diversity or trying to push immigrants with various cultural backgrounds to follow and fit in with the standards of society.[22] However, at least in policy, the South Korean government has made a move toward multiculturalism: the introduction of the New Nationality Law and immigrant integration policies are the latest steps forward, but definitely not the last. More comprehensive and systematic cooperation from national and local governments, as well as civil-society organizations and individuals, should be developed further in order for dual citizenship to bring full-fledged social benefits for every actors involved.

10.6 Conclusion

Dual citizenship policy represents both transnationalization of citizenship and a nationalist project for securing state authority. Bloemraad notes:

> dual citizenship inhabits a curious place. On the one hand, it undermines traditional citizenship by allowing, and even promoting, mutual belonging, claims-making, rights and responsibilities. [...] On the other hand, dual nationality reinforces the centrality of nation-states because they continue to be the bodies that grant citizenship. (2004, p. 393)

Behind the increasing number of countries recognizing dual citizenship in recent years, there is a growing interest in the diasporas on the side of the state authority. It has resulted in various policy changes, including dual citizenship policy attempting to encourage not only remittances and investments from emigrants, but also the return of the educated and skilled ones. It has also changed the image associated with emigrants from "betrayers" and "escapees" to "heroes" and "development partners," especially in developing countries (Guevarra, 2009; Whitaker, 2011). Each country has different reasons for recognizing or denying dual citizenship; in addition, the rules and practices of dual citizenship vary between those countries recognizing it. Although it is undeniable that economic and political interests are the strong driving forces behind the recognition of dual citizenship, attitudes toward dual citizenship vary between states depending on their political, economic, historical, social, and cultural background.

In the case of South Korea, the historical experience of having a large emigrant population as a consequence of colonization, decolonization, war, and economic difficulties, has prepared an abundant "resource"— namely overseas Koreans—for networking. It became especially attractive for the government following the economic crisis of the late 1990s. The growing numbers of immigrants, as well as such social problems as an aging population and declining birth rate, have also fueled the shift in migration and citizenship policies.

The New Nationality Law, with partial recognition of dual citizenship, represents the changing attitude of the South Korean state toward immigrants and the diasporas. It may become a springboard not only for resolving social problems and labor shortages, but also for recognizing the value of social diversity and realizing multiculturalism. However, in reality, South Korea's immigration policies, including dual citizenship, still have many limitations and inadequacies in achieving the ideal.

Who benefits, then, from dual citizenship in South Korea? For the government, it is an attempt to attract skilled and talented individuals from abroad, as well as to generate economic gains from overseas Koreans through their investments and other transnational activities. However, these expectations seem quite difficult to fulfill, given the social and legal obstacles, such as persistent ethno-racial nationalism and suspicion against cultural diversity, or exclusion from the dual citizenship policy of foreign-born Koreans under the age of 65 and male citizens who have not completed their military service. Such obstacles make dual citizenship an impractical and questionable option in the eyes of diaspora Koreans. The scope of South Korean transnational nationalism encompasses South and North Koreans, Koreans adopted abroad, and overseas Koreans around the world trying to reconstitute globally the nation (Park, 1996). The New Nationality Law may provide further institutional infrastructures for this reimagining of the nation beyond territorial boundaries, and then dual citizenship will become an arena where competing interests and identity-claims come into play. In fact, diaspora communities are not homogeneous, but consist of individuals and groups from different backgrounds with varying needs and interests. It is therefore an extremely difficult task for the government to balance and manage their interests with those of native citizens and other immigrant groups, because policies favorable for the diasporas or immigrants may cause opposition from native citizens. Without tackling this issue, however, a series of policies for the diasporas will not bring about any successful outcomes; and that is applicable to non-Korean immigrants as well.

Highly skilled migrants may stay without being naturalized in order to maintain their ability to move easily to other countries for better opportunities, or to avoid the military service obligation for their children, for instance. On the other hand, though, dual citizenship has the advantage of securing rights and status for low- or semi-skilled migrants. However, other than as migrant brides, obtaining Korean citizenship is not easy for low-skilled migrants, since they often encounter difficulties in satisfying the residential and work requirements for naturalization. Moreover, the still narrow concept of "national belonging" in South Korea on many occasions prevents them from being regarded as equal members of society even after obtaining Korean citizenship, which may make dual citizenship unappealing to immigrants. It is, therefore, possible to say that the dual citizenship policy of South Korea has not yet realized its potential benefits for any of the actors involved, due to its partiality and limits.

However, this is not to devalue the dual citizenship policy. Together with the multicultural policies introduced in South Korea, it has at least contributed to raising the question of diversity within the category of "Korean," as well as exposing the existence of various immigrant groups already living as members of the state, local communities, and families. As Lim points out, tolerance of cultural diversity and the transition to a multicultural society cannot be automatically achieved with mere policy introduction (Lim, 2009). In order for the dual citizenship policy to be beneficial for all stakeholders, from the state to individual migrants, there is a need for developing awareness of and respect for cultural and ethnic diversity. Various tasks are left for the society including further advocacy and awareness-raising, multicultural education at schools, legal regulations on corporate discrimination and hate speech, removal of educational obstacles for minorities, broader communication and dissemination of information at national and local government offices through multilingual media, and so on. Such efforts are especially important in countries like South Korea and Japan, where ethno-racial nationalism is persistent. The recognition of dual citizenship can contribute to foster a multicultural society. But such a potential will not simply be realized through policy implementation from the above. It is also and even more important to question about exclusive relationship between an individual and a political community and to recognize flexible and diverse forms of affiliations in order to go beyond the narrowly defined national and ethnic politics of belonging.

Notes

1. Citizenship and nationality are quite often used interchangeably. Nationality is the legal bond between a person and a state. It denotes formal membership

and gives rise to rights and duties for the individual and the state concerned. While this legal bond is also commonly referred to as citizenship, the latter is, however, a set of rights and duties that can, in some cases, be partially granted to an individual regardless of their nationality, and it does not necessarily overlap with the scope of nationality. However, to enter into a comprehensive discussion of the widely accepted definitions for these two terms—citizenship and nationality—is beyond the scope of this paper, given the broad debate surrounding these two terms. Although this paper uses "dual citizenship" rather than "dual nationality," it is still important not to conflate these two since understanding these as two distinct legal statuses may enable us to have a better understanding of an individual's legal status, political belonging, and social identity/identification.
2. This does not mean that dual citizenship had not become an issue before the Convention. In the 19th century, acquisition of nationality was already a matter of interstate cooperation for the US and European countries to resolve the competing claims of military conscription (Koslowski, 2001, p. 206).
3. While the modern meaning of the term "diaspora" is originally based on the Jewish experience of dispersion and a promise of future return, the term has come to be used in a broader sense in recent years without the catastrophic connotations (Cohen, 1997), referring to emigrants and their descendants living outside their countries of origin or ancestry while still maintaining a connection with those countries. However, what the term implies is more than just denoting emigrants and their descendants. The usage of the term here is to denote not just emigrants and their communities who maintain links with their "homeland," but also those subjects with whom state authorities actively engage in order to build a network for development. In other words, emigrants are treated as "diaspora" when they are recognized by the state authorities as the subject of interpellation and are incorporated into a sort of "center–outer" relationship against their homeland.
4. For details about South Korea's immigration policies, see S. Lee (2005).
5. The policy recognized, for instance, the real estate ownership of first-generation emigrants, and increased the limit of the amount of property that could be taken out of the country, which overseas Koreans had been calling for.
6. The Overseas Koreans Act granted partial citizenship to overseas Koreans, including legal residency, possession of land, and freedom to work in the country. It was the Korean emigrants and their descendants in the US who raised the initial idea of the Act, asking for equal treatment of former citizens living abroad in property succession and acquisition of real estate. Although the Act excluded Korean Chinese from the definition of overseas Korean at first, it was judged as unconstitutional in 2001 and was amended in 2004 to include Korean Chinese and Koreans in the former USSR countries.
7. The EPS enabled employers, especially small and medium businesses, to legally hire the migrant workers needed for their business, while securing basic rights for the workers under labor relations laws, and even putting obligations on employers to pay for "insurance," which covered the cost of returning and, if necessary, unpaid wages at the time of departure. The system was modified in 2008 to allow non-skilled workers to change their visa status to a permanent type by fulfilling certain criteria, such as five years of employment in the country and a good skill level. It was the first comprehensive program for the employment of foreign workers with conditions

equal to those of Korean workers, and it also contributed to reducing the number of undocumented migrant workers (Kong et al., 2010).
8. The law transformed the previous registration system, under which the household was the basis of registering an individual's address, represented by the head of the household. Under the new system, an individual could choose their own address for registration. The new system also allowed a married couple to give their child the mother's family name, which was previously restricted to the father's family name, and for the child to change their family name in the case of divorce or remarriage of a parent.
9. For details of the Multicultural Family Support Act, see Ministry of Gender Equality and Family website, http://english.mogef.go.kr/eng_laws/laws_12.html, accessed July 8, 2013.
10. See for instance work of Global Overseas Adoptees' Link (G.O.A.'L), http://goal.or.kr/, accessed August 10, 2013. G.O.A.'L launched its Dual citizenship Campaign in 2007 to raise awareness about adoptees and dual citizenship in South Korean society, and published a report in 2010 (Global Overseas Adoptees' Link, 2010).
11. "Overseas birth" means an act of traveling to another country with the aim of giving birth to a child there merely to obtain foreign citizenship.
12. *Hi Korea: e-government for foreigners*, http://www.hiKorea.go.kr/pt/main_kr.pt, accessed February 15, 2012.
13. Residential visa (F-2), Permanent Resident visa (F-5), and Overseas Koreans (F-4). A Residential visa (F-2) is granted to spouses of Korean nationals or permanent residents, and it allows a stay of three years only. It is also granted to foreign workers and investors upon satisfying certain requirements. Foreign residents are able to apply for a Permanent Resident visa (F-5) after residing in South Korea for three years with F-2 status. Those who came with an employment visa may apply for F-2 status by fulfilling certain requirements, and those who married a Korean national can obtain F-2 status upon marriage, and will be able to change to F-5 status after a stay of three years, whereby they will have the same rights as Korean citizens. However, the Korean government explicitly announced that it would provide "a high-investment foreigner and a foreigner of superior ability in specified fields" with a stable residency qualification, job security, and preferential treatment for F-5 status if they were going to obtain F-2 status and satisfy certain educational and financial criteria. F-5 status is to be offered immediately to foreign investors who have resided in Korea for at least three years, invested more than USD 500,000, and hired at least five Korean nationals. It is also granted to professional and skilled foreigners who are specialists in the fields of science, education, culture/art, physical culture, and business administration.
14. Introducing the concept of "the domestic abroad," Varadarajan (2010) analyzes the recent policies of the Indian state for its diaspora population. According to Varadarajan, there were two simultaneous, ongoing processes behind the Indian state embracing the concept of people of Indian origin abroad as "the domestic abroad," through such policy changes as the recognition of dual citizenship. It was necessary for the Indian state to bring in more foreign investment in the aftermath of the currency crisis of 1991. However, the succeeding neoliberal economic reforms were, in the

eyes of the bourgeoisie and political representatives, "imposed by external forces, a fact that was symptomatic to the loss of the sovereignty and the legitimacy of the Indian state" (Varadarajan, 2010, p. 20). In order to resolve this dilemma, engaging with Indian diaspora became essential for not just economic development but also the representation of the Indian state in international society.

15. While there are many studies on the cross-border activities of diaspora Koreans, the publications (in Korean) of the Research Center for Overseas Korean Business and Culture (Chonnam University, South Korea) are useful resources for understanding the economic and cultural activities of overseas Koreans.
16. South Korea Ministry of Justice, *Trends in Nationality Statistics*, http://www.index.go.kr/egams/stts/jsp/potal/ stts/PO_STTS_IdxMain.jsp?idx_cd=1760, accessed February 15, 2012.
17. During the period from January 2011 to March 2013, 12,011 foreigners who were naturalized through marriage, became dual citizens after making an oath of not exercising their foreign citizenship within South Korea Ministry of Justice, *Trends in Nationality Statistics*, http://www.index.go.kr/egams/stts/jsp/potal/ stts/PO_STTS_IdxMain.jsp?idx_cd=1760, accessed February 15, 2012.
18. "13 Korean adoptees obtain dual citizenship," *The Korea Herald*, April 19, 2011. http://www. Koreaherald.com/view.php?ud=20110419000739, accessed August 30, 2013.
19. The rate of international marriages has increased since 2000, reaching about 13% in 2005. The major countries of origin for these brides are China (Korean Chinese), Vietnam, the Philippines, and Cambodia, and many of them are married to Korean men working in agriculture and fisheries.
20. For further information on the service of the Multicultural Family Support Center, see a Portal Supporting Multicultural Households, http://www.livein Korea.kr/global/contents/contents_view.asp?idx=28, accessed July 8, 2013.
21. *The First Basic Plan for Immigration Policy, 2008–2012*, http://immigration.go.kr/HP/IMM/icc/basicplan.pdf, accessed January 21, 2012, and the *2nd Basic Plan for Immigration Policy, 2013–2017*, http://www. immigration.go.kr/HP/COM/bbs_03/ShowData.do, accessed September 1, 2013. See also *Building a Multicultural Society Together*, http://www.moj.go.kr/HP/TIMM/imm_07/image/bro_eng.pdf, accessed September 1, 2013. All published by the Korean Immigration Service.
22. For examples of recent studies on migrant integration in South Korea, see Y. L. Kim (2010), B. Lee (2010), and Y. O. Kim (2012).

References

Ang, I. (2001). Undoing diaspora: Questioning global Chineseness in the era of globalization. In I. Ang, *On not speaking Chinese: Living between Asia and the West* (pp. 75–92). London: Routledge.

Appadurai, A. (1996). *Modernity at large: Cultural dimensions of globalization*. Minneapolis: University of Minnesota Press.

Bauböck, R. (2003). Towards a political theory of migrant transnationalism. *International Migration Review, 37*(3), 700–723.
Bloemraad, I. (2004). Who claims dual citizenship? The limits of postnationalism, the possibilities of transnationalism, and the persistence of traditional citizenship. *International Migration Review, 38*(2), 389–426.
Bloemraad, I., Korteweg, A., & Yurdakul, G. (2008). Citizenship and immigration: Multiculturalism, assimilation, and challenges to the nation-state. *Annual Review of Sociology, 34*, 153–179.
Carlos, M. R. D. (2012). Lost in transition: Current issues in Japan's labor migration. In P. Kent, M. R. D. Carlos, A. Uyar & S. Park (Eds), *Policy dialogue and governance of migration: Comparative cases from Europe and Asia-Pacific, Research Series 1* (pp. 21–31). Shiga: Afrasian Research Centre, Ryukoku University.
Cho, H. (2011, April). Immigration policy and settlement patterns of migrants in South Korea and Singapore: Understanding ethnic and socio-economic class settlement behaviors in Asia. Paper presented at the PSA Conference, London, UK.
Chung, A. -Y. (2008). Kankoku no zaigai douhou ijuu roudousha [Overseas Korean immigrant workers in South Korea]. *Ritsumeikan Studies of Language and Culture, 26*, 77–96.
Cohen, R. (1997). *Global Diasporas: An introduction.* Seattle: University of Washington Press.
Faist, T. (2007). Introduction: The shifting boundaries of the political. In T. Faist, & P. Kivisto (Eds), *Dual citizenship in global perspective: From unitary to multiple citizenship* (pp. 1–23). New York: Palgrave Macmillan.
Faist, T. & Kivisto, P. (Eds) (2007). *Dual citizenship in global perspective: From unitary to multiple citizenship.* New York: Palgrave Macmillan.
Faist, T. & Gerdes, J. (2008). *Dual nationality in an age of mobility.* Washington, DC: Migration Policy Institute. Retrieved from http://www.migrationpolicy.org/trans atlantic/docs/ Faist-FINAL.pdf.
Global Overseas Adoptees' Link (2010). *Dual citizenship: Guidebook to dual citizenship for Korean adoptees.* Seoul: Global Overseas Adoptees' Link.
Guevarra, A. R. (2009). *Marketing dreams, manufacturing heroes: The transnational labor brokering of Filipino workers.* NJ: Rutgers University Press.
Hollifield, J. F. (2008). The politics of international migration: How can we "bring the state back in"? In C. Brettell & J. F. Hollifield (Eds), *Migration theory: Talking across disciplines.* (2nd edn, pp. 183–237). New York: Routledge.
Hübinette, T. (2009). Imagining a global Koreatown: Representations of adopted Koreans in Sky's music video eternity and Lee Jang-soo's feature film Love. *Norsk tidsskrift for migrasjonsforskning, 10*(2), 45–65.
Kibria, N. (2002). Of blood, belonging and homeland trips: Transnationalism and identity among second-generation Chinese and Korean Americans. In P. Levitt & M. C. Waters (Eds), *The changing face of home: The transnational lives of the second generation* (pp. 295–311). New York: Russell Sage.
Kim, Y. L. (2010). A study on sociocultural adaptation of immigrant workers in Korean society. *OMNES: The Journal of Multicultural Society, 1*(1), 107–129.
Kim, Y. O. (2012). Social integration of married migrant women in Korea: Between policies and experiences. *OMNES: The Journal of Multicultural Society, 3*(1), 78–101.

Kong, D., Yoon, K., & Yu, S. (2010). The social dimensions of immigration in Korea. *Journal of Contemporary Asia, 40*(2), 252–274.

Koslowski, R. (2001). Demographic boundary maintenance in world politics: Of international norms on dual nationality. In M. Albert (Ed.), *Identities, borders, orders: Rethinking international relations theory* (pp. 203–223). Minneapolis: Minnesota University Press.

Koslowski, R. (2006). International migration and globalization of domestic politics: A conceptual framework. In R. Koslowski (Ed.), *International migration and globalization of domestic politics* (pp. 5–32). London: Routledge.

Lee, B. (2010). Incorporating foreigners in Korea: The politics of differentiated membership. *OMNES: The Journal of Multicultural Society, 1*(2), 35–64.

Lee, S. (2005). The realities of South Korea's migration policies. In T. Akaha & A. Vassilieva (Eds), *Crossing national borders: Human migration issues in Northeast Asia* (pp. 191–214). Tokyo: United Nations University Press.

Lee, Y.-J., Seol, D.-H., & Cho, S.-N. (2006). International marriages in South Korea: The significance of nationality and ethnicity. *Journal of Population Research, 23*(2), 165–182.

Lee, Y. M. & Park, K. H. (2008). Negotiating hybridity: Transnational reconstruction of migrant subjectivity in Korea town, Los Angeles. *Journal of Cultural Geography, 25*, 245–262.

Lim, T. (2009). Who is Korean? Migration, immigration, and the challenge of multiculturalism in homogenous societies. *The Asia-Pacific Journal* (Vol. 30-1-09, July 27). Retrieved form http://www.japanfocus.org/-Timothy-Lim/3192

Low, L. (2011). The political economy of Singapore's policy on foreign talents and high skills society. *National University of Singapore* (December). Retrieved from http://research.nus.biz/ Documents/Research%20Paper%20 Series/rps0136.pdf.

Ministry of Justice, South Korea (2012). Churipgug-oegugin-jeongchaek-tonggye-yeonbo 2012 [Korea Immigration Service Statistics 2012]. Retrieved from http://www.moj.go.kr/HP/COM/bbs_03/BoardList.do.

Ong, A. (1999). *Flexible citizenship: The cultural logics of transnationality*. Durham, NC: Duke University Press.

Park, H. O. (1996). *Segyehwa*: Globalization and nationalism in Korea. *The Journal of International Institute, 4*(1). Retrieved from http://hdl.handle.net/2027/ spo.4750 978.0004.105

Portes, A. (2003). Theoretical convergence and empirical evidence in the study of immigrant transnationalism. *International Migration Review, 37*(3), 874–892.

Sassen, S. (1996). *Losing control? Sovereignty in an age of globalization*. NY: Columbia University Press.

Soysal, Y. (1994) *The limits of citizenship: Migrants and postnational membership in Europe*. Chicago, IL: University of Chicago Press.

Varadarajan, L. (2010). *The domestic abroad: Diasporas in international relations*. Oxford: Oxford University Press.

Vertovec, S. (2004). Migrant transnationalism and modes of transformation. *International Migration Review, 38*(3), 970–1001.

Whitaker, B. E. (2011). The politics of home: Dual citizenship and the African diaspora. *International Migration Review, 45*(4), 755–783.

Yeoh, B. S. A. & Lin, W. (2012). Rapid growth in Singapore's immigrant population brings policy challenges. *Migration information source*. Retrieved from http://www.migrationinformation. org/Profiles/display.cfm?ID=887.

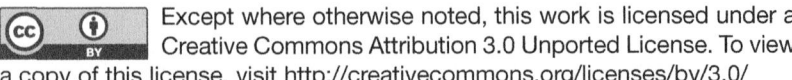 Except where otherwise noted, this work is licensed under a Creative Commons Attribution 3.0 Unported License. To view a copy of this license, visit http://creativecommons.org/licenses/by/3.0/

OPEN

11
"Global *Jinzai*," Japanese Higher Education, and the Path to Multiculturalism: Imperative, Imposter, or Immature?

Julian Chapple

11.1 Introduction

Japanese society has, at various times throughout its history, been led in different directions by state policy makers' catch phrases. The final societal destination of these slogans has changed to suit the needs of the times, but their reoccurrence and importance can neither be denied nor overlooked. Phrases and slogans such as *sonnō-jōi* (Revere the Emperor, Expel the Barbarians), *fukoku kyōhei* (Enrich the Country, Strengthen the Military), *tōyō no dōtoku, seiyō no gakugei* (Eastern Ethics, Western Science), *wakon yōsai* (Western Learning, Japanese Spirit), *bunmei kaika* (Civilization, Enlightenment) and *dastua nyūō* (Leave Asia, Join the West) are all examples of "battle cries" behind which society was rallied in order to rid itself of some seemingly corrupting influence or to adopt systems in order to make a radical change in direction. More recently, while arguably less provocative in nature, catch phrases have continued to be employed to focus national attention on goals deemed important by the nation's state-makers today. Here, words like *kindaika* (modernization), *ōbeika* (Westernization), *kokusaika* (internationalization), and *gurōbaruka* (globalization) have adorned official documents and the media reflecting the needs or goals of each respective period (Chapple, 2002).

While by no means solely limited to the education sector, as education is often considered the "cornerstone of all social systems" (Ministry of Education, Science and Culture 1999, 2), it is here that these national slogans and phrases have been utilized most successfully and have influenced the greatest number of policies and people. Since its inception in 1873, Japan's highly centralized modern education system has been used to disseminate official state philosophy well beyond the confines of the classroom, designed to change society in often dramatic and drastic ways. The fact that it remains comparatively top-down and uniform has contributed to the successful spread and social-consciousness permeation of slogans and their goals. It is through the education system that the government's ideals are promulgated and therefore a vehicle that reflects policy directives which are not always as simplistic or innocuous as their succinct slogans make them appear.

In the same vein as terms from eras gone by, one of the keywords in higher education in Japan today relates to the development of so-called "global *jinzai*" (global personnel or human resources). This chapter, through an examination of the background and goals of this latest term, aims to assess whether it represents a prerequisite for something worthwhile in Japanese society, is merely a guise serving some alternative purpose, or is in fact an (unsophisticated) attempt to achieve something beyond its reach. Through an examination of the situation, goals and actions taken in the name of fostering global *jinzai*, much can be learned of the (real?) motives behind the phrase. Ostensibly arising from a need to interact with larger numbers of non-Japanese in various situations and localities, global *jinzai* can be interpreted as Japan's equivalent attempt at what is often referred to as "global competence" in other countries, in order to deal with an increasingly interconnected world outside and a growing multicultural society at home.

The chapter argues that while outwardly the motives and goals of creating globally competent human resources and fostering internationalization appears seemingly straightforward (Knight & Altbach, 2007), different groups have somewhat differing—at times even contradictory—agendas. Thus, rather than functioning as a potential pathway towards multiculturalism, the global *jinzai* slogan is merely a vehicle for long sought after reform (particularly with regard to the English language and universities in general) reflecting a reality of Japanese society. In short, what is really being discussed are the fundamental changes in educational philosophy and structure required to enable development in a "globally competent" direction. Finally, it concludes by questioning whether this ongoing push really will, or can, lead to the expectations that many have, given the entire debate's immaturity and deficiencies in terms of being capable of fostering global citizens able to adapt to a more multicultural society.

11.2 What are global *jinzai*?

To understand what is generally referred to by the term global *jinzai* requires an appreciation of the situation facing Japanese society today. As in times past, which resulted to slogan-led plans, global *jinzai* is born out of a need to react to the external environment. In this case it is the twin forces of a desire to increase Japan's political presence on the global stage and strengthen its economic position internationally in the face of growing, diversified, and rapidly changing competition. Like all developed nations, the ability to be able to sell products in today's dramatically evolving world requires skills and abilities different from those of even just a few years ago. Consequently, education aimed at fostering globally competent human resources is something that most countries are today actively seeking.

This fact is evidenced through a quick Internet search, which reveals over 10 million hits related to the term "global *jinzai*" in Japan. It is used and discussed in the media as if its goals are clear and its focus defined. Yet, in spite of its seemingly constant recent media use, "global *jinzai*" continues to remain somewhat of a vague term, something akin to the term "leadership" in English, "a term which everybody knows, but for which there are countless definitions" (Pollock, 2012, p. 1). However, unlike slogans of the past, global *jinzai* encompasses a number of measurable qualities making it unique, a point addressed later.

One seemingly all-encompassing definition of global *jinzai* is the following, from the Joint Business-Academia Committee for the Promotion of Global *Jinzai* Development, which claims that global *jinzai* are:

> people who, in today's competitive and cooperative world, can—*while maintaining their sense of Japanese identity*—possess a broad worldview based on both general and specialized education, have communicative and cooperative abilities to build relationships which go beyond values, cultures and different languages, and that have the ability to create new values and the desire to contribute to society now and in future generations. (Author's translation and emphasis added)[1]

Another even more quantifiable definition can be found in the mid-term report (released in June 2011) of the Japanese Ministry of Economy, Trade and Industry (METI)'s Council on the Promotion of Global Human Resources, which claims that global *jinzai* comprise three categories (METI, 2011). The first is language proficiency and communication skills, and is the most detailed. The second category encompasses features such as an independent (*shutaisei*) active (*sekkyokusei*) attitude, a spirit of challenge, a harmonious (*chōwasei*) and flexible (*jyūnansei*) spirit, and a sense of commitment (*sekininkan*) and responsibility (*shimeikan*). The third category is the requirement for cross-cultural understanding and, once again, cultural identity as a Japanese.

While at first glance these both appear to be well-prepared definitions, they do pose a number of concerns. Explained this way, global *jinzai* is an outward-looking concept (similar to Japan's version of the concept of internationalization, *kokusaika*) and fails (perhaps purposely) to examine the requisite systemic changes required domestically. In other words, by focusing attention on the capabilities required for work abroad, the debate about the changes required to accept greater diversity within Japan are in effect quietly overshadowed and even nullified. Hence, acceptance of, and policies towards, multiculturalism are not seen as things that need to be considered. Global *jinzai* requires an international curriculum and it is here too that the link with internationalization is again apparent. Yet the difference seems to be an overwhelming feeling that by sending students abroad such talent can be fostered; it is not something that can be easily nurtured domestically. This most likely stems from the fact that multiculturalism is seen as something that exists in other settings (rarely in Japan) and therefore the required special skills can only be fostered overseas.

A second point of concern is that language skills can at least be "measured" using standardized achievement tests, while the other two categories are subjective and consequently extremely difficult to both foster and gauge. This probably explains why they are usually overlooked for the more easily identifiable "language ability" and there is such scant information regarding how exactly to foster them. This point will also be returned to later.

A third point of concern is the final category of cross-cultural understanding and cultural identity "as a Japanese" which reads almost as an oxymoron. While naturally understanding one's cultural identity is an important prerequisite and base for cross-cultural understanding, it is dubious to assume that this is something that can be taught at higher educational levels. Surely these are things that should take place at the lower levels of the educational ladder (if at all), and the need to reiterate it speaks volumes of the desire to protect the status quo. Similarly, the assumption that one's identity as a Japanese is a fixed concept that is required to be stressed first almost contradicts the very philosophy behind the entire global *jinzai* process itself. Yet, at a symposium organized by the *Sankei Shimbun* newspaper in 2012, three of the four expert panelists mentioned the need to understand and promote Japanese identity (*Sankei Shimbun*, 2012). Hence the term is at risk of being hijacked by those with agendas which may be opposed to the concept of internationalism. In short, global *jinzai* may merely represent another way of strengthening Japanese identity in reaction to a perceived outward threat. If not, one would expect there to be clear action and results suggesting the contrary. Evaluated this way, the slogan fits the mold of similar slogans of the past and falls into a kind of "sanctioned, but confined reform" category (i.e. educational reform sanctioned by the government but which falls within clearly stipulated confines—in this case firmly stressing and retaining "Japaneseness" as a prerequisite). However, ensuring that the promotion of a global mindset is predicated on the maintenance and reassurance of a Japanese identity is a very un-nuanced reality of what an individual is, and not only points to an ongoing heavy dose of social control, but is also a reflection of insecurity in allowing a total opening to the world. In other words, the development of global citizens (detailed later), which I argue is a more useful, important, and necessary goal of internationalization, is virtually untenable in Japan under present restrictions.

In other fields in Japan we can find different definitions: for example, those from both the Japan Business Federation (*Keidanren*) and the Council on Competitiveness Nippon (COCN), which do not include references to Japanese identity. However, this is likely because they are solely concerned with skills like negotiating with customers and business management and are merely reflections of what most other countries refer to by the concept of global *jinzai* and are beyond the scope of this chapter. Thus, the concept being pushed by MEXT appears to mask a few ulterior motives.

It is also interesting to note that, as mentioned, the development of skills deemed necessary for productivity in this global age are by no means the sole domain of Japanese educators. Rather, it is truly itself a global trend. However, when compared with definitions of what skills a globally competent person should have, the inadequacy of the predominant definitions in Japan is striking. In addition to mastering a foreign language and a different culture and geography, fluency in things like e-commerce, the Internet, knowledge of political and economic systems of other countries, and familiarity with global issues are also often stated as important (Ouyang & McAlpine, 2013). What is more, rarely do non-Japanese definitions of global competency skill requirements make much reference to an individual's sense of cultural and national identity as a prerequisite for functioning in a multicultural setting.

11.3 Background—why now?

Why has there been such an interest in the concept of global *jinzai* of late? After all, other than the slogan itself, nothing in the content of the concept is particularly ground-shaking or revolutionary. For decades now, Japan's leaders have been singing a similar tune and preaching the need for greater collective international skills. In 1997, for example, a special committee on education formed within the Japan Business Federation submitted a report entitled "Fostering Human Resources Capable of Contributing to the Global Society."[2] Claiming that dealing with a globalizing society is now a "matter of urgency," the report outlined four requirements of such human resources, namely: independence, respect for and understanding of difference, foreign language abilities to communicate with non-Japanese people, and specialist skills. Almost two decades later virtually the same skills are still considered a matter of urgency. So what exactly is different this time?

Until recently, an impressive image of Japanese businessmen traveling the world as a part of their jobs has permeated the media. Today, however, with a decline in the number of young Japanese studying abroad, and the world becoming more interdependent than ever before, there is seemingly a lack of Japanese willing (and perhaps able) to venture abroad in order to forward the nation's economic hopes. It is these twin factors—an increasingly "inward-looking mentality" of young Japanese coupled with the greater and diversifying international desires and needs of Japanese manufacturers and leaders—that has rekindled this entire debate recently.

11.3.1 An inward-looking trend

Since peaking at 82,945 students studying overseas in 2004, with the exception of the number of Japanese leaving to study in China and India (which has shown an increase), the overall number has been on the decline. The latest available statistics show that the number dropped 3.1% from the previous year (the sixth continuous year-on-year drop) to 58,060 in 2010 (*Nihon Keizai Shimbun*, 2013b). There are a number of reasons that have contributed to this decline. Firstly, the financial costs of study abroad (particularly in OECD nations) have risen dramatically over the past two decades. A second factor is language ability. While many students study abroad to improve their foreign language skills, usually that is all they are able to accomplish in the time away. In other words, taking regular classes at an overseas university, joining an internship program, or other such activities are usually out of the question. Thirdly, and related to the second point, due to increasing language requirements, the required educational level and corresponding academic motivation of Japanese students are also contributing factors. Fourthly, many Japanese universities are not well prepared to deal with students who do study abroad in terms of providing academic recognition of their study. Finally, a growing number of students ironically actually see study abroad as a disadvantage in finding employment in Japan, given the narrow and limited recruitment timeframe and differences in academic calendars. In short, the attitude towards study abroad—and indeed career planning itself today in Japan—is in flux, resulting in a growing gap between societal (particularly parental) expectations and those of the business world.

In a survey conducted in March 2013 by the Institute for a Global Society, 50% of high school students and 55% of university students surveyed responded that they felt it was too late for them to become globally active citizens, even if they started receiving education now to learn how to deal with a globalizing world (*The Japan Times*, 2013).

11.3.2 Future demand for global *jinzai*

As new technologies make rapid economic growth and development possible in more remote places and on an unprecedented scale, more than ever before developed nations need to keep pace in order to avoid being left behind. Based on present trends, Japan may be unable to take advantage of emerging growth in the newly expanding BRICs (Brazil, Russia, India, China) or VISTA (Vietnam, Indonesia, South Africa, Turkey, Argentina) regions without greater numbers of globally competent employees. Furthermore, Japan can no longer rely on a model in which only a handful of top, elite executives are responsible for global business success. Given the nature of the evolving global economy it is no longer only the large multinationals that require more globally competent staff, even "domestically-focused companies and small businesses are feeling the need to become more global" (Pollock, 2012, p. 1). And, for Japan to be able to play a greater, more proactive role—commensurate with its economic size—on the world stage, helping towards the solution of global problems, a much larger cross-section of society needs to be aware, interested, and involved in global issues on a regular basis.

Yet, at present, according to a survey of Japanese companies published in 2012, sponsored by Japan's Ministry of Education, Culture, Sports, Science and Technology, only around 1.68 million Japanese can be classified as globally competent *jinzai* (MEXT, 2012). It is estimated that demand for global *jinzai* by Japanese companies will grow by a massive 240% over the next five years (from 2012 and 2017), equating to around 8.7% of the entire employed population (*ibid.*). The good news is that, according to the aforementioned survey, 30% of university students and 40% of high school students said they want to become an active participant in the global society, but they just do not know how to do it (*The Japan Times*, 2013). Hence the urgency this time is greater than at any time in previous decades.

11.4 Extenuating reasons: An imposter in the policy?

However, there are other reasons behind the push for global *jinzai* than the above-mentioned predominantly business-oriented ones. A brief examination of these, and their respective agendas, reveals a familiar feature of educational policy in Japan that could be termed "Trojan horse change."

In addition to the concerns voiced in the business world, the global *jinzai* debate reflects a common sense of urgency within Japan that higher education is no longer serving the needs and goals of society, and consequently that Japan is being rapidly left behind. With Japan's eighteen-year-old-population rapidly declining, the need to seek alternative sources to contribute to the overall student pool has also become an important task. Foreign students have been targeted as one such possible source. To this end, in 2008 the government set a target of 300,000 international exchange students in Japan (a figure equivalent to approximately 10% of the entire Japanese student population) by 2020, a proposal more daring than its predecessor of 100,000 by 2000 (which was not in fact achieved until 2003 and then only as the result of an easing of regulations related to application and visa procedures).

Still, more pessimistic voices point out that 45.8% of private four-year universities were unable to fulfill their student quotas and had to rely on students from Asia to make up the shortfall or risk bankruptcy (Sawa, 2013). What is more, Japanese companies today are not only recruiting or relying solely on Japanese students. "There was a shared understanding between the Japanese business sector and the government that Japan needed to recruit talented students to succeed in international competition" (NIER, 2011, p. 3). Further, today, those students are being actively sort globally. Thus, global *jinzai* represents a "Trojan horse" attempt at university reform in order to increase international student numbers, internationalize the curriculum and faculty as well as to hopefully boost international rankings in the long-term (MEXT has set a goal of having ten Japanese universities ranked in the top 100 worldwide by 2020).

Yet Japan is competing in an increasingly competitive and expanding market, not only for global talent but also for international students. According to the OECD (2012), over the past three decades the number of international students has increased fivefold from 0.8 million worldwide in 1975 to 4.1 million in 2010. Not only is Japan's popularity as a destination a questionable factor (not being an English-speaking country, where by far the majority of students are heading), the figures also reveal that other countries' students are more active than Japanese students, meaning that they are becoming globally competent employees in greater numbers and contributing to their respective countries' growth and development. In short, Japan is facing intense competition on various fronts (NIER, 2011). Reform is recognized as a matter of urgency, but is not something that can easily be achieved.

11.5 Nothing more than English?

Returning to the fact that, of the three identified core components of global *jinzai*, only language skills are measurable, it is only here that anything resembling policies or plans actually exists at present. This likely stems from the reality that nationwide English language abilities are still not where the Japanese government would like them to be. In international TOEFL rankings in Asia, Japan is 27th out of 30 nations, and scores for other tests are not much different. Consequently, the global *jinzai* discussion comes at a crucial time for Japan, with other debates pertaining to English (i.e. foreign language) education in elementary schools, teacher licensing, and so forth also coming to the fore. In other words, global *jinzai* provides a useful smokescreen behind which discussions and even changes, particularly related to English language, can be ushered in under a sense of imperative.

In a recent concrete proposal, MEXT has announced that it plans to develop 100 "Super Global High Schools" from spring 2014, which will represent a new type of high school tasked with fostering global leaders who can deal with the world (Oka, 2013). These schools will place greater emphasis on English and other foreign languages while at the same time stressing problem analysis and problem-solving abilities as well as educating about culture and history. Perhaps the most striking feature of the proposal is that they will be classed as "exceptional schools" in terms of the national curriculum guidelines, and thus when necessary will not be bound by traditionally rigid rules.

Yet what such a policy proposal reveals in reality is, firstly, MEXT's lack of imagination (Super English Language High Schools [SELHis] were created in 2003 in an effort to improve the English language ability of Japanese high schools students, but have not led to striking results), and, secondly, once again it is really only English that is important. The fact that these schools will be an exception and not the norm points to the fact that it is after all only the elite who are being fostered. Finally, indicating that they may even be exempt from national curriculum restrictions, meaning they are stepping outside the norm in terms of what they offer, reflects the extent of the restriction that the present curriculum poses. Surely, if the goal was to foster Japanese with global competencies, then such options should be the norm offered to all the population. Furthermore, there is no public discussion about the role of languages other than English in the national curriculum, even though Japanese society today is far from the monolingual one it portrays itself as (Lie, 2004; Maher & Yashiro, 1995).

11.5.1 Aiming for the top: Global *jinzai* and university reform?

If we examine the action plans towards creating such global talent, as laid out by MEXT in its recently published proposals for reforming universities in order to make them "an engine for social change" (MEXT, 2012, p. 11), there are in fact scant references to the issue of global *jinzai*. Five goals and two plans are listed, the majority of which are aimed at institutional change, and this, again, probably ultimately reflects MEXT's real motive behind the debate on global *jinzai*.[3] Radically trying to change Japan's universities by first raising public and business awareness of the gap between present and desired higher education is an effective tool, followed by incentives to change.

The results to date, however, have been far from stunning. The much heralded "Global 30"[4] presently number only 13, and other than these, most universities are either struggling or see little incentive to radically internationalize their campuses other than the usual cosmetic changes. In reality, even a full implementation of the proposals that MEXT is suggesting is hardly likely to lead to any significant advance in overall standings of Japan's higher educational institutions on any global index. Further, it is unrealistic to expect universities to shoulder the burden of creating such future labor alone. It requires a concerted change in the compulsory education curriculum in general, greater emphasis on career education and more system-wide flexibility.

In order for global *jinzai* to become a driving force for educational reform at the top, changes are required, particularly in terms of educational quality, content, and the system itself. Firstly, faculty must themselves become more "globally competent," experienced, or at the very least, *inclined*.

This is not necessarily the case. University teachers in Japan are often criticized for being insular and inward-looking. Some are even opposed to having students study abroad (*Nihon Keizai Shimbun*, 2012). Unlike in many other developed countries, where competition and deregulation have led to enormous—at times incredulous—changes, today in Japan the notion of promotion based on seniority and lifetime employment, hinder greater openness and innovation (*Nihon Keizai Shimbun*, 2013a). Further, a lack of commitment by university leaders means that this trend will likely continue for the immediate future. Actively advertising internationally is one option, yet it requires a system in place to accommodate such talent as well as the ability for them to offer classes in, once again, English. Yet the creation of such a system is predicated on acquiring consensus and recognition among the Japanese populace that their country is now a multicultural society. This in turn requires an education system that actively acknowledges such a concept and educates accordingly. As a recent editorial in The Japan Times (2013) stated:

> Unfortunately, even when the curriculum is globalized and when broadening experiences like study abroad are undertaken, the teaching methods at most universities, as well as secondary schools, remain mired in one-way, teacher-centered approaches that do not help students acquire confidence, communication skills or a broader understanding that they need for engaging in international situations.

In an effort to bring greater clarity to the needs of global *jinzai*, a number of reports have already been released. A mid-term report released by the LDP's Financial Reform Group recommends doubling the present number of native English speaking teachers in Japan to 10,000 within three years, and to be able to send one to every elementary, junior, and senior high school in the country within ten years (*Nihon Keizai Shimbun*, 2013c). Similarly, as mentioned above, MEXT recommends increasing the number of foreign faculty in Japan's universities (although no concrete plans or details have been made yet) in plans which resemble the *oyatoi gaikokujin* (hired foreigners) project of the Meiji era, and consequently the hope of it leading to lasting changes is remote. Once again, the focus is on English and the concern is about reforming universities and on general language skills in particular.

In terms of systematic changes, a number of issues are pertinent. The development of global *jinzai* requires an international curriculum, and it is here too that the link with internationalization is again apparent.

Yet the difference seems to be an overwhelming feeling that by sending students abroad can be fostered such talent; it is not something that can be easily nurtured domestically. This most likely stems from the fact that multiculturalism is seen as something that exists in other settings but rarely in Japan, and special skills are required for people to be able to adequately deal with it. Such skills can only be fostered overseas. A commitment to making classes of an international standard and offering flexibility in academic calendars (the likes of the touted "Gap Year Project," Ashizawa, 2012) are two possible options. Here "international standard" does not mean to imply that present levels are necessarily low, rather that the systems supporting the curricula are not international. For example, the numbering of classes (to facilitate cross crediting) is undertaken by only around 7% of the nation's universities (*Nihon Keizai Shimbun*, 2012). Because global *jinzai* requires intercultural communication abilities and a greater understanding and acceptance of diversity (a fundamental of multiculturalism), there is also an urgent need to internationalize campuses in Japan to provide for such learning opportunities for those students unable (or unwilling) to study abroad, or for those who return to further hone their skills. More use of dual degrees, offering greater diversity in international programs (volunteer abroad, international internships, and so on) could be faculty- or university-wide possibilities. Meanwhile, at the class level, providing greater evidence of student learning which is internationally compatible (learning outcome assessment, portfolios, etc.) is another option.

Without doubt, the fostering of global *jinzai* has become a foundation stone of numerous policy initiatives and even the driving force behind the creation of some new faculties. Yet global *jinzai* refers to multi- and interdisciplinary skills usually acquired from disparate departments. Rather than new faculties, it would be more appropriate to give greater consideration to the offering of courses or qualifications that span disciplines and/or departments. Further, to lead to the fostering of global citizens, a much more transparent, focused, and open curriculum is required than exists at present. This leads on to a final question: is the ongoing push for global *jinzai*—however its goals are defined—an outdated and inadequate policy nowadays anyway?

11.6 Conclusion

The global *jinzai* slogan appears to be one aimed at pressing society to become more outward-looking and, in particular, English language-focused. Put simply, state goals like economic development and domestic growth require Japan to interact on a greater scale internationally. People are required to change, which inherently requires a reexamination of the role of the individual in society. Global *jinzai* must be players for "Corporate Japan" on a global stage, yet be able to think and act as individuals in one-on-one exchanges. Thus, global *jinzai* should ultimately lead to changing business structures in Japan that will in turn affect the education system and consequently all aspects of society. In short, in order to create global *jinzai*, the fundamentals of education, particularly its ultimate goals and the aims of state-making, will need to be reevaluated. The long-standing traditional group model is unlikely to support, or lead to, the creation of such human capital, because the world today is more complex than textbooks lead us to believe.

As a policy driver, global *jinzai* represents a massive push for Japan. Perhaps it may eventually even become a kind of "black ships" event for education in Japan, reminiscent of the fleet accompanying Commodore Perry that heralded in the modern age for Japan and its increasing interaction with other nations. That possibility remains, but, as I have attempted to outline, at present it is difficult to see it emerging. Whether global *jinzai* actually becomes a touchstone for change or merely joins the scrapheap of used slogans remains to be seen. And it may even be a moot point in the long term.

The ideal encapsulated in the term "global *jinzai*," despite the cosmopolitan and universal image it portrays, is fast becoming more and more irrelevant. Ouyang and McAlpine point out that the ultimate goal of educational internationalization is global citizenship—"the most important political and philosophical concept since the idea of the free, equal individual with rights" (Ouyang & McAlpine, 2013, p. 10)—and that global competency alone is not necessarily likely to achieve this. Thus, in spite of the best efforts by Japan's educational policy leaders and experts, the entire debate relating to global *jinzai* is highly unlikely to lead to any fundamental change. In this sense as well, it is therefore an imposter that misleads by association with trendy phrases and ideas.

> In contrast to global competency defined as a set of skills and knowledge useful in a globalised economy and labour market, global citizenship refers to individuals empowered by a broader knowledge of the wider world that contributes to their intellectual abilities of problem-solving and critical thinking, and most importantly *a strong sense of social responsibility from an unbiased global perspective*. (Ouyang & McAlpine, 2013, p. 10. Italics added)

Thus, as Ş. İlgu Özler (2013, p. 13) claims, "we need a new cosmopolitan vision, with a common human identity and a sense of global citizenship displacing our understanding of relations between citizens of 'foreign' countries." To achieve such a condition requires states to embrace the situation in which they are willing to relinquish their hold on nationalistic educational ideals so as to allow their citizens to see the bigger and, I would argue, more important, picture. If Japanese society is to embrace multiculturalism, the trend towards global *jinzai* offers potential and possibilities towards creating a required social and mental framework. However, multiculturalism or global citizenship are not the ultimate goal of many who promote the global *jinzai* debate. Once the ultimate goal of global *jinzai* is explained thus, it becomes easier to understand why, in spite of discussions, symposiums, policies, plans, and ongoing debates, in this undeveloped immature state it will likely never realize its full potential under present circumstances in Japan.

Notes

1. Author's translation. For the full report, see: http://www.jsps.go.jp/j-tenkairyoku/data/meibo_siryou/h23/ sankou06.pdf.
2. Author's translation. For the report see: Nikkeiren Kyōiku Tokubetsu Iinkai 1997.
3. The five goals are: improving foreign language ability through the use of entrance exams and classes, increasing overseas study and exchange opportunities, strengthening teachers' global educational ability, offering flexibility in entrance and graduation times, and increasing the number of foreign teachers.
4. The Global 30 (G30) project aims to contribute to the globalization of Japanese higher education by selecting 30 universities to act as centres of globalization by predominantly offering courses in English for international students.

References

Ashizawa, S. (2012). *Why now? Global jinzai and gap year*. Paper presented at Meiji University Research Institute of International Education Inaugural International Symposium Series 3, Tokyo. Retrieved from http://www.britishcouncil.jp/sites/ britishcouncil.jp/files/edu-ashizawa-meiji-university.pdf.

Chapple, J. (2002). Japan's policy of internationalisation: Prospects for a multicultural society (Ph.D. dissertation). Victoria University of Wellington, New Zealand.

Knight, J. & Altbach, P. (2007). The internationalization of higher education: Motivations and realities. *Journal of Studies in International Education*, 11, 290–305.

Lie, J. (2004). *Multiethnic Japan*. Cambridge: Harvard University Press.

Maher, J. C. & Yashiro, K. (Eds) (1995). *Multilingual Japan*. Clevedon, UK: Multilingual Matters.
Ministry of Economy, Trade and Industry [METI] (2011). *Mid-term report from the council on the promotion of global human resources*. Retrieved from http://www.meti.go.jp/policy/ economy/jinzai/san_gaku_kyodo/sanko1-1.pdf.
Ministry of Education, Culture, Sports, Science and Technology [MEXT] (2012). *Daigaku kaikaku jikkō puran*. [The plan to change universities]. Retrieved from http://www.mext.go.jp/b_menu/houdou/24/06/__icsFiles/afieldfile/2012/06/25/1312798_01.pdf.
Ministry of Education, Science and Culture (1999). *Japanese government policies in education, science, sports and culture 1999: Educational reform in progress*. Tokyo: Ministry of Education, Science, Sports and Culture Japan.
NIER [National Institute for Educational Policy Research] (2011). International student policy in Japan. In *Education in Japan*. Retrieved from http://www.nier.go.jp/ English/EducationInJapan/Education_in_Japan/Education_in_Japan_files/201203IntlSt.pdf
Nihon Keizai Shimbun (2012, December 21). Jinzai kyōsō kokkyō naku uchimuki kaeru kōki ni [A good opportunity to change from unward-looking].
Nihon Keizai Shimbun (2013a, January 18). Kyōin kōsō "uchimuki" yabure [It's faculty who need to break the "inward-looking" mentality].
Nihon Keizai Shimbun (2013b, February 9). Kaigai ryūgaku 6nen renzoku gen [The number of students studying abroad falls for the 6th straight year].
Nihon Keizai Shimbun (2013c, April 21). Gaikokujin kyōin 1man nin ni [Increase the number of foreign faculty to 10,000].
Nikkeiren K. T. I. (1997). *Gurōbaru shakai ni kōken suru jinzai no ikusei o* [Towards to development of human resources capable of contributing to a global society]. Tokyo: Nihon Keiei sha dantai remei Kyoiku bu.
OECD (2012). How many students study abroad and where do they go? In *Education at a glance 2012: Highlights, OECD publishing* (pp. 24–27). Retrieved from http://dx.doi.org/ 10.1787/eag_ highlights-2012-9-en.
Oka, Y. (2013, August 16). Kokusaijin yōsei ni "global kō" monkashō 100 ko shitei e [To develop international people MEXT plans to select 100 "global schools"]. *Asahi Shimbun*. Retrieved from http://www.asahi.com/edu/articles/TKY201308140432.html
Ouyang, G. & McAlpine, S. (2013). Global competency is not enough: Attaining global citizenship. In *EAIE summer forum: Discussing international education: Social responsibility* (pp. 8–10). Amsterdam: European Association for International Education.
Ş. İlgu Özler (2013). Global citizenship versus diplomacy: Internationalisation of higher education with a collective consciousness. In A. Labi (Eds), *Weaving the future of global partnerships* (pp. 13–18). Amsterdam: European Association for International Education.
Pollock, S. (2012). Cultivating "global jinzai" critical to Japan's international success. *Turnstone Ventures*. Retrieved from http://www.turnstoneventures.com/cultivating _global_jinazi.html.
Sankei S. (2012, August 12). Sankangaku kyōdō de gurōbaru jidai ni tekiō [Government, industry and universities working together to adapt to the global age].
Sawa, T. (2013, June 24). Commentary: Top students shunning Japan. *The Japan Times*.

The Japan Times (2013, June 16). Editorials: Too many inward-looking students. Retrieved from http://www.japantimes.co.jp/opinion/2013/06/16/editorials/too-many-inward -looking-students/#.Ucf7F81bBD.

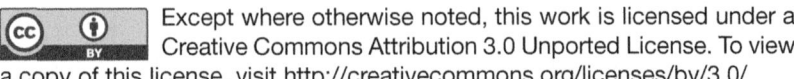 Except where otherwise noted, this work is licensed under a Creative Commons Attribution 3.0 Unported License. To view a copy of this license, visit http://creativecommons.org/licenses/by/3.0/

OPEN

Afterword

William S. Bradley and Kosuke Shimizu

Introduction

The chapters in this edited collection comprise a significant representation of research that was carried out at the Afrasian Research Centre of Ryukoku University in the past three years. While most of the authors are based in Japan and the majority of the material focuses on Japanese transnational and internationalization processes and movements, the connection of people, language, and politics in and to the wider region entailed that we look beyond the borders of Japan to the Asia-Pacific in framing many of the discussions both in individual chapters and in the collection as a whole. Some of these movements operate at a basic level such as the emigration of Japanese to the United States (Honda, Chapter 3), the immigration of foreigners to Japan and other countries (Carlos, Chapter 9), or the integration of foreign (often Asian) children into diversifying school systems (Gunderson, Chapter 4) or foreign domestic (often Asian) workers into Europe and elsewhere (Karatani, Chapter 8). In other cases, the processes are less obviously movements within national systems, as with language policies in Japanese education (Nagamine, Chapter 6 and Takakuwa, Chapter 7) or across international systems as with the language of International Relations (Shimizu, Chapter 5). In all cases, however, the phenomena under study cannot simply be reduced to one-way processes or even two-way phenomena of transfer and reception or resistance. The multiple levels of multicultural circulation require increasingly sophisticated theoretical models of understanding human activity that transcend national borders in the 21st century.

Partly for these reasons, we proposed the use of an interactive multiculturality in our introduction as a move beyond a more static multiculturalism which has come under increased scrutiny and critique in recent years. We have not made a greater effort to define this term partly from the perspective that no single term is going to solve the problems that have been identified with the current limitations of multiculturalism in theory and practice. New volumes on multiculturalism have been published with increasing urgency, it would seem, just as the term has come under greater fire in the social imaginary in many parts of the world and from politicians eager to make their national credentials secure. We acknowledge that others have used multiculturality and other such terms and will continue to use new terminology in an attempt to correct perceived shortcomings of a multiculturalism that is too dependent on culturalism. In the afterword we would like to reiterate two themes that have threaded these chapters even where they were not explicitly addressed throughout. First, what can the emphasis on the Asia-Pacific add to our understanding of a global multiculturalism and second whether it is time for multiculturalism to be replaced by other types of theoretical understandings.

Emphasis on the Asia-Pacific

Related to our discussion of the problem of methodological nationalism in the introduction is the question of what kind of regional understanding is supposed by the terminology Asia-Pacific. While, as noted above, many of the chapters have contributed to discussions of border crossing, questions can be raised, notably in the Japanese context, as to the degree that there is a firmly shared understanding of Japan's historical and political contributions to a region as amorphous as the Asia-Pacific. Indeed as several of the chapters have made clear, a broader understanding of multiculturalism in Japan as similar to other East Asian countries (Bradley, Chapter 2) or an understanding of what is entailed by further internationalization of Japanese young people as global resources (Chapple, Chapter 11) is not broadly conceived and shared across Japanese society. These connections of Japan and the Asia-Pacific through multiculturalism will likely continue to grow in the future, however, in ways that can be tracked at levels that are not civilizational in scale but consist instead of the less highlighted movements of people, developments in language policies, and other types of political and economic exchanges some of which have been detailed in this volume.

In a recent contribution to the multiculturalism literature, Crowder (2013) reviewed arguments concerning global cultures other than Western Europe and North America. He contends that this can be argued to be the genesis of liberal multiculturalism based on immigration in the post-World War II period. Noting Islam and Confucianism as two of the largest regional cultural groupings, which might challenge a universalism of human rights (as a key component of most versions of multiculturalism), he further examines what he terms the "Asian values debate." Citing multiple authors, Crowder (2013, pp. 183–189) notes some tendencies to see Confucian influences in East Asian contexts leading to favoring strong state authorities, family (as opposed to individual) values, and deference to socioeconomic rights over civil and political human rights. Without providing a point-by-point critique of such arguments (in fairness to Crowder, he is also citing others as much as positing such differences himself), we find such generalized understandings of East Asia lacking viable specificity. Let us give one example from our collective chapters. There are pressures and demands driving the changes in South Korean nationality laws to allow for dual citizenship (Park, Chapter 10), which exist in Japan equally, but have played out differently according to factors that could not be reduced to civilization analysis such as Confucian understandings in our opinion. It is for this reason that the diversity that we have assembled in these chapters is not meant to provide distinctive Asian examples of some form of multiculturalism that counters the Western European and North American multiculturalism (just as there is variety in such groupings as well). It is rather to illustrate the overlaps and divergences in problems of multicultural society in global contexts. We expect that the chapters here will contribute to understandings of migration, language, and politics in the wider global context not only East Asia or the Asia-Pacific.

Multiculturalism and new terminology

Finally we return to the problem of multiculturalism and multiculturality. We respect arguments that would like to move beyond the fixed ways of thinking about multiculturalism, multiculturalism beyond culture, if it can be imagined in our contemporary world. We called attention to this problem in the introduction and we conclude here with a similar set of ideas. The essential problem with multiculturalism as is has been theorized in past decades (and parodied by its critics) is not emphasis on diversity and tolerance but emphasis on problems based on essentialist readings of culture and identity. This argument is made repeatedly by many of the recent treatments of multiculturalism. Whether multiculturality as a term will come to stand for a process approach of understanding diversity across and within societies and even within individuals themselves is debatable. However, we remain convinced that there are the twin needs of humans for belonging to localized ethnic groupings but at the same time to become increasingly open to a globalized identity of humans facing similar challenges of ameliorating environmental risk, creating new modes of conflict reconciliation, and challenging the divisions and injustice of inequality in societies and a harshly unequal world. This evidently means that new models and understandings of a reinvigorated set of multicultural policies, negotiations, and processes will be a central theme of global politics for years to come. We hope with humility to have contributed to such understanding with this volume while aware that more nuanced theorizing and research will be required to meet the challenges noted above.

Reference

Crowder, G. (2013). *Theories of multiculturalism*. Cambridge: Polity Press.

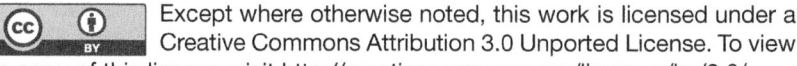

Except where otherwise noted, this work is licensed under a Creative Commons Attribution 3.0 Unported License. To view a copy of this license, visit http://creativecommons.org/licenses/by/3.0/

OPEN

Index

Abrams, D. 76, 77
access; citizenship 163, 167, 170, 177, 179, 184, 186; labor market 163, 167
acculturation 64, 65; and nation of origin 64; and reasons for immigrating 64; and age on entry 64; and amount of prior schooling 64; and economic status 64; and difficulties related to travel 64; and trauma related to war 64; and immigration status 64
administrator 101, 110, 111
Afrasian Research Center 1,
aging; population 163; population, Japan 183; society 127
anti-discrimination law 35
apprenticeship of observation 109
Arendt, H. 4, 95
Asia-Pacific 229–30
Asian EFL contexts 102, 110
assimilation 127
attention to facts and details (*see* significant cultural variables)
Australia; citizenship 177, 179; multiculturalism policies 167–8, 171–3, 177–9; Nurse Licensure Exam 171–2; nurse migration 167–9, 170–3, 177–9
awareness-raising; reflection-type activities 111
axial coding 104

banking view of teaching 67
Banting, K and Kimlycka, W. 166, 167
Basic Interpersonal Communicative Skills (BICS) 100
Belkin, G.S. 78
bilateral agreement 168; UK-Philippines 168
boomerang effect 151, 155

Brewer, M.B. 75, 77
Brown, W. 5
Buchan J. 163, 177
Buchan, Jobanputra and Goug 163, 177

candidate nurses, Japan 180–1
case-study approach 102
category diagram 104
chiki shakai 32
citizenship 170, 176, 190–211; Australia 177, 179; dual 175, 179, 190–211; global 225–6; Japan 182; UK 177, 182; USA 182
civilization 2
coalition government of the Liberal Democratic Party and the New Komeito Party 107
Cognitive Academic Language Proficiency (CALP) 100
cognitive style 66; analytic; methodical 66; reflective 66; global 66; relational 66; intuitive 66; assertiveness/compliance 66; dominance/submission 66; direct/indirect communication styles 66
communicative activities 108, 109
concentration camp 48, 50–4
concept map 104, 114
Condon, J.C. Jr. 63, 76
contact time 121, 122
context-sensitive, locally appropriate approaches 110, 112
country of origin 67
Course of Study; the 100, 108
critical incidents 106
critical mass of ESL numbers (*see* cultural inclusion and exclusion)
Crowder G. 230
cultural anthropology 2,
cultural inclusion and exclusion 66, 69, 70–3, 75–6, and model 74–5

cultural patterns 63; and race 63; and ethnicity 63; and socioeconomic status 63; and economy 63; and gender 63; and religion 63; and political philosophy 63.
culture 2, 63–6; the universal 63; the ecological 63; the national 63; the regional 63; the racio-ethnic 63; sociolinguistic definitions 63; anthropological definitions 63; ethnolinguisic definitions 63, views of teaching and learning 63; micro-view of 63, 64; macro-view of 63, 64
culture shock 64; and motivation 64; and ego permeability 64; and social distance 64; and psychological distance 64; and assimilation 64

de facto foreign language education 111
DelFattore, J. 69, 76
Democratic Party 107
descriptive ways of teaching 102, 111, 112
diversity 45–6, 54, 56–8
Dovidio, J.F. 76
Duff, P. 65, 75, 76

East Asian multiculturalism 36–7
Eddy, C. 66, 77
Ellis, R. 64, 76
English 82; as a Foreign Language (EFL) 100; as a Second Language (ESL) 109; education 100, 106, 108, 111; language 214–15, 221–4, 226; proficiency 106, 107
epistemology 7
Esses, V.M. 75, 76
exchange students 220, 226
exclusion (*see* cultural inclusion and exclusion)

family; reunification 163, 167, 177–9, 181, 184; (*also see* family structures)
family structures 66; roles of family members 66; child–rearing practices 66; gender roles 66; adult-child interactions 66; educational expectations 66; expression of emotions 66; conversational rules 66; child-rearing practices 66; individual responsibility 66; spirituality 66
feminization 140
first and second language (*see* significant cultural variables)
focus group questions (*see* focus groups)
focus groups 73–4; focus group questions 73
focus on grades (*see* significant cultural variables)
foreign; children 118, 129, 130, 131; Language Activities 119; language education 118, 119, 120, 121, 124, 128, 129, 132; Languages 119, 120, 121; students 130, 131
Foucault, M. 87
Freire, P. 67, 76

gaikokujin (foreigners) 223
generalization 102, 113
geographical scales 147
global competitiveness 99
global de-householding 141, 142, 156
global householding 139, 141, 142, 156
globalization 213, 226
Green D. 35
grounded theory 101, 104
Grounded Theory Approach (GTA) 101, 103, 104
Gunderson, L. 62, 64, 65, 66, 67, 70, 71, 73, 77

Hall, S. viii
Helmer, S. 66, 77
Hogg, M.A. 76, 77
Honey, P.J. 69, 77
household 138–9, 141
human security 143
Hamashita, T. 7, 93
history 44–6, 48, 50–1, 56–7
Huntington S 3, 91

identity; Japanese 215;
    cultural 215–17, 226
imagination 147, 157
Imamura, H. 93
inclusion (*see* cultural inclusion and
    exclusion)
in-depth interview 101, 103
individual differences (*see* cultural
    variables)
Indonesia 84
insecurity 146, 156
instrumental motivation 122
integration 45–6, 48, 54, 57–9;
    migrant 162, 166–7
integrative motivation 122
interculture 66; multiple
    intercultures 66
internal internationalization 128, 129
International Convention one the
    Protection of the Rights of All
    Migrant Workers and Members of
    their Families (ICMW); the 152
International English Language
    Testing System (IELTS) 178
international relations 6
*International Relations of the
    Asia-Pacific* 84
internationalization 216–17, 223, 225
Ireland, nurse migration 168, 169, 176
Iwabuchi, K. viii–x

Jackson, L.M. 76
Japan; as one nation 27;
    monoethnic 30
Japan 84; aging population 183;
    Business Federation
    (*Keidanren*) 217–18;
    candidate nurses 180–1;
    International Corporation of
    welfare Services (JICWELS) 180;
    Nurse Licensure Exam 164, 180–1;
    as one nation 27; monoethnic 30
    -Philippines Economic Partnership
    Agreement (JPEPA) 162, 164, 180,
    183
Japanese; EFL contexts 100, 102,
    110; immigrants 44–51, 53, 56–9;
    language instruction 130, 131;

society 118, 124, 129; way of
    teaching English 110
Japaneseness 217

Kachru, B. 87
Kingdom of Saudi Arabia (KSA), nurse
    migration 168, 170
Kivisto, 24
Kluckhohn, C. 63, 77
Korean 190–211; adoptee 195,
    201, 208–10; American 201, 202,
    210; Chinese 202, 207, 209, 210;
    in Japan 201, 202; in the former
    USSR 201, 202, 207; Overseas
    194–6, 199–202, 205, 207–9
Kroeber, A.L. 63, 77
Kwak J.H. 35
Kymlicka, W. 25

Labor 155
Laborers 155, 156
language; awareness 110;
    policy 127; socialization 65
Larson, D.N. 63, 77
Li, G. 68, 77
linguistic sensibilities 110
loyalty 47–8, 50–3, 56

mainstream culture 62, 65
Malaysia 84
Marques, J.M. 76, 77
Mazlish, B. 2,
member checking 104, 112
migrant; economic resources 169;
    final 162–3, 165, 169,
    171–3, 177, 181–3; human
    resources 163, 168–9,
    183; political (citizenship)
    resources 163, 168–70
    resources 168–70; social network
    resources 169–70; transferrable
    resources 169, 181–2;
    transit 162–3, 169, 171–3,
    176–8, 181–3
Migration; 'back door' 183; circular
    pattern 163–5, 183; 'front
    door' 183; 'side door' 183;
    revolving door 183

Ministry of Education, Culture, Sports, Science and Technology (MEXT) 1, 100, 217, 219–23
Ministry of Internal Affairs and Communications (Japan) 32
minorities 45–6, 53, 56–7
Mishra, V. 23, 25, 32
modernism 7
Modood, T. 166
Morris-Suzuki 27, 31
multicultural discourse 44–6
multicultural education 44, 46, 56
multicultural; model, the 62, 66–75; society 118, 121
multiculturality 5, 139, 229, 230, 231
multiculturalism 44–50, 54–9, 62, 201, 203–6, 210, 211, 214, 216, 224–6; Australia policies 167–8, 171–3, 177–9; crisis of 23, 26; critics of 24, 25–6, 31–2; definition 24–6; education 34; end of 23–4; in Japan 22–3; liberal 21; local 29, 32, 36, 37; political participation 34–5; private initiative 184; Singapore policies 164, 167–9, 171–2; top-down 162, 164, 184
multilingual society 128, 132
multiracialism 62
Murdock, G.P. 63, 77
Murphy, M. 24–5, 26

Nagayoshi K. 31
narrative 46, 49, 54
nation 47, 54, 57
nation-state 6
national; attachment 75; conformity 99; identity 51, 57; interest 47; -level of standardization 99
National curriculum guidelines 100
nationalism 198, 199, 201, 205, 206, 211
Nationality 190–200, 202–7, 209–11

native speakerism 105
Naturalization 195, 197, 201, 203, 206
needs analyses 110, 111
Nishida, K. 82, 92, 94–5
No-No Boy 51–2, 57
non-Western 6
non-Western 81, 83
number of foreign residents (Japan) 27–8
Nurse Licensure Exam; Australia 171–2; Japan 164, 180–1; Singapore (Singaporean Nursing Board Exam) 172; USA 171
nurse migration; Australia 167–9, 170–3, 177–9; Ireland 168, 169, 176; Kingdom of Saudi Arabia 168, 170; Philippines 162–84; Singapore 172–6; UK 168–70, 176–7; USA 177
nurse recruitment; Japan 180, 182–3; Philippines 168–70; Singapore 173–4
Nye, J. Jr 4

Ochs, E. 65, 77
open coding 104
Orientalism 84
overall numbers and inclusion/exclusion 70–2; individual differences 72
overseas domestic workers (ODW) 149

paradigm model 104
particularization 102, 113
Patterson, T.C. 2
Paul, A.M. 165, 177
permanent residency visa; Australia 178; Japan 181–2; Singapore 175–6
Pickett, C.L. 75, 77
place of nothingness 92, 94
place reputation 177
pluralism 55–6
policy making 101, 107, 111, 112

236 Index

policy maker   101, 110, 111, 112
political dialogue and discourse pertaining to education   112
political tactics   112
post-Western   83
Power geometry   147, 150
practical knowledge   105, 108, 109, 110, 111
prescriptive ways of teaching   111
Primary power rule   150
professional identities   106
properties and dimensions   104
process-oriented information   111
Public Sector Nurses and Midwives' Enterprise Agreement, Australia   178

qualitative research   102
quality of teachers   99

ratio of native English to ESL speakers (*see* cultural inclusion/exclusion)
Reid, J.M.   66, 72, 77
relationality   91–4
resiliency (*see* resilient students)
resilient students   72
retention; Japan   164, 182–3; nurse 163, 170
retrogression policy; USA   171
Richard-Amato, J.   64, 77
Roesingh, H.   72, 77
rote memorization (*see* significant cultural variables)
Ryukoku University   1

Said, E.   87
Scarcella, R.C.   66, 72, 77
Schieffelin, B.B.   65, 77
schooling (*see* cultural variables)
Schumann, J.   64, 65, 77
second language socialization (*see* language socialization)
Security   144
selective coding   104
self-esteem   106, 107
Semenya, A.H.   76
sense of distance   107

senior high school   100, 107, 108, 110, 111
September 11   viii
Shiga, Japan   62
Shih, C.Y.   93
significant cultural variables   66–72; country of origin   67; family   67–9 (see also family structures); first and second languages   69–70; L1 teaching and learning practices   70; rote memorization   70; attention to facts and details   70; teacher-centered instruction   70; focus on grades   70
Singapore   62; dependency ratio celling   174; employer sponsorship   176; foreign worker's levy   174–5, multiculturalism policies   164, 167–9, 171–2; nurse migration   172–6; Nursing Board   174, 176
Smalley, W.A.   63, 77
Smith, B.   77
Social location   147, 150
Social Science Citation Index   84
socialization (*see* language socialization)
soft power   4
sojourners   62
Sole responsibility   149
stakeholders   101, 111
stepping stone   163, 165, 174
stepwise migration; Filipino nurses   162–84
subjectivity   90, 92
super-diversity   26
Swan, M.   77

tabunka kyōsei   22, 27, 29, 31, 33, 37, 39n18
Talmy, S.   65, 75, 76
teacher; centered instruction (*see* significant cultural variables); -centered textbook-based grammar translation method   108, 109, 111; educator   100, 101, 110, 111, 112

Index 237

teachers' resistance 105, 107, 108
teaching and learning (*see* significant cultural variables)
Thailand 84
tolerance 45–6, 57, 59
tributary system 82, 93
totalitarianism 4
Trafficking 151
Transnationalism 191, 198, 201, 210–11
Tule Lake Camp 51–2

Uchida, Y. 69, 76
United Nations Commission on Human Rights 35
University 218–20, 222–4

Vertovec, S 25
Vontress, C.E. 63, 78

Westphalia System 89
work-stay immigrants 62
World Englishes 86

 Except where otherwise noted, this work is licensed under a Creative Commons Attribution 3.0 Unported License. To view a copy of this license, visit http://creativecommons.org/licenses/by/3.0/

The manufacturer's authorised representative in the EU is Springer Nature Customer Service Centre GmbH, Europaplatz 3, 69115 Heidelberg, Germany. If you have any concerns regarding our products, please contact ProductSafety@springernature.com

Printed and bound by CPI Group (UK) Ltd, Croydon, CR0 4YY
23/03/2026
02076663-0018